Around the World Low-Fat & No-Fat Meals in Minutes

More than 300 Delicious, Easy, and
Healthy Recipes from 16 Countries
in 30 Minutes or Less

M.J. Smith, R.D.

and

Michele Gaffney-Rabik

CHRONIMED
PUBLISHING

ISBN 1-56865-474-X

Cover Design: Terry Dugan Design
Text Design: David Enyeart

Printed in the United States of America

Dedications

This book is dedicated to my wonderful friends from Gourmet Club, who started 12 years ago in Guttenberg and have tasted their way around the world. Thanks for the company and the costumes and, most importantly, the cuisine.

M.J. Smith

This book is dedicated to my family. To my husband, Russ, and sons, Tyler and Zachary, who love to eat a variety of foods and are always willing to try something new, as long as I still make tacos, hamburgers, and macaroni and cheese! And to my Mom and Dad for buying me my first Easy-Bake oven at age four, even though I started requesting it at age two!

Michele Gaffney-Rabik

Acknowledgments

Thank you to Katie Schuster, who in a thoroughly cheerful and efficient manner, did whatever she was asked (in between her senior college classes and another part-time job) to get this manuscript ready.

M.J. Smith

A special thank you to a wonderful friend, Julie Adams, who was there for me no matter what, whether it be to do dishes piled high in the test kitchen, run to the grocery store, pack boxes, or just listen. Thanks, Julie, you're one in a million!

Also, thank you to M.J. for your perseverance through printer jams, blizzards, and the hectic pace of being a wife and mom and writing a book!

Michele Gaffney-Rabik

About the Authors

M.J. Smith is a Registered Dietitian and author of 7 previous cookbooks. She lives in Guttenberg, Iowa, a picturesque and historic Mississippi River community. Her writing office is located just across from Lock and Dam 10 where eagles soar in the winter and barges are towed in the summer. Ms. Smith has been featured in national magazines, including *Good Housekeeping* and *Shape*. All of her books start with a "low fat, in minutes" theme which she has perfected during her nearly 20 years of counseling individuals about quick and healthy cooking. She is married to Andy Smith, a family physician. Testing recipes in her home kitchen marries well with her responsibility of mothering their two school-age children. Look for her other books in any bookstore: *All-American Low-Fat Meals in Minutes, 60 Days of Low-Fat Low-Cost Meals in Minutes, 366 Low-Fat Brand-Name Recipes in Minutes, The Miracle Foods Cookbook, Year-Round Low-Fat & No-Fat Holiday Meals in Minutes, Cooking with Angels,* and the soon to be released *Diabetic Low-Fat & No-Fat Meals in Minutes.* M.J. Smith met Michele Rabik while browsing in a large supermarket. They became friends fast when they discovered their mutual love of fine cooking and good beer. Ms. Smith invites readers' comments at her e-mail address: mjsmithrd@worldnet.att.net.

Michele Gaffney-Rabik is a free-lance caterer and home economist. Michele has worked in all aspects of the food industry. Besides being a cookbook author, she has worked in product development, marketing, consumer relations, food service and dried fruit sales. Originally from Iowa, she and her husband, Russ, and children, Tyler and Zachary, lived in California in the wine country for several years, then decided to return to their roots in Iowa. The next project came along as two food connoisseurs decided to combine their ideas and recipes from around the world.

Notice: Consult Health Care Professional

Readers are advised to seek the guidance of a licensed physician or health care professional before making any changes in prescribed health care regimens, as each individual case or need may vary. This book is intended for informational purposes only and is not for use as an alternative to appropriate medical care. While every effort has been made to ensure that the nutrition information is the most current available, new research findings, being released with increased frequency, may invalidate some data. Some recipes contain wines and spirits. Readers are advised to seek guidance of a licensed physician concerning benefits and risks of moderate alcohol consumption.

Contents

Introduction

Around-the-World-Flavor Without the Fat

Around the world flavor without the fat is as simple as learning how to buy a perfect Persian melon and just slicing it.

This cookbook is pure cultural diversity with a uniform soul—16 world cuisines connected by low-fat/no-fat flavor. Written by a Registered Dietitian and a gourmet cook, this is not fast or frozen food. It is about savoring the simplicity of fresh ingredients and spices without the fat. It is also about experimenting with a new cooking method or maybe picking up a fun piece of international cookware. This journey begins and ends with two contradictory ingredients: explicit directions and unending encouragement to improvise. For this book is a journal of our own extended travels with food. And while our best secrets and shortcuts are shared, there will always be room for your own dash of flavor and fun.

We aim to knock you over with the first section of menus and recipes from around the world. Notice how we literally span the continents eastward from America to South America to Europe, Africa, Asia, and finally to Australia. At the beginning of each chapter, there are menus and tips for understanding the unique flavor and style of the cuisine. We did more than update our world geography skills writing this book, we scoured restaurants and grocery stores for the best low-fat foods and ingredients.

We developed our recipe format from some new and authoritative research conducted in the test kitchens of the National Live Stock and Meat Board. The format allows the reader to evaluate recipe ingredients and preparation steps at a glance. "Hands on" time as well as marinating, cooking/baking and chilling times are listed first. The recipe ingredient list includes options and substitutions. Directions are short and concise, yet specific. They tell what not to do (such as do not overcook) as well as what to do. If you have never made Beef Burgundy, you can look over our recipe in a few seconds and decide if you have the time and ingredients. We think any recipe in this book is very approachable for today's low-fat cook who wants to be creative, without spending all night in the kitchen.

Minding your low-fat/no-fat lifestyle will be nothing less than a barrel of fun with this book as your Friday night or Saturday afternoon companion.

Also, don't miss our Around the World Food Product, Restaurant, Spice, and Glossary Guides, which follow the recipes.

Using Food Exchange Plans

If you are using a food exchange plan for weight control or diabetes, look to the end of each recipe for the food exchange values. These exchange group values are based on the Exchange Lists for Meal Planning, a system developed and published by the American Dietetic Association and the American Diabetes Association. Exchange values for recipes using a combination of fruits, vegetables, or grains are based on the food exchange group that most closely matches the final nutrient profile. The Exchange Lists for Meal Planning were revised in 1995. The change concerned the arrangement of the various food lists into three broad groups based on their nutrient content and supports the concept of monitoring total carbohydrate consumption. The revised document can be purchased inexpensively from the American Dietetic Association at 1-800-877-1600, extension 5000.

Around the World Appetizer Buffet

Cheesy Dip & Carrot Sticks
with Reduced-Fat Crackers
Mexican Ceviche
Caribbean Black Bean Dip
With Reduced-Fat Tortilla Chips
British Isles Devils on Horseback
French Stuffed Mushrooms
Scandinavian Marinated Salmon
Italian Antipasto
Eastern European Pickled Fish
Middle Eastern Hummus

Around the World Dessert Buffet

Strawberries With Raspberry Sauce
Black Forest Cherry Cake
Fruit Soup
Cottage Cheese Torte
Honey Orange Biscotti

Chapter One

USA

Including the American South

Suggested All-American Menu

Crispy Oven Chicken
Creamy Coleslaw
Smashed Potatoes
Strawberry Pie
Chocolate Milk

American South Menu

Shrimp Creole
Red Beans and Rice
Hurricane

Add Fun, Subtract Expense

Throw a picnic in February by getting out the thermos jug and the red checked tablecloth and dressing up an ordinary hamburgers-on-Friday-night supper.

Check out *The First American Cookbook*, by Amelia Simmons (published by Dover Publications, Inc., New York, 1958). It is wonderful after-dinner reading with directions like these for stuffing and roasting a turkey: "one pound soft wheat bread, 3 ounces beef suet, 3 eggs, a little sweet thyme, sweet marjoram, pepper and salt and some add a gill of wine; fill the bird therewith and hang down to a steady solid fire and roast until a steam emits from the bread."

In the fall, oodles of apples fill market bins across America with seasonal shades of red, green, and yellow. Treat yourself to a new variety such as York, Fuji, Imperial, Stayman, Newtown Pippin, or Northern Spy.

Whenever you eat corn, say a thank-you to the first American citizens, the Indians. This first gift from the Native Americans to the country's first European settlers produced recipes for johnnycakes, hoecakes, pumpkin pie, Indian pudding, corn bread, succotash, cornmeal mush, and hasty pudding.

Europeans have long regarded Americans as gross and uneducated eaters. Most of us need to slow down and work at enjoying dinner conversation.

American cooking may have become a melting pot of diverse cuisines using herbs and spices from all over the world; however, nothing beats a fresh Maine lobster, some shrimp from off the coast of Texas, or a good old Midwest meat and potatoes dinner. To top it off, let's travel to the American South where good ol' home cookin' is at its best! Imagine yourself in New Orleans where you can get both Creole cooking, which marries French, African, and Spanish cuisines, and Cajun cooking, which is very hot and spicy. Both cuisines include lots of chopped onions, bell peppers, and celery, and a unique spice, file' powder, which is ground sassafras leaves.

America does have a few native spices, including dill, chives, mustard, parsley, garlic, and basil.

KENTUCKY LEMONADE

A cool refresher on a hot summer day

Preparation time: 5 minutes
Standing time: 30 minutes
6 servings—8 ounces each

1/2 cup fresh mint leaves
1 cup lemon juice
1/2 cup sugar
1/2 cup water
1 quart chilled ginger ale

1. Place mint leaves in the bottom of a 2-quart pitcher.

2. Combine lemon juice, sugar, and water; pour over mint leaves. Let stand 30 minutes.

3. Just before serving, stir in ginger ale. Serve over crushed ice.

126 calories per serving: 0 fat, 0 protein,
33 g. carbohydrate, 0 cholesterol, 11 mg. sodium.
For exchange diets, count 2 fruit.

MARDI GRAS PUNCH

A tasty nonalcoholic punch that is easy to prepare

Preparation time: 5 minutes
20 servings—6 ounces each

1 quart chilled apple cider
6-ounce can thawed frozen orange juice
6-ounce can thawed frozen lemonade
2 quarts chilled ginger ale or 2 quarts chilled sugar-free lemon
   lime soft drink
4 cups rainbow sherbet

1. In a large punch bowl, stir together apple cider, orange juice, and lemonade.

2. Add ginger ale.

3. Just before serving, scoop sherbet into balls and spoon into punch.

153 calories per serving: 0 fat, 1 g. protein,
35 g. carbohydrate (27 g. with sugar-free soft drink),
4 mg. cholesterol, 35 mg. sodium.
For exchange diets, count 2 1/2 fruit
(2 fruit with sugar-free soft drink.)

CHOCOLATE MILK

An all-American favorite!

Preparation time: 1 minute
2 servings—8 ounces each

2 cups skim milk
1 tablespoon chocolate syrup

1. Combine milk and syrup; mix thoroughly.

109 calories per serving: 0 fat, 9 g. protein,
18 g. carbohydrate, 4 mg. cholesterol, 140 mg. sodium.
For exchange diets, count 1 skim milk.

HURRICANE

The original Hurricane is made with passion fruit syrup, which may be difficult to find. Any of the combination fruit juices at your local grocer will work well in this refreshing beverage, which is very popular in New Orleans.

Preparation time: 2 minutes
2 servings—6 ounces each

2 ounces dark rum
2 ounces light rum
8 ounces pineapple-orange-banana juice
2 teaspoons lime juice

1. Shake ingredients thoroughly with 2 cups of crushed ice. Strain into a chilled glass.

93 calories per serving: 0 fat, 0 protein,
7 g. carbohydrate, 0 cholesterol, 0 sodium.
For exchange diets, count 1 1/2 fruit.

CHEESY DIP

A fix-quick dip! Especially good with carrot sticks.
Preparation time: 5 minutes
8 servings—2 tablespoons each

3 ounces reduced-fat cream cheese
8-ounce jar Cheez Whiz
1 cup fat-free mayonnaise

1. In a medium bowl, combine all ingredients; refrigerate, or serve immediately with fresh carrots or reduced-fat wheat crackers.

63 calories per serving: 4 g. fat, 3 g. protein,
4 g. carbohydrate, 12 mg. cholesterol, 444 mg. sodium.
For exchange diets, count 1/2 skim milk, 1/2 fat.

DILL DIP FOR VEGETABLES

Preparation time: 20 minutes
Chilling time: 30 minutes
8 servings—1/4 cup dip each

Dill dip:
1 cup reduced-fat mayonnaise
1 cup nonfat sour cream
2 tablespoons dry onion soup mix
1 tablespoon dried dill weed
assorted fresh vegetables for dipping (For something different,
   try strips of yellow squash, asparagus tips, red pepper rings,
   radish roses, brocciflower tops, whole fresh pea pods, or whole
   baby carrots.)

1. In a small mixing bowl, combine first 4 ingredients. Cover and refrigerate at least 30 minutes. Serve with fresh vegetables. This dip stays fresh for up to 5 days.

69 calories per serving: 2 g. fat, 2 g. protein,
9 g. carbohydrate, 0 cholesterol, 315 mg. sodium.
For exchange diets, count 1/2 starch, 1/2 fat.

MOM'S FAVORITE SUGAR-FREE MUFFINS

Preparation time: 20 minutes
Baking time: 20 minutes
18 servings—1 muffin each

1 cup chopped dates
1/2 cup raisins
1/2 cup chopped dried pitted prunes
1/2 cup apple juice
1/2 cup water
1/2 cup reduced-fat margarine
1/4 teaspoon salt
1/2 cup liquid egg substitute
1 teaspoon vanilla
1 cup flour
1 teaspoon baking soda
1/2 cup chopped walnuts

1. Preheat oven to 350° F.

2. In a medium saucepan, stir together dates, raisins, prunes, apple juice, and water. Bring to a boil, and boil for 5 minutes. Stir in margarine and salt; set aside to cool.

3. Stir in egg substitute and vanilla; mix well. In a small bowl, mix flour and baking soda together just until mixed; add to batter. Fold in nuts.

4. Line muffin cups with papers, and fill 2/3 full.

5. Bake at 15 to 20 minutes or until done. Turn off oven, and leave muffins in oven for 2 minutes.

154 calories per serving: 7 g. fat, 4 g. protein,
23 g. carbohydrate, 0 cholesterol, 83 mg. sodium.
For exchange diets, count 1 starch, 1/2 fruit, 1 fat.

OVERSIZED OATMEAL ROLLS

This recipe was developed in my early days as a home economist for a cereal company. Everyone stopped by the test kitchen for a sample whenever the aroma wafted through the office.

Preparation time: 20 minutes; Rising time: 2 hours
Baking time: 18 minutes
16 servings—1 roll each

1 cup quick oats
1/2 cup margarine
21/3 cups hot water (120-125° F.)
2 packages active dry yeast
1/3 cup packed brown sugar
1 tablespoon sugar
1/4 teaspoon salt
4 1/2 cups flour
1 cup whole wheat flour
nonstick cooking spray

1. In a large bowl, soften oats and margarine in hot water; let cool until lukewarm. Add yeast, sugars, and salt to oat mixture; mix well. Let stand 5 minutes.

2. In a medium bowl, combine flours; stir into oat mixture. Dough will be slightly sticky. Do not knead. Cover; let rise in a warm place for about an hour.

3. Roll dough into 2-inch balls. Place on baking sheets coated with cooking spray. Let rise until double, about an hour.

4. Bake in preheated oven at 350° F. for 15 to 18 minutes. Remove from baking sheets; cool slightly on wire racks.

240 calories per serving: 6 g. fat, 6 g. protein,
40 g. carbohydrate, 0 cholesterol, 110 mg. sodium.
For exchange diets, count 3 starch.

NEW ENGLAND FISH CHOWDER

This main dish will warm you up on a wintry day.

Preparation time: 15 minutes
Cooking time: 50 minutes
8 servings—1 1/2 cups each

2 pounds halibut fillets
2 cups water
3 cups diced potatoes
1/2 teaspoon salt
2 slices diced lean bacon
1 cup chopped onion
1/2 cup shredded carrot
1/2 cup chopped celery
4 cups skim milk
1 bay leaf
1/4 teaspoon black pepper

1. In a medium saucepan, bring halibut and water to a boil; reduce heat and simmer, covered, for about 10 minutes or until fish flakes easily with a fork. Remove fish from broth; set aside.

2. Add potatoes and salt to broth; cover and boil 8 minutes or until potatoes are almost tender.

3. In a large skillet, saute' bacon, onion, carrot, and celery about 5 minutes; drain thoroughly.

4. Flake fish. Add fish, bacon mixture, milk, bay leaf, and pepper to potatoes and broth. Slowly bring to a boil. Reduce heat; simmer 15 minutes.

271 calories per serving: 4 g. fat, 31 g. protein,
27 g. carbohydrate, 41 mg. cholesterol, 307 mg. sodium.
For exchange diets, count 1 starch, 2 vegetable, 4 very lean meat.

VEGETABLE SOUP

Preparation time: 15 minutes
Cooking time: 25 minutes
4 servings—2 cups each

1/2 pound lean ground beef or lean beef stew cubes
1/2 cup chopped onion
2 ribs celery, diced
1/2 cup fresh mushrooms, sliced thin
1 teaspoon basil
1 teaspoon dill weed
1/4 teaspoon celery salt
1 large carrot, sliced thin
6 cups no-added-salt chunky tomatoes
2 medium potatoes, peeled and cubed

1. In a large stockpot, brown ground beef or stew meat with onion, celery, and mushrooms. Drain off any fat from meat.

2. Add all remaining ingredients to the stockpot, and bring to a boil. Reduce heat to a simmer for 20 minutes or until carrots and potatoes are tender.

250 calories per serving: 7 g. fat, 17 g. protein,
27 g. carbohydrate, 42 mg. cholesterol, 67 mg. sodium.
For exchange diets, count 2 lean meat, 1 vegetable, 1 1/2 starch.

CLASSIC CHILI

Serve leftover chili over spaghetti and call it Cincinnati-style!

Preparation time: 15 minutes
Cooking time: 35 minutes
8 servings—1 1/2 cups each

1 pound lean ground beef
1 teaspoon oregano
1/2 teaspoon thyme
1 large onion, chopped
1 green pepper, chopped
1/2 teaspoon monosodium glutamate
2 minced garlic cloves
1 tablespoon paprika
1 tablespoon chili powder
1 teaspoon cumin
2 16-ounce cans no-added-salt chunky tomatoes
2 16-ounce cans kidney beans
8-ounce can no-added-salt tomato sauce
1/2 ounce unsweetened chocolate, grated (optional)

1. Brown ground beef in a Dutch oven; drain well.

2. Add the next 9 ingredients, and cook over medium heat for 8 minutes, stirring, until vegetables are cooked through.

3. Add tomatoes, beans, and tomato sauce. Bring mixture to a boil. Stir in grated chocolate, if desired. Reduce heat, and simmer for at least 20 minutes.

242 calories per serving: 8 g. fat, 18 g. protein,
26 g. carbohydrate, 42 mg. cholesterol, 318 mg. sodium.
For exchange diets, count 2 lean meat, 2 vegetable, 1 starch.

CREAMY COLESLAW

Preparation time: 15 minutes
8 servings—1 cup each

Salad:
1 pound shredded cabbage and carrots
2 stalks celery, finely diced
4 green onions, diced
1 firm ripe tomato, seeded and chopped

Dressing:
1/2 cup reduced-fat mayonnaise
1/4 teaspoon lemon pepper
2 tablespoons sugar
1 tablespoon vinegar
1 teaspoon celery seed
1 tablespoon prepared horseradish or 1 teaspoon yellow mustard
(optional)

1. In a large salad bowl, combine vegetables.

2. In a shaker container, mix ingredients for dressing. Pour dressing over salad; mix. Refrigerate for up to an hour or serve immediately. Omit the tomato if you want to refrigerate leftovers for the next day.

104 calories per serving: 6 g. fat, 4 g. protein,
10 g. carbohydrate, 13 mg. cholesterol, 91 mg. sodium.
For exchange diets, count 2 vegetable, 1 fat.

TYLER'S SPINACH SALAD

My oldest son Tyler, an aspiring cook, created this salad.

Preparation time: 15 minutes

4 servings—2 cups each

1 bunch fresh spinach
2 slices cooked, crumbled bacon
1/2 cup minced celery
1/2 cup shredded carrots
1/4 cup sliced mushrooms
1/3 cup low-calorie French dressing
1/3 cup reduced-fat croutons

1. Tear spinach leaves into bite-size pieces into a large salad bowl. Add bacon, celery, carrots, and mushrooms; toss to mix.

2. Pour dressing over top; toss lightly. Top with croutons. Serve immediately on chilled plates.

86 calories serving: 4 g. fat, 3 g. protein,
11 g. carbohydrate, 5 mg. cholesterol, 287 mg. sodium.
For exchange diets, count 1 vegetable, 1 fat.

GRANDMA'S GELATIN SALAD

We ask Grandma 'Great' to bring this
favorite to all our holiday get-togethers.

Preparation time: 15 minutes
Chilling time: 4 hours
12 servings—1/12 pan each

Gelatin salad:

    2 3-ounce packages sugar-free lime Jello
    2 cups boiling water
    8-ounce can drained, crushed pineapple, reserving juice
    water
    1 cup shredded cabbage
    1 cup shredded carrots
    1/2 cup chopped celery
    1/4 cup chopped green pepper
    1/4 cup sliced stuffed green olives
    1/4 cup chopped black walnuts
    2 tablespoons chopped pimiento

Topping:

    3-ounce package fat-free cream cheese
    1/4 cup fat-free mayonnaise
    1 tablespoon skim milk (additional milk may be added for
      thinner consistency)

1. In a medium bowl, stir together gelatin and boiling water until completely dissolved.

2. Add enough cold water to reserved pineapple juice to make 2 cups. Add to gelatin; mix well.

3. Stir in remaining ingredients except topping, and pour into an 11" x 9" pan; refrigerate 4 hours or until firm.

4. In a small bowl, combine all ingredients for topping. Spread over gelatin.

---

66 calories per serving: 3 g. fat, 3 g. protein,
8 g. carbohydrate, 0 cholesterol, 119 mg. sodium.
For exchange diets, count 2 vegetable, 1/2 fat.

CREAMY POTATO SALAD

The buttermilk makes it just like Grandma used to make!

Preparation time: 30 minutes
8 servings—1/2 cup each

Salad:

      6 cups cooked diced potatoes (4 large potatoes)
      1/4 cup sliced green onion
      2 hard-cooked eggs, coarsely chopped

Dressing:

      1/2 cup reduced fat mayonnaise
      1/4 teaspoon celery seed
      1 teaspoon prepared mustard
      1 tablespoon vinegar
      1 teaspoon sugar
      2 tablespoons buttermilk
      1/4 teaspoon salt
      1/2 teaspoon white pepper

1. Combine potatoes, onion, and eggs in a salad bowl.

2. Whisk dressing ingredients together in a small bowl. Pour dressing over potato mixture, and carefully stir with a large spoon.

---

89 calories per serving: 3 g. fat, 2 g. protein,
12 g. carbohydrate, 30 mg. cholesterol, 82 mg. sodium.
For exchange diets, count 1 starch.

MUFFALETTA

A melt-in-your-mouth meal in a sandwich.

Preparation time: 15 minutes
16 servings—1 wedge each

Olive salad:
> 7-ounce jar chopped artichokes, drained
> 1/2 cup sliced pitted black olives
> 1/2 cup chopped roasted red pepper
> 1/4 cup chopped celery
> 1/4 cup sliced stuffed green olives
> 1/4 cup chopped onion
> 1/4 cup shredded low-fat mozzarella cheese
> 1/4 cup fat-free Italian dressing

Sandwich loaf:
> 1 round loaf sourdough bread
> 1/4 cup fat-free Italian salad dressing
> 4 ounces sliced low-fat turkey breast
> 4 ounces sliced reduced-fat salami
> 4 ounces light Swiss cheese

1. In a medium bowl, combine all ingredients for olive salad.

2. Slice off the top third of bread in one piece; remove soft bread from inside bottom piece, leaving a crust shell. Brush Italian dressing inside bread shell and on cut side of bread top.

3. Spoon olive salad into bread shell. Layer meats and cheese over salad. Replace bread top. Cut into wedges, and serve at room temperature.

> 143 calories per serving: 4 g. fat, 9 g. protein,
> 19 g. carbohydrate,15 mg. cholesterol, 494 mg. sodium
> (To reduce sodium, choose reduced sodium salad dressing and salami.)
> For exchange diets, count 1 lean meat, 1 starch.

TUNA & NOODLE CASSEROLE

Preparation time: 15 minutes
Baking time: 30 minutes
8 servings—1 1/2 cups each

6 ounces noodles of choice
4 ounces fresh mushrooms, sliced thin
1/2 cup green onion, chopped fine
1 tablespoon margarine
1 small can sliced water chestnuts, drained
2 6-ounce cans water-packed tuna, drained
nonstick cooking spray
13-ounce can reduced-fat cream of mushroom soup
1/4 teaspoon marjoram
1/4 teaspoon thyme
1/4 teaspoon salt (optional)
1/2 teaspoon white pepper
1 tablespoon lemon juice
1/2 cup chow mein noodles

1. Preheat oven to 350° F.

2. Cook noodles according to package directions. Do not overcook.
Meanwhile, sauté mushrooms and onions in margarine.

3. Combine cooked noodles, sautéed vegetables, water chestnuts,
and tuna in an 8" square baking dish that has been sprayed with
cooking spray.

4. Combine soup, marjoram, thyme, salt, pepper, and lemon juice.
Fold into the tuna mixture. Top with chow mein noodles.

5. Bake for 30 minutes or cook in the microwave for 18 to 20 minutes or until bubbly. This recipe can be assembled and frozen, then
thawed and baked later.

205 calories per serving: 4 g. fat, 16 g. protein,
26 g. carbohydrate, 0 cholesterol, 368 mg. sodium.
For exchange diets, count 2 lean meat, 1 vegetable, 1 starch.

BREAKFAST EGG BAKE

Preparation time: 15 minutes
Baking time: 40 minutes
8 servings—3 x 3 inch square each

12 slices of white or French bread, crust removed
nonstick cooking spray
4 ounces cubed lean ham
2 cups skim milk
8 eggs or 2 cups liquid egg substitute
1/4 cup minced onion
1/2 teaspoon dry mustard
1/4 teaspoon paprika
1/4 teaspoon salt
2 ounces low-fat cheddar cheese, shredded
1 tablespoon dried parsley

1. Preheat oven to 400° F.

2. Cut bread into cubes, and spread over the bottom of a 7" x 11" or 9" x 12" pan that has been sprayed with cooking spray. Sprinkle ham on top of the bread.

3. Using a mixer or blender, combine milk, eggs, onion, mustard, paprika, and salt. Pour over ham. Sprinkle with shredded cheese and parsley.

4. Bake for 35 to 40 minutes, or refrigerate overnight and bake in the morning.

235 calories per serving: 9 g. fat, 18 g. protein,
22 g. carbohydrate, 270 mg. cholesterol with eggs
(19 mg. with egg substitute), 432 mg. sodium.
For exchange diets, count 2 lean meat and 1 1/2 starch.

BEST EVER BURGERS

Preparation time: 20 minutes
Grilling time: 15 minutes
8 servings—1 burger each

2 pounds lean ground beef, pork, or turkey

1. Form 8 patties from ground meat. Grill 2 inches from medium flame for 6 minutes on each side. Serve with rolls and toppings from choices below.

Boston variety:
16 slices Boston brown bread
1 cup baked beans
4 bacon strips, cooked and diced
1/4 cup chili sauce

English variety:
8 toasted English muffins
1 large red onion, cut into rings
8 leaves romaine lettuce
1/2 cup chutney

Spa variety:
8 whole-grain buns
1 cup green pea pods
1 cup chopped broccoli
1 cup bean sprouts

Midwest variety:
8 bakery rolls
8 leaves iceberg lettuce
8 slices fresh tomato
1/2 cup dill pickle slices
1/4 cup chopped white onion

German variety:
16 slices rye bread
1 cup drained sauerkraut
1/2 cup nonfat sour cream

Nutrition information on next page

Best Ever Burgers (continued)

Note: Nutrient analysis is based on lean ground beef.

....

Boston:
420 calories per serving: 10 g. fat, 36 g. protein,
46 g. carbohydrate,98 mg. cholesterol, 890 mg. sodium.
For exchange diets, count 4 lean meat, 2 starch, 2 vegetable.

....

English:
376 calories per serving: 11 g. fat, 37 g. protein,
33 g. carbohydrate,114 mg. cholesterol, 414 mg. sodium.
For exchange diets, count 4 lean meat, 2 starch.

....

Spa:
304 calories per serving: 8 g. fat, 34 g. protein,
22 g. carbohydrate,94 mg. cholesterol, 284 mg. sodium.
For exchange diets, count 4 lean meat, 1 starch.

....

Midwest:
340 calories per serving: 8 g. fat, 34 g. protein,
32 g. carbohydrate, 94 mg. cholesterol, 573 mg. sodium.
For exchange diets, count 4 lean meat, 1 1/2 starch.

....

German:
354 calories per serving: 8 g. fat, 36 g. protein,
33 g. carbohydrate, 94 mg. cholesterol, 800 mg. sodium.
For exchange diets, count 4 lean meat, 1 1/2 starch.

HOMEMADE KETCHUP

This ketchup may be made 10 days ahead.
It's perfect for a homestyle barbecue!

Preparation time: 10 minutes
Cooking time: 1 hour
24 servings—1 tablespoon each

4 (28-ounce) cans whole tomatoes, drained
2 1/2 cups chopped onion
1/2 cup chopped green pepper
4 minced garlic cloves
1/2 cup brown sugar
1 cup cider vinegar
1 teaspoon whole cloves
1 teaspoon whole allspice, crushed
1 cinnamon stick
1 teaspoon celery seed
2 teaspoons dry mustard
1 teaspoon paprika
1/8 teaspoon hot pepper sauce
1 teaspoon salt (optional)

1. In a large, heavy kettle, cook tomatoes, onion, green pepper, and garlic over low heat, covered, for about 30 minutes or until vegetables are soft.

2. Press mixture through a food mill fitted with a medium plate. Place puree into kettle with brown sugar and vinegar. Simmer, stirring frequently, until mixture is reduced by half, about 20 minutes.

3. Tie cloves, allspice, cinnamon, and celery seed in a cheesecloth bag, and add to tomato mixture along with mustard and paprika. Simmer about 10 minutes or until very thick, stirring frequently.

4. Discard cheesecloth bag. Add hot pepper sauce and salt, if desired.

------

56 calories per serving: 0 fat, 1 g. protein,
14 g. carbohydrate,0 cholesterol, 239 mg. sodium.
For exchange diets, count 1 fruit.

THANKSGIVING TURKEY AND DRESSING

Follow these tips for turning out a perfect bird.

Preparation time: 15 minutes
See chart for roasting time

Purchase: Allow 3/4 to 1 pound of turkey per person to be served. This method ensures plenty of white and dark meat to suit individual taste and allows for some leftovers.

Preparation for roasting: Thaw a frozen turkey, breast side up, in its unopened wrapper on a tray in the refrigerator. Estimate at least one day of thawing for every 6 pounds of turkey. Do not thaw at room temperature. Remove original plastic wrapper from thawed or fresh turkey. Remove neck and giblets from body cavity. Rinse the turkey inside and out with cool water, and pat dry with paper towels. Stuff turkey lightly if desired. Return legs to tuck position. Insert a meat thermometer into the deepest part of the thigh. Place turkey, breast up, on a flat rack in a shallow pan. Brush skin with vegetable oil. Place in preheated 325° oven. When skin is golden brown, shield the breast loosely with a tent of foil to prevent overbrowning. Roast to an internal temperature of 180° in the thigh, 170° in the breast, and 160° in the stuffing. Begin checking for doneness 30 minutes before anticipated end of cooking.

GENERAL GUIDELINES TO ESTIMATE COOKING TIME:

Weight of Turkey	Roasting time in Hours	
	STUFFED	UNSTUFFED
10-18 lb.	4-4/12	3-3 1/2
18-22 lb.	4 1/2-5	3 1/2-4
22-24 lb.	5-5 1/2	4-4 1/2
24-29 lb.	5 1/2-6 1/2	4 1/2-5

When appropriate temperature has been reached, remove turkey from the oven, cover, and allow to rest at room temperature 20 to 30 minutes before carving.

Nutrients per 4-ounce serving of roast turkey without skin:
186 calories per serving: 6 g. fat, 33 g. protein,
0 carbohydrate, 86 mg. cholesterol, 79 mg. sodium.
For exchange diets, count 5 very lean meat.

DRESSING
Preparation time: 20 minutes
Baking time: 45 minutes
12 servings—3/4 cup each

nonstick cooking spray
4 cups fresh bread crumbs
1/2 cup skim milk
1 cup no-added-salt chicken broth
1 medium onion, diced
1 tablespoon margarine, melted
1/2 pound turkey sausage, browned and drained
2 ribs celery, diced fine
1/4 cup raisins
1/4 cup cranberries
1 teaspoon sage

1. Preheat oven to 350° F.

2. Spray a 2-quart casserole dish with cooking spray. Combine all ingredients in the casserole dish.

3. Cover and bake for 35 minutes. Add additional broth if the mixture becomes dry. Remove cover to brown the top for an additional 10 minutes of baking.

If desired, stuff dressing inside the turkey just before roasting, and follow the roasting time on the chart.

177 calories per serving: 5 g. fat, 8 g. protein,
21 g. carbohydrate, 14 mg. cholesterol, 186 mg. sodium.
For exchange diets, count 1 lean meat, 1/2 fruit, 1 starch, 1/2 fat.

CRISPY OVEN CHICKEN

Preparation time: 10 minutes
Baking time: 40-50 minutes
4 servings—4 ounces each

2 egg whites, whipped
1 1/2 cups evaporated skim milk
1 teaspoon poultry seasoning
3 cups crushed cornflakes (crush in a zippered plastic bag)
1 pound skinless, boneless chicken pieces
nonstick cooking spray

1. Preheat oven to 400° F.

2. Combine egg whites, milk, and seasoning in a shallow mixing bowl. Whip for 2 minutes.

3. Dip chicken in milk mixture, then shake in the bag with the cornflakes and place on a baking sheet that has been sprayed with cooking spray. Bake for 40 to 50 minutes.

215 calories per serving: 9 g. fat, 21 g. protein,
7 g. carbohydrate, 66 mg. cholesterol, 230 mg. sodium.
For exchange diets, count 3 lean meat, 1/2 bread/starch.

SHRIMP CREOLE
Preparation time: 10 minutes
Cooking time: 35 minutes
8 servings—1 cup each

1 tablespoon reduced fat margarine
1 tablespoon olive oil
1 cup chopped onion
1 cup chopped celery
1/2 cup chopped green pepper
1 teaspoon thyme
1 minced garlic clove
1 bay leaf
3 cups chopped tomatoes
2 tablespoons tomato paste
1/2 teaspoon salt
1/4 teaspoon black pepper
3/4 pound raw shelled and deveined shrimp
1/4 cup fresh parsley

1. In a large skillet, heat margarine and olive oil; add onion, celery, green pepper, thyme, garlic, and bay leaf. Saute' just until vegetables are soft.

2. Add tomatoes, tomato paste, salt, and pepper; bring to a boil.

3. Add shrimp; reduce heat to simmer. Simmer, stirring occasionally, for 30 minutes.

4. Add parsley; simmer for 2 minutes. Serve over rice.

102 calories per serving: 4 g. fat, 10 g. protein,
9 g. carbohydrate,65 mg. cholesterol, 281 mg. sodium.
For exchange diets, count 1 lean meat, 2 vegetable.

SMASHED POTATOES

This potato side dish complements anything from baked chicken to grilled hamburgers.

Preparation time: 5 minutes
6 servings—3/4 cup each

4 large potatoes, cut, and cooked with the skins on (still warm)
2 tablespoons fat-free cream cheese
2 tablespoons low fat buttermilk
2 tablespoons thinly sliced green onion
1/2 teaspoon garlic salt
1/4 teaspoon black pepper

1. Place potatoes in a large saucepan. Cover potatoes with water. Bring to a boil; cover and simmer for about 30 minutes, or until potatoes are cooked through.

2. As soon as potatoes are done, combine all ingredients, and smash with a potato masher until almost smooth. If potatoes are dry, add additional buttermilk.

154 calories per serving: 0 fat, 4 g. protein,
35 g. carbohydrate,0 cholesterol, 209 mg. sodium.
For exchange diets, count 2 starch.

RED BEANS AND RICE

A favorite in the southern United States and throughout Latin America.

Preparation time: 15 minutes
Cooking time: 2 1/2 hours
8 servings— 3/4 cup each

---

2 cups water
1 cup dried red kidney beans
2 slices cubed lean bacon
1/2 cup chopped onion
1/2 cup chopped celery
1/4 cup chopped green pepper
1 minced garlic clove
1 cup uncooked medium-grain rice

1. In a large saucepan, heat water and beans to boiling; boil 2 minutes. Cover, remove from heat, and let stand 1 hour. Add additional water to cover beans if necessary.

2. Heat to boiling; reduce heat. Cover and simmer about 1 hour or until beans are soft. Drain and reserve liquid.

3. In a medium skillet, cook remaining ingredients except rice until vegetables are tender and bacon is crisp. Drain well.

4. If necessary, add water to reserved liquid to make 2 cups. Add reserved liquid, bacon mixture, and rice to beans in large saucepan. Heat to boiling, then reduce heat. Cover and simmer 15 minutes. Do not lift cover or stir.

5. Remove from heat; fluff lightly with a fork. Cover and let steam an additional 10 minutes.

....

79 calories per serving: 1 g. fat, 1 g. protein,
13 g. carbohydrate,2 mg. cholesterol, 47 mg. sodium.
For exchange diets, count 1 starch.

SAUTÉED SWEET CORN

A native American staple.

Preparation time: 10 minutes
Cooking time: 10 minutes
8 servings—1/2 cup each

1 1/2 tablespoons reduced-fat margarine
1/4 cup chopped onion
1/4 cup chopped green bell pepper
2 tablespoons chopped red bell pepper
3 cups fresh corn kernels
1/4 teaspoon salt
1/4 teaspoon black pepper
1/8 teaspoon paprika

1. In a large skillet, melt margarine over low heat. Add onion, green pepper, and red pepper; sauté just until vegetables are soft.

2. Add corn; stir-fry 2 to 3 minutes. You may need to add 1 to 2 teaspoons of water if the mixture looks dry.

3. Season with salt, pepper, and paprika.

107 calories per serving: 2 g. fat, 3 g. protein,
23 g. carbohydrate, 0 cholesterol, 100 mg. sodium.
For exchange diets, count 1 1/2 starch.

REUNION BAKED BEANS

Preparation time: 10 minutes
Slow cooker time: 2-3 hours; Conventional oven time: 45 minutes
8 servings—3/4 cup each

4 slices bacon, diced, cooked crisp, and drained
16-ounce can red beans, well drained
16-ounce can red kidney beans, well drained
1/2 cup diced onion
1/2 cup diced celery
1/4 teaspoon garlic powder
1/2 cup catsup
1/2 teaspoon hot pepper sauce
Beano* (optional)

1. Combine all ingredients in a slow cooker or baking dish. Cover and slow cook on high for at least 2 hours or bake in conventional oven at 350° F. for 45 minutes.

*Beano is a liquid product available at most large grocery stores and pharmacies that reduces the gas-producing effects of dried beans, peas, and lentils. It's helpful for people who are just adding beans to their diet and are sensitive to gas-producing foods. The gastrointestinal tract eventually adapts to a high fiber diet and gas production lessens as legumes become part of the routine diet.

113 calories per serving: 2 g. fat, 8 g. protein,
19 g. carbohydrate, 2 mg. cholesterol, 554 mg. sodium.
For exchange diets, count: 1 starch, 1 very lean meat.

STRAWBERRY PIE

You can also use fresh peaches with peach gelatin in this recipe.

Preparation time: 15 minutes
Chilling time: 1 1/2 hours
8 servings—1 slice each

Crust:
　　1 reduced-fat prepared graham cracker crust
Filling:
　　4 cups sliced strawberries
　　3/4 cup sugar
　　1 cup water
　　3 tablespoons cornstarch
　　3 tablespoons corn syrup
　　3 tablespoons strawberry-flavored gelatin
Topping:
　　8 ounces 1% fat vanilla yogurt

1. Place sliced berries on the crust.

2. Combine sugar, water, cornstarch, and corn syrup in a saucepan. Boil for 2 minutes, stirring constantly.

3. Remove the pan from the heat, and stir in gelatin. Pour mixture over the berries. Chill for at least 1 1/2 hours.

4. Serve with vanilla yogurt. For best results, make this dessert within 4 to 18 hours of service.

194 calories per serving: 4 g. fat, 1 g. protein,
37 g. carbohydrate, 2 mg. cholesterol, 94 mg. sodium.
For exchange diets, count: 2 fruit, 1/2 starch, 1 fat.

CHOCOLATE CHIP COOKIES

Preparation time: 20 minutes
Baking time: 12 minutes
24 servings—1 cookie each

1/4 cup light corn syrup
1/4 cup brown sugar
1 tablespoon vegetable oil
2 whole eggs or 1/2 cup liquid egg substitute
1 teaspoon vanilla
1/2 cup nonfat sour cream
2/3 cup flour
1/2 teaspoon baking soda
1/2 teaspoon salt
1 1/2 cups quick cooking oats
2 tablespoons wheat germ
1/2 cup chocolate chips
nonfat cooking spray

1. Preheat oven to 375° F.

2. In a large mixing bowl, cream corn syrup, brown sugar, and oil
with an electric mixer on low speed until the mixture is smooth and
creamy.

3. Beat in eggs, vanilla, and sour cream.

4. In a medium mixing bowl, combine flour, soda, salt, oats, and
wheat germ. Fold dry ingredients into egg and sugar mixture. Fold in
chocolate chips.

5. Drop rounded tablespoons of dough on a baking sheet that has
been sprayed with cooking spray. Flatten cookies slightly with the
spoon. Bake for 12 minutes or until lightly browned. Cool cookies
slightly before removing them from the pan. Store cookies in the
freezer.

83 calories per serving: 2 g. fat, 2 g. protein,
14 g. carbohydrate,1 mg. cholesterol with egg substitute
(14 mg. with real egg), 21 mg. sodium.
For exchange diets, count 1 starch.

APPLE PIE

Preparation time: 20 minutes
Baking time: 1 hour
8 servings—1 slice each

9-inch unbaked pie crust
6 large baking apples, peeled and sliced thin
1/2 cup sugar
1/2 cup apple juice concentrate
1/2 cup flour
1 teaspoon cinnamon
1/4 teaspoon nutmeg
1/4 cup brown sugar
1/2 cup flour
1/4 cup butter-flavored reduced-fat margarine

1. Preheat oven to 350° F.

2. Prick crust with fork 6 to 8 times. Place sliced apples in the pie crust, and set aside.

3. In a small mixing bowl, mix together sugar, apple juice concentrate, 1/2 cup flour, cinnamon, and nutmeg. Toss with apples until they are well coated.

4. In the same mixing bowl, mix brown sugar, 1/2 cup flour, and margarine until crumbly. Sprinkle over the apples. Bake for 1 hour.

305 calories per serving: 9 g. fat, 2 g. protein,
56 g. carbohydrate,0 cholesterol, 203 mg. sodium.
For exchange diets, count: 2 starch, 1 1/2 fruit, 1 fat.

PUMPKIN PIE

Preparation time: 10 minutes
Baking time: 55 minutes
12 servings—1 slice each

9-inch reduced-fat prepared graham cracker crust, unbaked
16-ounce can solid pack pumpkin
13-ounce can evaporated skim milk
2/3 cup packed brown sugar
3 eggs or 3/4 cup liquid egg substitute
1 teaspoon pumpkin pie spice
1 teaspoon vanilla
1/4 teaspoon salt

1. Preheat oven to 375° F.

2. In a blender container or large mixing bowl, blend or beat all ingredients except crust until well blended. Pour into crust.

3. Bake on bottom rack of oven until a knife inserted 1 inch from the edge comes out clean, about 55 minutes. Cool on a wire rack.

198 calories per serving: 6 g. fat, 25 g. protein,
31 g. carbohydrate, 53 mg. cholesterol, 214 mg. sodium.
For exchange diets, count 1 starch, 1 fruit, 1 fat.

Chapter Two

Mexico

Suggested Mexican Menus

Sangria
Artichoke Salad With Cilantro
Chicken Tacos With Fruit Salsa
Mexican Rice

Tortilla Soup
Jalapeño Cornbread
Vegetable Burrito
Mexican Coffee

Add Fun, Subtract Expense

Enjoy roasted sweet corn sprinkled with lime juice.

Try to sort out all the different Mexican peppers on the market. Argbol chili peppers are slim, curved, 3 to 5 inch bright red pods that are almost as hot as cayenne peppers. Chili pizuin, also known as a bird's eye pepper, is small, red, and fiery hot and must be used with extreme caution. Chipotle peppers are considered a delicacy in Mexico for their rich smoky flavor. The serrano pepper is more pungent and spicy than the larger jalapeño. Authentic Mexican salsa includes tomatillos, a round, cherry-like fruit.

If tortillas are a family favorite, consider purchasing a terra-cotta tortilla steamer (about $18). Just soak the base in water, fill with tortillas, and heat in the microwave. The damp heat keeps tortillas soft and pliable throughout the meal.

Make your own salsa with a salsa machine. The hand-cranked processor whips up salsa in seconds, and there is only one container to wash.

Salsa and chip lovers, put a "baja bowl" on your wish list. This unique bowl with a beveled lip allows you to push more salsa onto each chip, and its angular design prevents spillage during dipping (about $15).

The prickly pear is a Mexican fruit that is available in the fall and is well suited for salads, jams, and jellies.

Try a margarita cocktail:
Stir 1 1/2 ounces tequila and 1/2 ounce triple sec with juice from 1/2 lemon or lime and crushed ice. Rub the rim of a cocktail glass with lemon or lime, then dip rim in salt, and fill the glass with mixture.

Try a Mexicola:
Mix 2 ounces tequila and the juice of 1/2 lime in a tall collins glass. Add ice cubes. Fill the glass with cola, and stir gently.

To create a Mexican-spiced meal at home, use cilantro, garlic, chili powder, cinnamon, oregano, chili peppers, and cumin.

MEXICAN HOT COCOA

This homemade hot chocolate with a hint of cinnamon will warm you on a wintry day. For a quick version, prepare instant hot cocoa as directed on package; add a drop of almond extract, and sprinkle with cinnamon.

Preparation time: 5 minutes
6 servings—6 ounces each

1/2 cup sugar
1/4 cup unsweetened cocoa
1/3 cup hot water
4 cups skim milk
2 teaspoons cinnamon
1/2 teaspoon almond extract

1. In a medium saucepan, stir together sugar and cocoa; add hot water. Bring to a boil over medium heat, stirring constantly. Stir constantly while boiling for 2 minutes.

2. Add milk and cinnamon; stir and heat through. Do not boil.

3. Remove from heat; add almond extract. Beat until foamy.

158 calories per serving: 1 g. fat, 8 g. protein,
29 g. carbohydrate, 3 mg. cholesterol, 93 mg. sodium.
For exchange diets, count 1 skim milk, 1 fruit.

MARGARITA

A must for a Mexican fiesta.
Preparation time: 5 minutes
2 servings—6 ounces each

Margarita:
1 ounce gold tequila
1 ounce orange-flavored liqueur
2 ounces sweet & sour mix
splash Rose's lime*
1 cup crushed ice

Glass:
2 lime slices with 1 small cut to center
coarse salt

1. In a blender, blend all ingredients for margaritas just until smooth.

2. Rub rims of 2 glasses with lime wheel; dip rims in salt.

3. Pour frozen margarita into prepared glasses. Garnish with lime wheel.

* A West Indian sweetened lime juice, packaged in a bottle and found in most supermarkets in the beverage section.

133 calories per serving: 0 fat, 0 protein,
10 g. carbohydrate, 0 cholesterol, 8 mg. sodium.
For exchange diets, count 2 fruit.

TEQUILA SUNRISE

A colorful drink for brunch.

Preparation time: 5 minutes
2 servings—6 ounces each

1 1/2 ounces tequila
6 ounces orange juice
10 ice cubes
1/2 ounce grenadine

1. Shake together tequila, orange juice, and ice cubes. Strain into 2 glasses, then add fresh ice cubes.

2. Slowly add grenadine. Colors will layer to look like a beautiful sunrise.

90 calories per serving: 0 fat, 2 g. protein,
10 g. carbohydrate, 0 cholesterol, 12 mg. sodium.
For exchange diets, count 1 1/2 fruit.

SANGRIA

Preparation time: 10 minutes
Chilling time: 30 minutes
8 servings—8 ounces each

1 liter red wine (may substitute no-alcohol red wine)
1/4 cup Grand Marnier (may substitute 1 tablespoon
  orange extract)
2 tablespoons brandy
1/4 cup fresh-squeezed orange juice
1 tablespoon sugar
2 large oranges, cut into thin slices, then cut in half
1 large lemon, cut into thin slices, then cut in half
1 large peach, cut into thin wedges
12-ounce bottle sparkling water
ice cubes

1. In a large pitcher, combine all ingredients except the sparkling water and ice cubes. Refrigerate for at least 30 minutes.

2. Add sparkling water just before serving. Pour into large clear goblets filled with ice cubes.

73 calories per serving: g. fat, g. protein,
8 g. carbohydrate, 0 cholesterol, 5 mg. sodium.
For exchange diets, count 1 fruit.

WHITE WINE SANGRIA

Traditional Sangria is made with red wine. This lighter version made with white wine complements a spicy Mexican meal.

Preparation time: 10 minutes
Cooking time: 5 minutes
Chilling time: 2 hours
12 servings—5 ounces each

1 cup orange juice
1/2 cup sugar
1.5 liter bottle white wine, nonalcoholic wine, or sparkling
  grape juice
1/4 cup lemon juice
1 orange, cut into thin slices, then cut in half
1 lime, cut into thin slices, then cut in half
1 lemon, cut into thin slices, then cut in half
1/2 cup lemon-lime soda

1. In a medium saucepan, combine orange juice and sugar. Cook over medium heat, stirring occasionally, until sugar is dissolved. Pour into a 2-quart pitcher.

2. Add all remaining ingredients except soda to orange juice mixture. Stir. Cover tightly and refrigerate 2 hours.

3. Just before serving, add soda. Serve over ice in tall glasses.

118 calories per serving: 0 fat, 0 protein,
12 g. carbohydrate, 0 cholesterol, 8 mg. sodium.
For exchange diets, count 2 fruit.

MEXICAN COFFEE

Use regular or decaffeinated coffee, depending on your preference.

Preparation time: 5 minutes
1 serving—1 cup each

1 ounce coffee-flavored liqueur
6 ounces hot coffee
2 teaspoons reduced-fat whipped cream

1. Place liqueur in a large mug. Add coffee; top with whipped cream.

121 calories per serving: 2 g. fat, 0 protein,
17 g. carbohydrate, 0 cholesterol, 2 mg. sodium.
For exchange diets, count 1 1/2 fruit.

GREEN CHILI SALSA

Try this salsa when fresh, ripe tomatoes aren't available.

Preparation time: 10 minutes
Cooking time: 20 minutes
12 servings—2 tablespoons each

2 tablespoons chopped onion
1 minced garlic clove
1 tablespoon olive oil
14 1/2-ounce can whole tomatoes, chopped (undrained)
1/2 cup water
4-ounce can chopped green chilies
2 teaspoons vinegar
1/2 teaspoon oregano
1/2 teaspoon salt
1 tablespoon chopped cilantro

1. In a medium skillet, cook onion and garlic in olive oil just until soft.

2. Stir in remaining ingredients except cilantro. Simmer 20 minutes, stirring occasionally.

3. Stir in cilantro.

23 calories per serving: 1 g. fat, 0 protein,
3 g. carbohydrate, 0 cholesterol, 175 mg. sodium.
For exchange diets, count 1 vegetable.

DIP OLÉ

This festive layered appetizer is served with tortilla chips.

Preparation time: 10 minutes
16 servings—1/2 cup each

16-ounce can fat-free refried beans
1 cup fat-free sour cream
1 cup taco sauce
3 cups shredded lettuce
1/2 cup reduced-fat cheddar cheese
1/2 cup chopped ripe tomatoes
1/4 cup chopped red onion
2 tablespoons sliced black olives

1. On a large round serving plate, spread refried beans. Spread sour cream evenly over beans. Spread taco sauce evenly over sour cream.

2. Layer remaining ingredients in the order listed.

76 calories per serving: 2 g. fat, 6 g. protein,
10 g. carbohydrate, 5 mg. cholesterol, 360 mg. sodium.
For exchange diets, count 1 skim milk.

PICO DE GALLO

My friend Toni Schuster shares this Mexican pleasure.

Preparation time: 15 minutes
12 servings—1/2 cup each

---

6 jalapeño peppers, seeded and chopped fine (note: always wear
  rubber gloves when working with hot peppers)
1 large yellow onion, chopped fine
4 medium fresh tomatoes, peeled, seeded, and chopped
3/4 teaspoon minced garlic
1/4 cup fresh cilantro, minced
2 tablespoons olive oil
3 tablespoons red wine vinegar

1. Combine all ingredients in a bowl. Cover and chill until serving.
Use as a topping on any Mexican dish or use as a dip with reduced-
fat taco chips.

....

40 calories per serving: 2 g. fat, 1 g. protein,
4 g. carbohydrate, 0 cholesterol, 132 mg. sodium.
For exchange diets, count 1 vegetable, 1/2 fat.

CHILI CON QUESO

A reduced fat, microwaveable version of hot, spicy cheese dip.
Serve with low-fat tortilla chips for a great hit at a Mexican party!

Preparation time: 5 minute
Cooking time: 4 minutes
30 servings—1 ounce each

1 pound light processed cheese product, cubed
10-ounce can diced tomatoes with green chilies
4-1/2-ounce can chopped green chilies

1. In a medium microwaveable, bowl combine all ingredients. Cook in the microwave on high for 4 minutes or until cheese is melted, stirring after each minute.

40 calories per serving: 2 g. fat, 3 g. protein,
2 g. carbohydrate, 0 cholesterol, 291 mg. sodium.
For exchange diets, count 1 lean meat.

BEAN DIP

Add more or less salsa to achieve the consistency desired.
Salsas vary in thickness depending on the tomatoes used.

Preparation time: 5 minutes
Cooking time: 5 minutes
8 servings—1/3 cup each

16-ounce can fat-free refried beans
1 cup salsa
1/4 cup minced onion

1. In a medium saucepan stir together all ingredients; heat through.

53 calories per 1/3 cup serving: 0 fat, 4 g. protein,
12 g. carbohydrate, 0 cholesterol, 529 mg. sodium.
For exchange diets, count 2 vegetable.

SALSA

This fat-free delight goes with everything from chips to grilled seafood. For hotter salsa, add more jalapeños. For less heat, remove seeds from jalapeño.

Preparation time: 5 minutes
6 servings—1/3 cup each

---

2 chopped large ripe tomatoes
1/4 cup chopped onion
1/4 cup chopped cilantro
1 finely chopped jalapeño pepper (note: always wear rubber gloves when working with hot peppers)
1 minced garlic clove
1 tablespoon lime or lemon juice
1/8 teaspoon black pepper
1/8 teaspoon salt

1. In a medium bowl, combine all ingredients; refrigerate, or serve immediately.

13 calories per serving: 0 fat, 1 g. protein,
3 g. carbohydrate, 0 cholesterol, 41 mg. sodium.
For exchange diets, count it as a free food.

CEVICHE

Only fresh fish can be used for this appetizer. You can use red snapper, oysters, halibut, or clams instead of shrimp and scallops—just omit step one.

Preparation time: 10 minutes
Cooking time: 2 minutes; Chilling time: overnight
10 servings—1/2 cup each

Seafood:
　　1 cup peeled, deveined fresh shrimp
　　1 cup fresh sea scallops
Sauce:
　　3/4 cup fresh lemon juice
　　1 cup chopped tomato
　　1/2 cup thinly sliced green onions
　　1 seeded, chopped jalapeño (note: always wear rubber gloves
　　　when working with hot peppers)
　　2 tablespoons chopped fresh cilantro
　　2 tablespoons ketchup
　　4 drops hot pepper sauce

1. In a large saucepan, bring about 2 cups of water (enough to cover seafood) to boil; add shrimp and scallops, and boil 1 1/2 minutes. Drain and cut into bite-size pieces.

2. Place seafood in a glass bowl. Add remaining ingredients, and stir to mix. Cover and refrigerate overnight.

3. Serve with tortilla chips or melba toast.

53 calories per serving: 1 g. fat, 9 g. protein,
3 g. carbohydrate, 42 mg. cholesterol, 107 mg. sodium.
For exchange diets, count 1 very lean meat, 1 vegetable.

SPINACH QUESADILLAS

The filling possibilities for this Mexican appetizer are endless.
Eat as is or pass the salsa!

Preparation time: 10 minutes
Cooking time: 5 minutes
8 servings—3 quesadillas each

---

1 cup thawed and drained frozen chopped spinach
1/4 cup thinly sliced green onions
1 minced garlic clove
2 teaspoons olive oil
8 fat-free flour tortillas slightly warmed in microwave
1/2 cup shredded hot pepper cheese

1. In a medium skillet, cook spinach, onion, and garlic in olive oil just until vegetables are soft.

2. Spoon spinach mixture equally on 4 tortillas. Divide cheese evenly over spinach. Top each with another tortilla.

3. Warm quesadillas one at a time for about 20 seconds in the microwave or just until cheese melts. Cut each into 6 pie-shaped wedges.

183 calories per serving: 6 g. fat, 7 g. protein,
21 g. carbohydrate, 0 cholesterol, 265 mg. sodium.
For exchange diets, count 1 vegetable, 1 starch,
1 very lean meat, 1 fat.

JALAPEÑO CORNBREAD

Preparation time: 10 minutes
Bread machine time: 4 hours, 10 minutes
Manual method: 2 hours, 30 minutes
24 servings—1/2 slice each

1/4 cup water
1 cup cream-style corn
2 ounces reduced fat shredded cheddar cheese
3 1/4 cups white bread flour
2 teaspoons sugar
3 tablespoons cornmeal
2 tablespoons nonfat dry milk powder
1 teaspoon salt
1 teaspoon yeast
1 tablespoon soft margarine
1/3 cup chunky salsa
1 medium jalapeño pepper, seeded, rinsed and finely chopped
(note: always wear rubber gloves when working with hot peppers)

1. Place first 10 ingredients in the order listed in a bread machine pan. Select "add bread" from menu, and push "start." Wait approximately 30 minutes for the beeper, then add salsa and chopped pepper.

2. Loaf will be done in 4 hours and 10 minutes using a Hitachi bread machine.

3. Serve this bread with a bowl of tortilla soup.

4. If you prefer making bread from scratch: gently mix 1/4 cup hot tap water with sugar, dry milk powder, yeast, salt, and margarine in a large mixing bowl. Allow mixture to rest 5 minutes. Stir in creamed corn and cheese, then gradually add flour and cornmeal, working the mixture to a smooth dough. Fold in salsa and chopped pepper. Knead for 10 minutes, then cover and allow dough to rise for 1 hour in a warm place. Punch the dough down, form a loaf shape and place in a loaf pan that has been sprayed with nonstick cooking spray. Allow dough to rise again, then bake in a preheated 350° oven for 25 minutes or until the top is browned. Cool for 15 minutes, then remove bread to a cooling rack.

111 calories per 1/2 slice serving: 3 g. fat, 3 g. protein, 18 g. carbohydrate, 2 mg. cholesterol, 116 mg. sodium. For exchange diets, count 1 starch, 1/2 fat.

TORTILLA SOUP

This soup is usually garnished with strips of fried tortillas.
Crumbled fat-free tortilla chips make a great substitute.

Preparation time: 10 minutes
Cooking time: 20 minutes
8 servings—3/4 cup each

14 1/2-ounce can undrained tomatoes

1 cup diced onion

2 tablespoons cilantro

1 minced garlic clove

1/4 teaspoon sugar

5 cups fat-free chicken broth

1/4 teaspoon cumin

1/4 teaspoon black pepper

1/2 cup shredded reduced-fat Monterey Jack cheese

1/2 cup crumbled fat-free tortilla chips

1. In a blender, combine tomatoes, onion, cilantro, garlic, and sugar; blend until chunky.

2. In a large saucepan, combine tomato mixture and chicken broth; simmer 20 minutes. Add cumin and pepper.

3. Pour hot soup into bowls. Sprinkle with cheese and tortilla chips. Serve immediately.

119 calories per serving: 3 g. fat, 7 g. protein,
16 g. carbohydrate, 10 mg. cholesterol, 489 mg. sodium.
For exchange diets, count 3 vegetable, 1 fat.

ARTICHOKE SALAD WITH CILANTRO-BASIL DRESSING

Preparation time: 10 minutes
8 servings—1/2 cup each

2 16-ounce cans artichoke hearts

Dressing:

3/4 cup cider vinegar

1/4 teaspoon salt

1 teaspoon freshly ground pepper

1 tablespoon sugar

1 tablespoon dried basil

1 cup fresh cilantro, chopped

1 teaspoon minced garlic

1/4 cup olive oil

Chopped fresh greens

1. Drain artichoke hearts, and cut into bite-sized pieces. Place in a salad bowl.

2. In a shaker container, combine the ingredients for the dressing. Pour over artichokes, cover, and refrigerate until serving. Serve on a bed of chopped fresh greens.

133 calories per serving: 5 g. fat, 5 g. protein,
17 g. carbohydrate, 0 cholesterol, 129 mg. sodium.
For exchange diets, count 3 vegetable, 1 fat.

BEEF TACOS

This is Tyler and Zachary's favorite supper.

Preparation time: 15 minutes; Cooking time: 25 minutes
10 servings—1 taco each

Meat filling:
    1 pound lean ground beef
    1/4 cup chopped onion
    1 minced garlic clove
    1 teaspoon minced jalapeño pepper (fresh or canned)
    1/2 cup tomato sauce
    1 tablespoon cooking sherry
    2 teaspoons brown sugar
    3/4 teaspoon chili powder
    1/2 teaspoon crushed oregano
    1/4 teaspoon salt
    1/4 teaspoon black pepper
    1/4 teaspoon ground cumin
    1/8 teaspoon cinnamon

Tacos:
    10 warmed fat-free flour tortillas or taco shells

Meat filling:
    1/4 cup fat-free sour cream
    2 1/2 cups shredded lettuce
    1/2 cup reduced-fat Cheddar cheese
    taco sauce

1. In a large skillet, brown beef; add onion, garlic, and jalapeño pepper. Cook 2 to 3 minutes until onion is soft; drain thoroughly.

2. Add remaining ingredients for meat filling. Simmer, stirring frequently, for about 15 minutes.

3. Fill each tortilla or taco shell with sour cream, meat filling, lettuce, and cheese. If using tortillas, roll up, tucking one end in so filling will stay inside. Pass the taco sauce.

244 calories per serving: 8 g. fat, 19 g. protein,
24 g. carbohydrate, 56 mg. cholesterol, 275 mg. sodium.
For exchange diets, count 1 starch, 2 lean meat, 2 vegetable.

VEGETABLE BURRITOS

A meatless entrée.

Preparation time: 10 minutes
Cooking time: 10 minutes
6 servings—1 burrito each

1 cup chopped zucchini
1/2 cup corn kernels
1/4 cup chopped onion
1/4 cup chopped mushrooms
1/4 cup water
1 teaspoon chili powder
1/2 teaspoon garlic salt
1/4 teaspoon cumin
1 cup drained black beans
1 cup cooked brown rice
6 warmed fat-free flour tortillas

1. In a medium saucepan, simmer zucchini, corn, onion, and mushrooms in water about 5 minutes. Add chili powder, garlic salt, and cumin, and simmer 5 additional minutes. Remove from heat.

2. Add beans and rice to vegetable mixture; stir to mix. Spoon equal amounts of the vegetable/rice mixture down the center of each tortilla; roll up, tucking the ends in.

3. Burritos may be warmed further in the microwave if desired. Serve with taco sauce or salsa.

196 calories per serving: 1 g. fat, 8 g. protein,
40 g. carbohydrate, 0 cholesterol, 349 mg. sodium.
For exchange diets, count 2 starch, 2 vegetable.

CHILI VERDE BURRITOS

Pork tenderloin and tomatillos give this main dish a Tex-Mex flair.

Preparation time: 15 minutes
Cooking time: 25 minutes
8 servings—1 burrito each

Chili Verde:
1/2 cup chopped onion
2 teaspoons reduced-fat margarine
3/4 pound cooked, cubed lean pork tenderloin
1 minced clove garlic
1/2 teaspoon salt
1/2 teaspoon cumin
3 finely chopped tomatillos (remove husks)
4-ounce can chopped green chilies
1 finely chopped green tomato
1 1/2 tablespoons sugar
1/2 cup fat-free chicken broth

Burritos:
8 warmed fat-free flour tortillas
1/2 cup fat-free sour cream
1 cup salsa

1. In a large skillet, cook onion in margarine until soft. Add pork and garlic; cook, stirring frequently, for 2 minutes.

2. Add remaining ingredients for chili verde, and simmer 20 minutes. Additional chicken stock may be added if necessary for desired consistency.

3. Spoon equal amounts chili verde onto flour tortillas; roll up, tucking the ends in. Top each with 1 tablespoon sour cream. Garnish with 2 tablespoons salsa.

256 calories per serving: 7 g. fat, 17 g. protein,
31 g. carbohydrate, 34 mg. cholesterol, 645 mg. sodium.
For exchange diets, count 2 starch, 2 lean meat.

CHICKEN AND
SOUR CREAM BURRITOS

You can make this dish the day before and refrigerate in a nonmetal pan.
Then just bake and add toppings!

Preparation time: 20 minutes
Baking time: 20 minutes
10 servings—1 burrito each

Chicken filling:
  3 cups cooked, shredded, boneless, skinless chicken breast
  1/2 cup chopped onion
  1-1/4-ounce package taco seasoning
  water

Sauce:
  10-3/4-oz. can reduced-fat cream of chicken soup
  1 cup nonfat sour cream
  4-ounce can chopped green chilies

Enchiladas:
  10 large fat-free flour tortillas
  1 cup shredded part-skim mozzarella cheese

Topping:
  1 cup shredded part-skim mozzarella cheese
  2 cups shredded lettuce
  1/2 cup chopped tomato
  1/4 cup chopped red onion

1. In a large skillet, combine chicken, onion, and taco seasoning mix. Add water according to package directions, and simmer according to directions on taco seasoning packet.

2. Preheat oven to 350°. In a medium bowl, stir together all ingredients for sauce. Place 1/3 of sauce mixture in bottom of 13" x 9" pan; set aside.

3. Assemble burritos by dividing chicken mixture and 1 cup mozzarella cheese evenly among tortillas; roll tortillas, and place on sauce in pan.

Chicken and Sour Cream Burritos (continued)

4. Pour remaining sauce mixture over burritos. Top with 1 cup mozzarella cheese. Bake for 20 minutes or until heated through. If made ahead and refrigerated, bake an additional 10 minutes.

5. Combine lettuce, tomato and onion. Place on top of burritos.

....

391 calories per serving: 11 g. fat, 38 g. protein,
33 g. carbohydrate, 85 mg. cholesterol, 807 mg. sodium
(To reduce sodium, choose reduced-sodium taco seasoning mix.)
For exchange diets, count 2 starch, 4 lean meat.

SPICY RED SNAPPER

Preparation time: 15 minutes
Cooking time: 20 minutes
8 servings—6 ounces fish each

2 tablespoons margarine
1 tablespoon olive oil
8 6-ounce red snapper fillets, thawed
1 large white onion, chopped fine
1/2 teaspoon minced garlic
juice of 2 limes
6 large tomatoes, peeled, seeded, and chopped
2 whole jalapeño peppers, seeded and chopped
1/4 teaspoon black pepper
1 bunch fresh cilantro, chopped

1. In a large skillet, heat margarine and olive oil over medium heat. Sauté red snapper fillets for 4 minutes on each side or until they are golden.

2. Remove the fish from the pan and transfer to a warm platter. Add onion and garlic to the pan, and cook for 3 minutes. Add lime juice, tomatoes, and jalapeños; stir. Reduce heat to low, and cook uncovered for 4 to 6 minutes.

3. Add black pepper to the pan, and return fish to the pan. Spoon some of the sauce over the fillets. Cover, and continue heating on low for 4 to 6 minutes or until fish is flaky. Transfer fish and sauce to a platter, and garnish with chopped cilantro.

243 calories per serving: 7 g. fat, 36 g. protein,
8 g. carbohydrate, 70 mg. cholesterol, 276 mg. sodium.
For exchange diets, count 5 very lean meat, 2 vegetable.

FAJITAS

Genuine fajitas are made from charbroiled beef skirt steak sliced very thin and served with flour tortillas. Other condiments generally served with fajitas are lettuce, tomato, sautéed onions and green peppers, and hot sauce. Many restaurants now serve chicken and seafood "fajitas." Although not authentic, they are equally delicious. Use the same marinade for seafood and chicken.

Preparation time: 15 minutes
Marinating time: 24 hours for beef;
30 minutes to 4 hours for seafood or chicken
Cooking time: 15 minutes
6 servings—1 fajita each

Marinade:

1/4 cup reduced-sodium soy sauce
2 tablespoons Worcestershire sauce
2 tablespoons lime juice
1 tablespoon dry red wine
1 tablespoon unsweetened pineapple juice
1 tablespoon olive oil
2 crushed garlic cloves
1/4 teaspoon black pepper
1/8 teaspoon hot pepper sauce

Fajitas:

1 pound beef skirt steak
1 cup sliced onion
1/2 cup sliced green pepper
6 fat-free flour tortillas

1. In a medium bowl, combine all ingredients for marinade; reserve 2 tablespoons.

2. Place steak in a dish; pour marinade over steak (except 2 tablespoons). Cover and refrigerate 24 hours. You must marinate for at least 24 hours to tenderize this tough cut of beef.

3. Pour reserved marinade over onion and green pepper slices. You may wrap mixture in foil and cook on the grill with the beef, or you may simmer slowly in a medium skillet about 5 minutes or until soft.

4. Cook meat on charcoal grill over hot coals about 5 to 7 minutes on each side, depending on thickness of meat. Cut beef across the grain into thin slices.

5. Serve meat and pepper and onion mixture with tortillas. Diners can wrap the meat and vegetables in the tortilla and roll it up like a burrito, or they can put one bite of meat and vegetables in a corner of the tortilla and eat and roll as they go.

197 calories per serving: 9 g. fat, 13 g. protein,
16 g. carbohydrate, 24 mg. cholesterol, 578 mg. sodium.
For exchange diets, count 1 starch, 2 lean meat.

CHICKEN MOLE

Mole is a Mexican sauce that varies from region to region. Two surprising ingredients that are usually found in mole sauce are chocolate and peanut butter. Reduced-fat peanut butter is used to ensure an authentic flavor.

Preparation time: 10 minutes
Cooking time: 15 minutes
2 servings—1 chicken breast half each

Chicken:
>   2 boneless, skinless chicken breast halves
>   1 teaspoon chili powder
>   1/4 teaspoon garlic salt
>   1/4 teaspoon black pepper
>   1 tablespoon olive oil

Sauce:
>   14-ounce can Mexican-style stewed tomatoes
>   1 teaspoon chili powder
>   1 teaspoon reduced-fat peanut butter
>   1/4 teaspoon cumin
>   1/4 teaspoon cinnamon
>   1/4 ounce unsweetened chocolate

1. Sprinkle chili powder, garlic salt, and pepper on chicken. Heat oil in a medium skillet. Add chicken and brown about 2 minutes on each side. Remove chicken; set aside.

2. Add all sauce ingredients except chocolate to skillet; stir and heat through. Add chocolate; simmer about 5 minutes or until sauce thickens.

3. Add chicken to sauce, and cook for about 4 minutes until chicken is just cooked through.

---

265 calories per serving: 10 g. fat, 30 g. protein,
13 g. carbohydrate, 73 mg. cholesterol, 745 mg. sodium.
For exchange diets, count 2 vegetable, 4 lean meat.

BEAN TOSTADA

A quick and easy after-school snack.
Preparation time: 5 minutes
1 serving—1 tostada each

1 tostada
2 tablespoons fat-free refried beans
1 tablespoon taco sauce
2 teaspoons reduced-fat Cheddar cheese
1 tablespoon shredded lettuce
1 tablespoon chopped tomato

1. Spread beans over tostada. Spread taco sauce evenly over beans; sprinkle with cheese. Cook in the microwave on high for about 1 minute or just until cheese melts.

2. Sprinkle lettuce and tomato over tostada.

157 calories per serving: 5 g. fat, 8 g. protein,
22 g. carbohydrate, 5 mg. cholesterol, 695 mg. sodium.
For exchange diets, count 1 starch, 1/2 skim milk, 1 fat.

CHICKEN TACOS WITH FRUIT SALSA

*These tacos are delightful for lunch. Plan ahead and grill chicken
breasts along with whatever you are making for dinner the night before.*

Preparation time: 15 minutes
Cooking time: 4 minutes
4 servings—1 taco each

Fruit salsa:

    1 large orange, peeled and cut into bite-size pieces
    1/4 cup chopped red onion
    1/4 cup chopped red pepper
    2 tablespoons cilantro
    1 tablespoon lime juice
    1/4 teaspoon chili powder
    1/4 teaspoon black pepper

Tacos:

    4 grilled boneless, skinless chicken breast halves
    1/4 cup reduced-fat Monterey Jack cheese
    4 slightly warmed fat-free flour tortillas

1. In a small bowl, combine all ingredients for fruit salsa.

2. Shred chicken. Place some shredded chicken on half of each tortilla. Sprinkle 1 tablespoon cheese over chicken on each tortilla. Fold tortilla over chicken mixture.

3. Heat a large nonstick skillet. Cook tacos about 2 minutes on each side or just until cheese is melted. Garnish each taco with fruit salsa.

280 calories per serving: 9 g. fat, 24 g. protein,
26 g. carbohydrate, 44 mg. cholesterol, 280 mg. sodium.
For exchange diets, count 3 lean meat, 2 fruit.

ENCHILADA PIE

A timesaving Mexican dish.

Preparation time: 15 minutes
Cooking time: 30 minutes
9 servings—1 square each

---

1 pound lean ground beef
1/3 cup chopped onion
8-ounce can tomato sauce
1 1/4-ounce package reduced-sodium taco seasoning
10 3/4-ounce can reduced-fat cream of chicken soup
1/2 cup skim milk
12 6-inch corn tortillas cut in half
2 cups reduced-fat Cheddar cheese

1. Preheat oven to 350° F.

2. In a large skillet, brown ground beef and onion; drain. Stir in tomato sauce and taco seasoning. Bring mixture to a boil; reduce heat and simmer 5 minutes. Remove from heat

3. In a medium bowl, stir together soup and milk. Spread half of the soup mixture in a 13" x 9" pan.

4. Place 12 tortilla halves over soup mixture in pan. Spoon meat mixture over tortillas. Top with remaining tortilla halves.

5. Spoon remaining soup mixture over tortillas. Top with cheese.

6. Bake for 30 minutes.

267 calories per serving: 12 g. fat, 16 g. protein,
0 carbohydrate, 76 mg. cholesterol, 110 mg. sodium.
For exchange diets, count 4 lean meat.

the Caribbean, Central & South America

Suggested Central/ South American Menu

Picadillo
Cuban Cornbread
Marta's Cuban Black Bean Soup
Coo-Coo

Suggested Caribbean Menu

Palm Heart Salad
Island Pork Tenderloin
Caribbean Peas and Rice
Bananas Flambé

Add Fun, Subtract Expense

Look for Jamaican ginger, a rich, heavy, sweet spice, perfect for barbecue recipes.

Jerk seasoning is a spice blend with a history that predates Columbus's visit to the new world. Use it with chicken and pork before grilling.

Guava is available in your produce market in the spring and summer and originates in Central America. Guava may be white, yellow, or pink and can be eaten fresh or juiced. Uniq fruit is native to Jamaica and, like its cousin the grapefruit, is available in the winter.

Try a Cuban Special

Shake 1/2 ounce pineapple juice, the juice of 1/2 lime, 1 ounce rum, and 1/2 teaspoon curacao with cracked ice. Strain into a 3-ounce cocktail glass. Garnish with a stick of pineapple and a cherry.

Try a Jamaica Glow Cocktail

Shake 1 ounce dry gin, 1/2 ounce claret, 1/2 ounce orange juice, and 1 teaspoon rum with cracked ice. Strain into a 3-ounce cocktail glass.

Mix a Jamaica Grand

Fill a 12-ounce collins glass with a small scoop of sherbet, 1 1/2 ounces brandy, and 1 ounce curacao. Fill the glass with carbonated water, and stir. Sprinkle nutmeg on the top for garnish.

Try a Cuban Cocktail

Shake the juice of 1/2 lime, 1/2 teaspoon powdered sugar, and 2 ounces rum with cracked ice. Strain into a 3-ounce cocktail glass.

Taste a Brazil Cocktail

Stir 1 1/4 ounces dry vermouth, 1 1/4 ounces sherry wine, 1 dash bitters, and 1/4 teaspoon absinthe substitute with cracked ice. Strain into a 3-ounce cocktail glass.

Caribbean cooking reflects a myriad of flavors from hot and spicy to warm and fruity with the abundance of tropical fruits. The Scotch bonnet pepper is used widely to heighten the heat and spice of jerk barbecue and other meat dishes. Substitute chopped hot chili peppers in your next marinade to liven it up.

Fresh garden and seafood markets are open at least twice weekly in most cities in the Caribbean. The aroma is delightful. Besides the fresh fruits and vegetables, the spices and herbs available are black and green peppercorns, coriander, nutmeg, mace, cinnamon, curry, saffron, cayenne pepper, allspice, ginger, cilantro, cloves, and chili powder. Experiment with a few spices at a time. Add small amounts to taste to your own barbecue sauce, soups, pastas, and main dishes. Create a whole new family favorite!

BLACK BEAN DIP

Serve this low-fat dip with fresh veggies or low-fat tortilla chips.

Preparation time: 5 minutes
8 servings—1/4 cup each

15-ounce can drained black beans
1 tablespoon chopped fresh cilantro
1 minced garlic clove
2 teaspoons lemon juice
2 teaspoons balsamic vinegar
1/2 teaspoon cumin
1/2 teaspoon chili powder
1/4 teaspoon black pepper
1/8 teaspoon salt

1. In a food processor, process all ingredients until smooth.

267 calories per serving: 0 fat, 3 g. protein,
8 g. carbohydrate, 0 cholesterol, 48 mg. sodium.
For exchange diets, count 2 vegetable.

MUENSTER ROLLS

These cheese rolls make any menu special.

Preparation time: 20 minutes
Baking time: 20 minutes
12 servings—1 roll each

12-ounce package hot roll mix
light beer
1 tablespoon margarine, melted
4 ounces Muenster cheese, shredded
nonstick cooking spray

1. Preheat oven to 350°F.

2. Empty hot roll mix into a medium bowl. Follow package directions for preparation of the dough, substituting light beer for the water. Amounts will vary slightly depending on the brand of roll mix you use.

3. Allow the dough to rest, covered, for 5 minutes. Roll out dough on a floured board into a circle.

4. Spread melted margarine over the dough. Sprinkle with cheese. Cut the circle into 12 wedges.

5. Roll each wedge up starting from the wide end. Tuck the point under, and place on a baking sheet that has been sprayed with cooking spray. Bake for 20 minutes or until golden brown.

159 calories per serving: 3 g. fat, 6 g. protein,
34 g. carbohydrate, 8 mg. cholesterol, 133 mg. sodium.
For exchange diets, count 2 starch.

BANANA BREAD

*Just a touch of coconut makes this South American
banana bread extra moist.*

**Preparation time: 20 minutes
Baking time: 1 hour
16 servings—1 slice each**

1 cup sugar
1/4 cup soft margarine
1/2 cup liquid egg substitute (or substitute 2 eggs)
1 1/2 cups mashed ripe banana (3-4 bananas)
1/3 cup water
1 2/3 cups flour
1 teaspoon baking soda
1/2 teaspoon salt
1/4 teaspoon baking powder
1/4 cup coconut
nonstick cooking spray

1. Preheat oven to 350° F.

2. In a large bowl, mix sugar and margarine. Add egg substitute, and
stir until blended. Add bananas and water; beat 30 seconds.

3. Stir in remaining ingredients, except coconut, just until moistened.
Fold in coconut.

4. Spray bottom only of a 9" x 5" x 3" loaf pan with cooking spray.
Pour batter into pan.

5. Bake for about 1 hour or until knife inserted in center comes out
clean.

6. Cool 5 minutes. Loosen sides from pan; remove loaf. Cool completely.

168 calories per serving: 4 g. fat, 3 g. protein,
30 g. carbohydrate, 0 cholesterol with egg substitute
(22 mg. cholesterol with eggs), 105 mg. sodium.
For exchange diets, count 2 starch.

CUBAN CORN BREAD

Preparation time: 15 minutes
Baking time: 45 minutes
24 servings—1 slice each

1/2 cup diced dried pineapple
2 teaspoons rum extract
1/3 cup sugar
1/3 cup soft margarine
2 eggs or 1/2 cup liquid egg substitute
1 cup coconut cream
1 cup yellow cornmeal
1 cup flour
1 1/2 teaspoons baking powder
1/2 teaspoon salt
1/2 teaspoon cinnamon
1/4 teaspoon cloves
1 cup dried coconut
nonstick cooking spray

1. Preheat oven to 375° F.

2. Mix pineapple and rum extract in a small bowl. In a large bowl, beat sugar and margarine together. Add eggs or egg substitute, and beat until well blended.

3. Stir in all remaining ingredients except the coconut until well blended. Fold in pineapple and rum mixture and coconut.

4. Pour batter into a loaf pan that has been sprayed with cooking spray. Bake for 45 minutes or until golden brown. Cool for 15 minutes, then remove from pan and cool on a wire rack.

135 calories per serving: 7 g. fat, 2 g. protein,
16 g. carbohydrate, 20 mg. cholesterol with real egg, 115 mg. sodium.
For exchange diets, count 1 starch, 1 fat.

MARTA'S CUBAN BLACK BEAN SOUP

This recipe came from a special friend who lived in Cuba.

Soaking time: overnight; Preparation time: 15 minutes
Cooking time: 2 1/2 hours

12 servings—1 cup each

Beans:
    1 pound black beans, washed
    6 cups water
Soup:
    water
    1 bay leaf
    6 whole allspice
    1 medium onion, chopped
    1 green pepper, chopped
    4 cloves garlic, minced
    1 tablespoon olive oil
    1/8 teaspoon oregano
    1/8 teaspoon cumin
    1/4 cup dry white wine
Optional:
    salt and pepper

1. Soak beans in water in a stockpot overnight.

2. Add additional water until the water level is 2 inches above the beans.

3. Add bay leaf and allspice, and bring the mixture to a boil. Reduce heat to simmer until the beans are soft, about 1 1/2 hours.

4. Sauté onion, green pepper, and garlic in the olive oil in a skillet until tender. Add vegetable mixture, oregano, cumin, wine, salt, and pepper to the beans. Continue cooking until they are creamy, about 1 hour.

....
59 calories per serving: 1 g. fat, 3 g. protein, 9 g. carbohydrate, 0 cholesterol, 1 mg. sodium. For exchange diets, count 2 vegetable.

MINTED QUINOA SALAD

Look for quinoa next to the rice or grains in your market.

Preparation time: 10 minutes
Cooking time: 20 minutes
8 servings—1 cup each

2 cups quinoa or rice
3 cups no-added-salt chicken broth
2 bunches fresh parsley, washed and minced
1 bunch fresh mint, washed and minced
1 fresh tomato, seeded and chopped
2 green onions, chopped fine
2 tablespoons olive oil
Juice of 2 lemons
Freshly ground black pepper

1. Place the quinoa in a fine strainer, and rinse well. Place in a large saucepan with chicken broth, and bring it to a boil. Reduce heat and simmer for 15 minutes.

2. Place the minced parsley and mint in a serving bowl. Add the tomato, green onion, olive oil, lemon juice, and black pepper.

3. Transfer cooked quinoa to the serving bowl. Toss and serve.

115 calories per serving: 5 g. fat, 3 g. protein,
16 g. carbohydrate, 0 cholesterol, 2 mg. sodium.
For exchange diets, count 1 starch, 1 fat.

PALM HEART SALAD

Preparation time: 15 minutes
8 servings—3/4 cup each

16-ounce can palm hearts, drained
6 ounces frozen peas, thawed and drained
16-ounce can diced beets, drained
1 small onion, minced
1 small cucumber, diced

Dressing:

1/3 cup reduced fat mayonnaise
2 tablespoons vinegar
1 tablespoon sugar
1 tablespoon skim milk
1/2 teaspoon salt
1/2 teaspoon pepper

Garnish:

2 tablespoons chopped black olives

1. Slice palm hearts into a large salad bowl. Add peas, beets, onion, and cucumber.

2. Combine ingredients for dressing in a small mixing bowl. Pour over salad; toss to mix. Garnish the salad with chopped black olives.

106 calories per serving: 4 g. fat, 4 g. protein,
16 g. carbohydrate, 0 cholesterol, 344 mg. sodium.
For exchange diets, count 1 starch, 1/2 fat.

PAPAYA AND PEPPER SALAD

Serve this as a side dish with jerked chicken.

Preparation time: 20 minutes

8 servings—1 cup each

1 red onion, peeled, halved and sliced thin
2 large oranges, peeled, cut in half and cut into sections
2 grapefruits, peeled, cut in half and cut into sections
1 ripe papaya, peeled, seeded and cut into thick slices
1 red pepper, cored, seeded and cut into thin strips
1 yellow pepper, cored, seeded and cut into thin strips

Dressing:

2 tablespoons lime juice
1/2 teaspoon Dijon-style mustard
1 tablespoon olive oil

1. In a large salad bowl, combine ingredients for the salad.

2. In a shaker container, combine ingredients for the dressing. Pour dressing over salad. Toss and serve.

67 calories per serving: 2 g. fat, 1 g. protein,
13 g. carbohydrate, 0 cholesterol, 6 mg. sodium.
For exchange diets, count: 1 fruit.

ISLAND PORK TENDERLOIN

Preparation time: 20 minutes; Marinating time: 30 minutes
Cooking time: 2 hours

8 servings—3 ounces meat and 1/4 cup sauce each

1 cup orange juice
1/4 cup lime juice
2 pounds lean boneless pork loin roast
3/4 teaspoon minced garlic
1 teaspoon oregano
1/2 teaspoon black pepper
1 large onion, chopped fine
2 ribs celery, sliced fine
1 large carrot, sliced thin
1 teaspoon salt
1/2 cup orange juice

1. In a zippered plastic bag, combine 1 cup orange juice and lime juice with pork loin. Place in the refrigerator for at least 30 minutes.

2. Preheat oven to 325° F.

3. Remove pork from juice. Rub meat with garlic, oregano, and pepper. Place on a rack in a shallow roasting pan. Insert meat thermometer. Discard the meat juices and bag.

4. Place onion, celery, carrot, and salt in an aluminum foil packet beside the pork roast. Roast the meat and vegetables for about 2 hours or until a meat thermometer registers 170° F. in the thickest part of the pork loin.

5. Place the vegetables in a blender along with 1/2 cup orange juice. Process until smooth.

6. Slice the pork loin, and serve the pureed vegetable sauce on the side.

203 calories per serving: 7 g. fat, 26 g. protein,
9 g. carbohydrate, 65 mg. cholesterol, 180 mg. sodium.
For exchange diets, count 3 lean meat, 2 vegetable.

PICCADILLO

This dish is very popular in the Caribbean and has become traditional holiday fare in the southern states. Serve with fat-free tortilla chips as a dip or roll up in a fat-free flour tortilla and serve as a burrito!

Preparation time: 15 minutes; Cooking time: 1 1/2 hours
20 servings—1/3 cup each

1/2 pound lean ground beef
1/2 pound lean ground pork
2 minced garlic cloves
1 cup water
1/2 teaspoon seasoned salt
1/2 teaspoon oregano
1/4 teaspoon black pepper
1/4 teaspoon cumin
3 peeled and diced tomatoes
6-ounce can no-added-salt tomato paste
1/2 cup raisins
1/4 cup chopped stuffed green olives
1/4 cup sliced green onion
1 tablespoon drained capers
1/2 teaspoon sugar
1/2 cup toasted slivered almonds

1. In a large skillet, brown beef, pork, and garlic; drain well.

2. Add water, salt, oregano, pepper, and cumin to beef mixture. Simmer, covered, for 30 minutes.

3. Add remaining ingredients except almonds. Cook over low heat, stirring occasionally, about 45 minutes or until thickened.

4. Add almonds; simmer an additional 10 minutes.

71 calories per serving: 3 g. fat, 3 g. protein,
8 g. carbohydrate, 18 mg. cholesterol, 100 mg. sodium.
For exchange diets, count 1 vegetable, 1 lean meat.

ROPA VIEJA

This Puerto Rican dish can be prepared with any leftover beef, even tough cuts. Shredding and stewing the meat makes it tender.

Preparation time: 15 minutes; Cooking time: 20 minutes
12 servings—3/4 cup each

---

1 tablespoon vegetable oil
1 cup chopped onion
1 cup chopped fresh tomato
3/4 cup chopped green pepper
2 minced garlic cloves
1 pound cooked, shredded flank steak
9-ounce can whole tomatoes
1 tablespoon capers
1/2 teaspoon black pepper
1/4 teaspoon salt
4 cups cooked rice

1. Heat oil in a large skillet; add onion, tomato, green pepper, and garlic. Sauté about 5 minutes.

2. Add steak, canned tomatoes, capers, pepper, and salt. Simmer 10 to 15 minutes, stirring occasionally.

3. Serve immediately over rice.

193 calories per serving: 6 g. fat, 12 g. protein,
22 g. carbohydrate, 26 mg. cholesterol, 112 mg. sodium.
For exchange diets, count 1 starch, 1 vegetable, 1 1/2 lean meat.

JAMAICAN JERK CHICKEN

The best jerk barbecue is made in barrels and cooked all day long on the streets in Jamaica. Jerk can be made from chicken, pork, or goat.

**Preparation time: 15 minutes; Marinating time: 6 hours
Cooking time: 10 minutes
8 servings—3 ounces each**

1 cup diced onion
1/2 cup sliced green onion
3/4 cup reduced-sodium soy sauce
1/2 cup red wine vinegar
1/4 cup brown sugar
1/4 cup chopped, seeded jalapeno pepper
2 tablespoons vegetable oil
2 tablespoons thyme
1 teaspoon black pepper
1/2 teaspoon ground cloves
1/2 teaspoon nutmeg
1/2 teaspoon allspice
1/4 teaspoon cinnamon
1/4 teaspoon crushed red pepper flakes
1 1/2 pounds boneless, skinless chicken breast, cut into strips

1. Place all ingredients except chicken in a food processor or blender. Process 10 to 15 seconds at high speed.

2. Place chicken in a dish; pour marinade over it. Cover and refrigerate 4 to 6 hours.

3. Remove chicken from marinade. Grill chicken on oiled grill over hot coals for 4 to 5 minutes on each side.

168 calories per serving: 6 g. fat, 22 g. protein,
13 g. carbohydrate, 45 mg. cholesterol, 1000 mg. sodium
(To reduce sodium, substitute 1/2 cup fat-free no-added-salt
chicken broth for 1/2 cup of the soy sauce.)
For exchange diets, count 3 very lean meat, 1 fruit.

JERKED SHRIMP

*Made famous in Jamaica, this recipe for jerk
can be adapted for poultry or pork.*

Preparation time: 10 minutes; Marinating time: 30 minutes
Broiling time: 8 minutes
8 servings—3 ounces each

---

1 teaspoon ground allspice
1 teaspoon minced garlic
1 teaspoon ground ginger
2 tablespoons brown sugar
1 teaspoon cinnamon
1/2 teaspoon chopped fresh jalapeño pepper (note: always wear
   rubber gloves when working with hot peppers)
1/8 teaspoon cayenne pepper
1/4 teaspoon black pepper
1/2 teaspoon salt
1 teaspoon olive oil
2 green onions, chopped
1/4 cup wine vinegar
2 tablespoons lime juice
2 pounds fresh or frozen shrimp, peeled and deveined

1. In a large zippered plastic bag, combine all ingredients except
shrimp. Shake well to mix. Add the shrimp to the bag, and shake to
coat. Refrigerate shrimp in the bag with mixture for at least 30 minutes.

2. Preheat broiler. Arrange shrimp on a large broiling pan. Broil for 3
to 4 minutes on each side or until cooked through.

> 130 calories per serving: 3 g. fat, 18 g. protein,
> 8 g. carbohydrate, 129 mg. cholesterol, 277 mg. sodium.
> For exchange diets, count 3 very lean meat, 1/2 fruit.

CARIBBEAN PEAS AND RICE

Preparation time: 10 minutes
Cooking time: 12 minutes
8 servings—3/4 cup each

2 slices bacon, diced and cooked crisp
16 ounces frozen peas
1 cup instant rice
2/3 cup water
1/4 cup orange juice
1/2 teaspoon ground thyme

1. Combine all ingredients in a medium casserole dish.

2. Microwave on high for 10 to 12 minutes, stopping to stir mixture twice. Fluff rice, and serve hot.

123 calories per serving: 3 g. fat, 5 g. protein,
19 g. carbohydrate, 4 mg. cholesterol, 127 mg. sodium.
For exchange diets, count 1 starch, 1 fat.

Coo-coo

A Caribbean combination of okra and cornmeal.

Preparation time: 5 minutes; Cooking time: 15 minutes
Baking time: 45 minutes
12 servings—2/3 cup each

1 cup water
1/2 teaspoon oregano
10-ounce package frozen cut okra
2 cups cornmeal
2 cups cold water
3 tablespoons reduced-fat margarine
1/2 teaspoon salt
nonstick cooking spray

1. Preheat oven to 350° F.

2. In a medium saucepan, bring 1 cup water and oregano to a boil; add okra. Cover and simmer about 8 minutes or until okra is crisp-tender. Do not drain.

3. In a medium bowl, combine cornmeal and cold water. Gradually add to okra, stirring constantly. Cook over medium heat 2 to 3 minutes or until mixture thickens, stirring occasionally. Stir in margarine and salt.

4. Pour into a 2-quart casserole which has been sprayed with cooking spray. Bake for 30 to 45 minutes or until set.

5. Invert onto a serving plate.

158 calories per serving: 3 g. fat, 4 g. protein,
31 g. carbohydrate, 0 cholesterol, 136 mg. sodium.
For exchange diets, count 2 starch.

BANANAS FLAMBÉ

An easy, yet impressive dessert.

Preparation time: 10 minutes
Cooking time: 2 minutes
6 servings—1/2 cup each

2 tablespoons reduced-fat margarine
2 tablespoons brown sugar
4 peeled bananas, halved and sliced crosswise
1/4 teaspoon cinnamon
1/4 cup dark rum
1/4 cup creme de banana
1 pint nonfat vanilla frozen yogurt

1. In a medium skillet, heat margarine and brown sugar, stirring frequently, until mixture forms a syrup, about 2 minutes. Add banana slices and cinnamon; stir gently until bananas are coated with syrup. Remove from heat.

2. Add rum and creme de banana to mixture in skillet; touch a match to the liqueur. Let flames subside for about 10 seconds. Douse flame.

3. Scoop frozen yogurt into serving bowls; spoon bananas over top. Serve immediately.

234 calories per serving: 2 g. fat, 3 g. protein,
51 g. carbohydrate, 0 cholesterol, 94 mg. sodium.
For exchange diets, count 3 fruit, 1 fat.

WHITE CAKE
WITH TROPICAL FRUIT COMPOTE

A variety of fruits makes this dessert especially colorful.

Preparation time: 15 minutes
12 servings—1/12 cake each

Cake:
 94% fat-free white cake mix

Fruit compote:
 2 cups cubed pineapple
 1 cup cubed banana
 1 cup cubed kiwi fruit
 1 cup cubed mango
 3 tablespoons fresh lime juice
 1 tablespoon sugar

1. Prepare and bake cake according to package directions.

2. In a large bowl, combine all fruits. Stir in lime juice and sugar.

3. Cut cake into squares. Spoon compote over top.

226 calories per serving: 2 g. fat, 4 g. protein,
49 g. carbohydrate, 159 mg. cholesterol, 312 mg. sodium.
For exchange diets, count 2 starch, 1 fruit.

Chapter Four

British Isles

Suggested British Isles Menu

Kidney Pie
Colcannon
Tomato Aspic
Raspberry Scones
Irish Coffee

Add Fun, Subtract Expense

Mace, fennel, basil, mustard, Worcestershire, thyme, curry, bay leaf, sage, and parsley are common spices in British cooking.

Grab some fennel from your cupboard and use it like the English do. They add it to almost all fish dishes and claim it as a remedy for digestive distress.

Mace is a widely available spice used by the English in place of nutmeg. Recognize it as the traditional flavor of doughnuts, fruitcake, and muffins. Try some mace in your favorite vegetable beef soup. You'll love the unique flavor.

Look for Irish oatmeal in your favorite gourmet shop. Slightly chewy, rich, and nutty in flavor, this chopped whole grain oatmeal will make breakfast a banquet.

The most primitive grinding tool, the mortar and pestle. is still a kitchen essential. The sets by Mason and Cash Potters of England are considered the best due to their vitrified ceramic grinding surface that does not stain, absorb odors, or leave traces of smashed garlic or ground oregano (about $30).

Taste a Blarney Stone Cocktail
Shake 2 ounces Irish whiskey, 1/2 teaspoon absinthe substitute, 1/2 teaspoon curacao, 1/4 teaspoon maraschino, and 1 dash bitters well with cracked ice. Strain into a 3-ounce cocktail glass. Garnish with orange peel and an olive.

Try an East India Cocktail
Shake 1 1/2 ounces brandy, 1/2 teaspoon pineapple juice, 1/2 teaspoon curacao, 1 teaspoon rum, and 1 dash bitters with cracked ice. Strain into a 3-ounce cocktail glass. Garnish with a twist of lemon peel and a cherry.

Try an Emerald Isle Cocktail
Stir 2 ounces dry gin, 1 teaspoon creme de menthe (green), and 3 dashes bitters with cracked ice. Strain into a 3-ounce cocktail glass.

Mix an English Rose Cocktail
Shake 1 1/2 ounces dry gin, 3/4 ounce apricot brandy, 3/4 ounce dry vermouth, 1 teaspoon grenadine, and 1/4 teaspoon lemon juice with cracked ice. Strain into a 4-ounce cocktail glass. Frost the rim of the glass by rubbing with lemon and dipping in sugar. Serve with a cherry.

Try a London Buck
Fill an 8-ounce highball glass with 1 ice cube, 2 ounces of dry gin, juice of 1/2 lemon, and ginger ale. Stir gently.

Taste a London Cocktail
Stir 2 ounces dry gin, 2 dashes orange bitters, 1/2 teaspoon simple syrup (2 parts water to 1 part sugar, cooked over low heat until clear), and 1/2 teaspoon maraschino with cracked ice. Strain into a 3-ounce cocktail glass. Garnish with a twist of lemon peel.

Try a London Special
Put rind of 1/2 orange into a 6-ounce champagne glass, then add 1 lump sugar and 2 dashes of bitters. Fill with chilled champagne, and stir gently. You may remove orange rind with a slotted spoon before drinking.

IRISH COFFEE

You must use Irish whiskey in this hot drink.

Preparation time: 5 minutes
2 servings—6 ounces each

1 ounce Irish whiskey
2 teaspoons sugar
10 ounces freshly brewed coffee
2 tablespoons reduced-fat whipped topping

1. Pour whiskey in 2 large coffee mugs. Add sugar, and stir to mix.
Fill with coffee. Top with whipped topping.

61 calories per serving: 1 g. fat, 0 protein
4 g. carbohydrate, 0 cholesterol, 0 sodium.
For exchange diets, count 1 1/2 fruit.

CHAMPAGNE JULEP

Preparation time: 10 minutes
4 servings—5 ounces each

1 tablespoon sugar
4 sprigs fresh mint
8 ice cubes
1 liter bottle champagne or nonalcoholic sparkling white grape
juice
1 fresh lemon, cut into wedges

1. Divide sugar and mint into 4 tall collins glasses.

2. Put 2 ice cubes in each glass, fill with champagne, and garnish with lemon wedges.

111 calories per serving: 0 fat, 0 protein
5 g. carbohydrate, 0 cholesterol, 10 mg. sodium.
For exchange diets, count 2 fruit.

DEVILS ON HORSEBACK

Preparation time: 15 minutes
Cooking time: 10 minutes; Baking time: 10 minutes
8 servings—2 prunes each

16 large dried prunes
1/3 cup red wine
1 bay leaf
1/4 cup chutney
8 slices turkey bacon

Garnish:
fresh greens

1. Preheat oven to 400° F.

2. Place prunes in a small saucepan. Add wine and bay leaf, and simmer over low heat for 5 to 10 minutes. Cool the prunes, and remove the pits.

3. Stuff each prune with 1/2 teaspoon of chutney. Then wrap one half-slice of bacon around each stuffed prune, secure it with a toothpick, and place it in a baking dish.

4. Bake for 10 minutes or until the bacon is very crisp. Drain on paper towels, then transfer to a serving platter lined with fresh greens.

118 calories per serving: 3 g. fat, 3 g. protein
18 g. carbohydrate, 10 mg. cholesterol, 248 mg. sodium.
For exchange diets, count 1 fruit, 1 fat.

SPINACH PESTO APPETIZER

This hot dish will be the hit of the appetizer table.

Preparation time: 20 minutes
Baking time: 40 minutes
20 servings—1/3 cup each

1/2 teaspoon minced garlic
1 cup loosely packed basil leaves, minced fine
10 ounces frozen spinach, thawed
1 cup coarse dry bread crumbs
4 eggs, beaten, or 1 cup liquid egg substitute
1 medium onion, chopped
1 teaspoon salt
1/4 teaspoon nutmeg
1/4 teaspoon ground black pepper
1 1/4 cups nonfat ricotta cheese
1/4 cup grated Parmesan cheese
1/4 cup chopped walnut pieces
nonstick cooking spray

1. Preheat oven to 375° F.

2. In a medium bowl, combine all the ingredients (except cooking spray). Mix well.

3. Press ingredients into an 8" square casserole dish that has been sprayed with cooking spray.

4. Bake for 40 minutes. Serve hot with reduced-fat wheat crackers.

79 calories per serving: 3 g. fat, 6 g. protein
7 g. carbohydrate, 34 mg. cholesterol with real eggs
(2 mg. with egg substitute), 213 mg. sodium.
For exchange diets, count 1 very lean meat, 1 vegetable.

SHRIMP AND MELON SALAD

Preparation time: 20 minutes
8 servings—2 cups each

2 small ripe cantaloupe
1 pound cooked shrimp
4 green onions, sliced thin
Dressing:
1/2 cup reduced-fat mayonnaise
2 tablespoons ketchup
1/2 teaspoon paprika
1 teaspoon lemon juice
1 teaspoon vinegar
1/2 teaspoon chili powder
Garnish:
fresh greens

1. Cut melons in half and scoop out balls, transferring them to a salad bowl. Add cooked shrimp and diced green onions to the bowl.

2. In a small bowl, combine the ingredients for the dressing, stirring to mix well. Pour dressing over the melon and shrimp, tossing to coat.

3. Serve melon and shrimp on a bed of greens on a pretty salad plate.

121 calories per serving: 5 g. fat, 12 g. protein
7 g. carbohydrate, 21 mg. cholesterol, 360 mg. sodium.
For exchange diets, count 1/2 fruit, 1 1/2 very lean meat.

IRISH BREAD
Preparation time: 20 minutes
Baking time: 1 1/4 hours
24 servings—1/2 slice each

4 cups flour
1/2 cup sugar
6 teaspoons baking powder
1 teaspoon salt
1/4 cup soft margarine
2 1/4 cups skim milk
2 cups raisins
2 tablespoons caraway seeds
nonstick cooking spray

1. Preheat oven to 350° F.

2. Sift the flour, sugar, baking powder, and salt into a large bowl.

3. Cut margarine into the flour mixture with a pastry blender or fork.

4. Stir in milk, raisins, and caraway seeds; blend well.

5. Spray a 9" x 5" x 3" loaf pan or skillet with nonstick cooking spray. Pour dough into prepared pan. Bake 1 to 1 1/4 hours or until done. Bread is done when a wooden pick inserted into the center of the loaf comes out clean.

163 calories per serving: 2 g. fat, 3 g. protein
33 g. carbohydrate, 0 cholesterol, 116 mg. sodium.
For exchange diets, count 2 starch.

BLUEBERRY TEA CAKES

Preparation time: 15 minutes
Baking time: 10 minutes
12 servings—1 tea cake each

16-ounce package reduced-fat blueberry muffin mix
1 1/2 teaspoons cornstarch
1/2 cup flour
1 egg or 1/4 cup liquid egg substitute
1/4 cup nonfat sour cream
1/2 teaspoon finely grated lemon peel

Topping:
2 tablespoons margarine
1/4 cup honey

1. Preheat oven to 400° F.

2. Open blueberries from the muffin mix, and drain the juice into a small saucepan. Add cornstarch, and stir until blended. Cook over low heat until mixture comes to a boil and thickens. Remove from heat, and stir in berries.

2. In a large mixing bowl, combine muffin mix and flour. Add egg, sour cream, and lemon peel. Stir until just moist.

3. Turn dough out onto a floured surface, and knead 10 times, then roll into a rectangle.

4. Cut dough into 12 squares, and place 2 inches apart on a baking sheet. Use your finger to indent each square. Use a teaspoon to fill the indentation with the reserved thickened blueberries.

5. Bake for 10 minutes. Remove from oven and cool on a wire rack.

6. In a small bowl, melt margarine and stir in honey. Serve on the side with warm tea cakes.

76 calories per serving: 2 g. fat, 2 g. protein
13 g. carbohydrate, 16 mg. cholesterol with real egg
(2 mg. cholesterol with egg substitute), 6 mg. sodium.
For exchange diets, count 1 starch.

RASPBERRY SCONES

Preparation time: 15 minutes
Baking time: 20 minutes
8 servings—1 scone each

2 cups flour
1/4 cup sugar
2 1/2 teaspoons baking powder
1/4 teaspoon salt
1/4 teaspoon nutmeg
1/3 cup soft margarine
1/2 cup skim milk
1 egg or 1/4 cup liquid egg substitute
2 teaspoons finely grated lemon peel
1 cup fresh raspberries
nonstick cooking spray

1. Preheat oven to 425° F.

2. In a large bowl, combine flour, sugar, baking powder, salt, and nutmeg. Cut in margarine with a pastry blender until the mixture is crumbly.

3. In a small bowl, beat together milk, egg, and lemon peel. Add egg mixture to the dry ingredients, and mix just until the dry ingredients are moist.

4. Gently stir in raspberries.

5. Gather the dough into a ball, and very gently knead the dough 8 times on a floured surface. Pat the dough into a 9" circle, and cut the circle into 12 wedges. Place wedges on a baking sheet that has been sprayed with cooking spray.

6. Bake for 20 minutes or until the tops of the scones are golden brown.

188 calories per serving: 4 g. fat, 5 g. protein
33 g. carbohydrate, 18 mg. cholesterol with real egg
(4 mg. cholesterol with egg substitute), 119 mg. sodium.
For exchange diets, count 1 fruit, 1 starch, 1 fat.

BARLEY BREAD

Look for barley flour in a food co-op.
Preparation time: 10 minutes
Bread machine time: 4 hours, 10 minutes
24 servings—1/2 slice each

1 1/8 cup water
2 cups white bread flour
1 cup barley flour
3 tablespoons molasses
2 tablespoons nonfat dry milk powder
1 teaspoon salt
3/4 teaspoon cinnamon
1 teaspoon yeast
1 tablespoon soft margarine

1. Measure ingredients in order listed, and add to bread machine pan. Push start.

2. Loaf will be done in 4 hours and 10 minutes using a Hitachi bread machine.

3. Serve this bread with all-fruit apricot or orange preserves.

4. If you prefer making bread from scratch: gently mix hot tap water with molasses, dry milk powder, yeast, cinnamon, salt, and margarine in a large mixing bowl. Allow mixture to rest 5 minutes. Gradually add both kinds of flour, working the mixture to a smooth dough. Knead for 10 minutes, then cover and allow dough to rise for 1 hour in a warm place. Punch the dough down, form a loaf shape, and place in a loaf pan that has been sprayed with nonstick cooking spray. Allow dough to rise again and bake in a preheated 350° oven for 25 minutes or until the top is browned. Cool for 15 minutes, then remove bread to a cooling rack.

75 calories per serving: 1 g. fat, 2 g. protein
14 g. carbohydrate, 0 cholesterol, 110 mg. sodium.
For exchange diets, count 1 starch.

MULLIGATAWNY

This soup recipe comes straight from Ireland!

Preparation time: 15 minutes
Cooking time: 35 minutes
8 servings—1 cup each

1 cup chopped, peeled apple
1 cup chopped onion
1/2 cup shredded carrot
1 tablespoon vegetable oil
1 tablespoon flour
1 teaspoon curry powder
4 cups fat-free no-added-salt chicken broth
1/3 cup chopped seedless grapes
1 tablespoon chutney
1 tablespoon chopped parsley
2 teaspoons lemon juice
1 teaspoon sugar
1/4 teaspoon black pepper

1. Sauté apple, onion, and carrot in oil for about 2 minutes; add flour and curry powder, and stir for 1 minute. Add chicken broth; bring to a boil and cook until thickened.

2. Add remaining ingredients. Bring to a boil, reduce heat, cover and simmer for 30 minutes, stirring occasionally.

53 calories per serving: 2 g. fat, 0 protein
9 g. carbohydrate, 0 cholesterol, 6 mg. sodium.
For exchange diets, count 2 vegetable.

COCK-A-LEEKIE SOUP

*This medieval soup was traditionally
garnished with prunes stuffed with hazelnuts.*

Preparation time: 15 minutes
Cooking time: 20 minutes
8 servings—1 1/2 cups each

nonstick cooking spray
1/2 pound boneless white meat chicken, cubed
1/2 teaspoon celery salt
1/2 teaspoon onion salt
1/2 cup pearl barley
2 quarts water
1 bay leaf
6 peppercorns
2 tablespoons dried parsley
6 leeks, cleaned well and sliced into "coins"

1. Spray a large Dutch oven with cooking spray. Add cubed chicken,
celery salt, and onion salt. Brown meat over medium heat until it is
no longer pink.

2. Add all remaining ingredients, and bring mixture to a boil. Reduce
heat to a simmer, and cook for 15 minutes or until leeks are tender.

61 calories per serving: 1 g. fat, 9 g. protein
3 g. carbohydrate, 29 mg. cholesterol, 289 mg. sodium.
For exchange diets, count 1 very lean meat, 1 vegetable.

BEEF BARLEY SOUP WITH VEGETABLES

Preparation time: 20 minutes
Simmering time: 1 hour
8 servings—1 1/2 cups each

1 1/2 pounds lean stew meat, trimmed and cut into chunks
12-ounce can beer
1 quart water
2 large white onions, chopped
4 large carrots, peeled and cut into chunks
2 white turnips, peeled and chopped
3 celery ribs, cleaned and cut into chunks
2 large leeks, cleaned and sliced
1/4 cup pearl barley
1/4 cup split green peas
1/2 teaspoon ground black pepper

1. Combine all ingredients in a large stockpot. Bring mixture to a boil, then reduce heat to a simmer. Simmer for 1 hour, then serve.

250 calories per serving: 9 g. fat, 28 g. protein
13 g. carbohydrate, 90 mg. cholesterol, 91 mg. sodium.
For exchange diets, count 3 lean meat, 1 starch.

SCOTCH BROTH

Preparation time: 15 minutes
Cooking time: 1 hour, 45 minutes
8 servings—1 cup each

1 pound boneless cubed lamb
6 cups water
1/2 cup barley
1/2 cup chopped onion
2 whole cloves
1 bay leaf
1/2 teaspoon salt
1/4 teaspoon black pepper
1 cup chopped carrot
1 cup diced rutabaga
1/2 cup chopped celery
1/4 teaspoon crushed dried rosemary
1/4 teaspoon crushed dried thyme

1. In a large saucepan, combine lamb, water, barley, onion, cloves, bay leaf, salt, and pepper. Bring to a boil; reduce heat. Cover and simmer for 1 hour.

2. Remove cloves and bay leaf. Add remaining ingredients. Cover and cook for 30 minutes more or until vegetables are tender.

145 calories per serving: 3 g. fat, 14 g. protein
15 g. carbohydrate, 36 mg. cholesterol, 195 mg. sodium.
For exchange diets, count 1 starch, 2 very lean meat.

TOMATO ASPIC

This stately salad complements red meat entrées.

Preparation time: 15 minutes
Chilling time: 3 hours
8 servings—1/8 slice of gelatin ring each

2 cups tomato juice
1 small onion, chopped
1 rib celery, chopped
2 tablespoons brown sugar
2 bay leaves
4 whole cloves
2 envelopes unflavored gelatin
1 cup cold water
1 cup cold tomato juice
3 tablespoons lemon juice
4 ribs celery, very finely chopped

Garnish:
fresh greens

1. In a small saucepan, combine 2 cups tomato juice, onion, celery, brown sugar, bay leaves, and cloves. Bring mixture to a simmer, and cook for 4 minutes.

2. In a medium bowl, soften gelatin in cold water. When gelatin is softened, stir in cold tomato juice. Place a strainer over the bowl and pour in hot tomato juice mixture, straining out the vegetables and whole spices. Discard the cooked vegetables and spices.

3. Add 1 cup cold tomato juice and lemon juice. Refrigerate for 30 minutes or until mixture is partially set.

4. Fold in celery and pour into a 5-cup ring. Chill until firm, about 2 1/2 hours. To unmold, dip mold in hot water for 30 seconds and then turn out onto a serving plate lined with fresh greens. Slice and serve.

42 calories per serving: 0 fat, 1 g. protein
11 g. carbohydrate, 0 cholesterol, 435 mg. sodium.
For exchange diets, count 2 vegetable.

PICKLED BEETS
Preparation time: 15 minutes
Chilling time: 30 minutes to 4 days
8 servings—1/2 cup each

2 1-pound cans sliced beets, drained
1 large yellow onion, sliced thin
1/2 cup vinegar
2 tablespoons sugar
1/8 teaspoon ground cloves
1/2 teaspoon salt
3 peppercorns
1/2 bay leaf

1. In a salad bowl, combine beets with onion.

2. In a shaker container, combine all remaining ingredients. Pour marinade over vegetables.

3. Marinate in the refrigerator at least 30 minutes or up to 4 days.

58 calories per serving: 0 fat, 2 g. protein
14 g. carbohydrate, 0 cholesterol, 198 mg. sodium.
For exchange diets, count 1 fruit.

SMOKED TURKEY AND BLUE CHEESE SALAD

Preparation time: 25 minutes
8 servings—2 cups each

Salad:

1 pound smoked turkey, cut into thin strips
1 small head lettuce, washed and shredded
1 bunch of green onions, washed and chopped fine
1/4 pound bean sprouts, washed and drained
4 ounces fresh mushrooms, cleaned and sliced thin
1 small cucumber, cut into thin slices
1 small ripe avocado, peeled and diced
4 cooked egg whites, chopped
1/4 cup croutons
1/4 cup raisins
4 strips bacon, diced and cooked crisp

Dressing:

8 ounces nonfat yogurt
2 tablespoons reduced-fat mayonnaise
2 ounces blue cheese, crumbled
1/2 teaspoon salt
1/2 teaspoon black pepper

Garnish:

sesame breadsticks

1. In a large salad bowl, combine ingredients for the salad.

2. In a small mixing bowl, combine ingredients for the dressing. Pour dressing over the salad, and toss to coat.

3. Garnish with sesame breadsticks

194 calories per serving: 10 g. fat, 20 g. protein
6 g. carbohydrate, 151 mg. cholesterol, 329 mg. sodium.
For exchange diets, count 1 vegetable, 2 lean meat, 1 fat.

SAVORY SEAFOOD SALAD

Preparation time: 20 minutes
8 servings—1 1/2 cups each

1 tablespoon margarine
1/4 teaspoon minced garlic
1 leek, cleaned well and sliced into "coins"
1 medium onion, peeled and chopped
4 cups cooked seafood (cooked crab, shrimp, salmon, or your
   favorite combination)
1/4 teaspoon salt
1/4 teaspoon pepper
1/4 teaspoon Tabasco sauce
1 small head lettuce, chopped
1 lemon, cut into 8 wedges

1. Melt margarine in a large Dutch oven. Sauté garlic, leek, and onion
in melted margarine until tender.

2. In a salad bowl, combine sautéed vegetables with seafood. Add
salt, pepper, and Tabasco. Refrigerate until serving time.

3. To serve, divide chopped lettuce among 8 salad plates. Spoon
seafood salad onto the lettuce, and garnish with lemon wedges.

124 calories per serving: 3 g. fat, 22 g. protein
4 g. carbohydrate, 81 mg. cholesterol, 491 mg. sodium.
For exchange diets, count 3 very lean meat, 1 vegetable.

CORNED BEEF AND CABBAGE

Preparation time: 15 minutes
Cooking time: 3 hours

**8 servings—3 ounces meat, 1 cabbage wedge,
and 2 tablespoons sauce each**

1 1/2 pounds corned-beef brisket, well trimmed
cold water to cover
1 small onion
4 whole cloves
1 bay leaf
5 peppercorns
1 medium head cabbage, cut into 8 wedges
Horseradish sauce:
1/2 cup nonfat sour cream
1/2 cup 50% reduced-fat mayonnaise
2 tablespoons prepared hot horseradish
1 tablespoon chopped parsley

1. Place trimmed brisket in a large Dutch oven. Cover with cold water. Add onions, cloves, bay leaf, and peppercorns.

2. Bring mixture to a boil, then reduce heat to a simmer for 3 hours. Skim off fat and foam from top of water.

3. Add cabbage wedges during last 10 minutes of cooking time.

4. In a small mixing bowl, combine ingredients for sauce.

5. Use a slotted spoon to remove cabbage wedges. Place them around the edges of a large platter. Slice the brisket, and layer slices of meat down the middle of the platter. Serve horseradish sauce on the side.

248 calories per serving: 12 g. fat, 28 g. protein
7 g. carbohydrate, 80 mg. cholesterol, 199 mg. sodium.
For exchange diets, count 4 very lean meat, 1 vegetable.

KIDNEY PIE

Preparation time: 20 minutes
Cooking time: 25 minutes; Baking time: 20 minutes
8 servings—1/8 pie each

---

2 strips bacon, diced
1/2 pound beef kidney, chopped into bite-sized pieces
1/2 pound sirloin steak, cut into 1-inch pieces
1/4 cup flour
1 cup red wine
2 small onions, diced
2 bay leaves
1/2 cup chopped parsley
1/2 cup chopped celery, including leafy tops
1 cup sliced mushrooms
1/4 teaspoon salt
1 teaspoon black pepper
1 teaspoon marjoram
nonstick cooking spray
1 1/2 cups reduced-fat baking mix, such as Bisquick Light
1/2 cup beef broth

1. Preheat oven to 375° F.

2. In a large skillet, cook bacon and kidney meat until bacon is crisp.

3. Roll chunks of sirloin steak in flour, then add to skillet and sauté for 3 minutes or until well browned. Add wine, onions, bay leaves, parsley, celery, mushrooms, salt, pepper, and marjoram. Cover and simmer mixture for 10 minutes.

4. Meanwhile, spray an 11" x 7" baking dish with cooking spray.

5. Use a fork to combine baking mix and beef broth in a small bowl. Mix just until liquid is absorbed—dough will be sticky.

6. Pour beef and vegetable mixture into the prepared baking pan. Use a spoon to dollop biscuit dough on top of beef and vegetable mixture. Bake for 20 minutes or until biscuits are golden brown.

244 calories per serving: 7 g. fat, 19 g. protein
28 g. carbohydrate, 159 mg. cholesterol, 111 mg. sodium.
For exchange diets, count 1 vegetable, 1 1/2 starch, 2 lean meat.

PINEAPPLE CHUTNEY

This refreshing relish is good with pork or poultry.

Preparation time: 15 minutes
Cooking time: 10 minutes; Chilling time: 1 hour
8 servings—1/4 cup each

3/4 cup sugar
1/2 cup vinegar
1 teaspoon ginger
1/2 teaspoon cumin
1/8 teaspoon salt
1 large onion, coarsely chopped
3/4 cup dried apricots, quartered
1/2 cup raisins, chopped
8-ounce can crushed pineapple, drained

1. In a 2-quart saucepan, combine sugar, vinegar, ginger, cumin, and salt.

2. Bring the mixture to a boil, then stir in onions, apricots, and raisins. Reheat to boiling, then reduce heat and simmer for 5 minutes.

3. Fold in crushed pineapple. Chill for at least 1 hour.

78 calories per serving: 0 fat, 1 g. protein
20 g. carbohydrate, 0 cholesterol, 11 mg. sodium.
For exchange diets, count 1 1/2 fruit.

GOLDEN FRUIT CHUTNEY

Serve with pork or chicken.

Preparation time: 15 minutes
Cooking time: 30 minutes
16 servings—1/4 cup each

1 firm banana, diced
1 apple, diced
1 large onion, chopped
1/4 teaspoon minced garlic
8-ounce can pineapple tidbits in juice
1/2 cup brown sugar
1/2 cup golden raisins
1/4 cup lime juice
1 teaspoon ground ginger
1 tablespoon mustard seed
1/2 teaspoon chili powder
2 teaspoons finely grated orange peel

1. In a medium saucepan, combine all ingredients. Simmer uncovered for 30 minutes. Chill in a covered container.

72 calories per serving: 0 fat, 1 g. protein
17 g. carbohydrate, 0 cholesterol, 4 mg. sodium.
For exchange diets, count 1 fruit.

COLCANNON

Preparation time: 15 minutes
Cooking time: 8 minutes
8 servings—1 cup each

3 cups shredded cabbage
1/4 cup sliced green onions
2 tablespoons water
1/8 teaspoon salt
6 medium peeled and cooked potatoes, still warm
1/3 cup skim milk
1 tablespoon reduced-fat margarine
1/2 teaspoon salt
1/4 teaspoon black pepper

1. In a covered microwaveable casserole dish, cook cabbage, onions, water, and 1/8 teaspoon salt on high for 6 to 8 minutes or until vegetables reach desired doneness.

2. Mash potatoes until there are no lumps. Beat in milk. Add margarine, salt, and pepper.

3. Stir in cabbage-onion mixture.

123 calories per serving: 1 g. fat, 4 g. protein
26 g. carbohydrate, 0 cholesterol, 238 mg. sodium.
For exchange diets, count 1 starch, 2 vegetable.

IRISH BLARNEY POTATOES AND CABBAGE

A delightful and unique appetizer.

Preparation time: 20 minutes
Baking time: 30 minutes
12 servings—2 potatoes each

12 cooked new potatoes with skin on
2 cups finely shredded cabbage
1/4 cup water
1/4 teaspoon salt
1/8 teaspoon black pepper
1 cup shredded lean corned beef
10-ounce package cooked, chopped spinach
1/4 cup sliced green onions
1 tablespoon fat-free mayonnaise
1 tablespoon spicy yellow mustard
1/8 teaspoon hot pepper sauce
11-ounce can reduced-fat cream of mushroom soup
1/4 cup reduced-fat cheese of your choice

1. Preheat oven to 350° F.

2. Cut potatoes in half; scoop out center leaving the shell intact. Set aside. Reserve potato pulp for another use.

3. In a medium microwaveable dish, place cabbage, water, salt, and pepper. Cover and microwave on high for 7 minutes.

4. In a large bowl, stir together corned beef, spinach, onions, mayonnaise, mustard, and pepper sauce. Stuff mixture into potato shells. Mix extra meat filling with cabbage and mushroom soup.

5. Spread cabbage-corned beef mixture in bottom of a 13" x 9" pan. Press stuffed potatoes on cabbage mixture in pan so potatoes will stay meat side up.

6. Sprinkle with cheese. Cover pan with aluminum foil. Bake for 30 minutes.

215 calories per serving: 6 g. fat, 12 g. protein
32 g. carbohydrate, 20 mg. cholesterol, 307 mg. sodium.
For exchange diets, count 1 lean meat, 2 starch.

Chapter Five

France

Suggested French Menus

Salad Niçoise
French Bread
Bouillabaisse
Cherries Jubilee

Asparagus Soup
Rosemary Bread
Beef Wellington
Herbed Potatoes
Your Favorite Fruit Sorbet

Add Fun, Subtract Expense

In a moment of almost serious despair, former French President de Gaulle said: "How is it possible for people to govern themselves in a land where there are more than 400 different kinds of cheese?" Cheese is an important part of any hot meal in France and the French eat two hot meals each day. Cheese is served before the main course, the dessert or fruit. Perhaps the most famous cheese is Roquefort, the blue-streaked sheep's cheese that comes from the village of the same name in southwestern France. The nutrition advantage of this cheese is that it takes just a small amount to flavor a large recipe.

Bread and water is no joke in France. French office workers pick up a baguette and a bottle of mineral water from corner vendors at lunch time and enjoy the street scene.

Crisco Savory Seasonings is a flavorful blend of seasonings and canola oil. Try Lemon Butter, Roasted Garlic, or Classic Herb to sophisticate your seafood, vegetables, or potatoes.

Add French chervil to your spice cupboard. This sweet herb imparts a delicate flavor to marinated cold vegetable salads. It is not suited for hot dishes, as heat quickly consumes its flavor.

Shallots are a member of the onion family and grow as a cluster rather than a single bulb. The flavor is a cross between an onion and garlic, but more delicate, sweet, and complex. Used heavily in northern French cooking, they are worth finding in the grocery store.

Add tarragon to tuna or chicken salad for a French twist.

For perfect chocolate mousse for two, buy a mini springform pan. These 4-inch pans are perfect for half recipes and are super easy to release (about $9).

If Dijon mustard is always on your table, ask for a porcelain mustard pot. It is dishwasher safe and comes with a matching server (about $9).

For crepes or pancakes, use a crepe pan. For fat-free cooking, insist on a 4-layer nonstick surface with an aluminum inner core for even heat diffusion (about $30).

Add a touch of France to your breakfast with a Bistro coffee pot. These glass carafes come with a press and stainless steel filter for rich coffee flavor (4-cup pot is about $15).

What about the French paradox? The popular theory is that the rate of heart disease among the French is low, even though their diet is high in fat, because they drink red wine every day. Current health recommendations stress a maximum of one serving (5 ounces) of wine for women and two servings of wine for men daily.

Try a Napoleon Cocktail
Stir 2 ounces dry gin, 1/2 teaspoon curacao, and 1/2 teaspoon Dubonnet with cracked ice. Strain into a 3-ounce cocktail glass.

Try a Panama Cocktail
Shake 1 ounce creme de cacao, 1 ounce sweet cream, and 1 ounce brandy with cracked ice. Strain into a 4-ounce cocktail glass.

To add a French touch to an ordinary dish, substitute part of the fat, broth, or other liquid in your recipe with wine. White wine complements chicken, seafood, white sauces, and sautéed mushrooms. Red wine gives robust flavor to beef burgundy, stews, and spaghetti sauce.

Add dill or celery seed to pasta salads and cottage cheese. Thyme, garlic, savory, bay leaf, and tarragon are also spices the French use quite liberally.

STUFFED MUSHROOMS

Preparation time: 10 minutes
Baking time: 7 minutes
8 servings—4 mushroom caps each

1 pound fresh mushrooms
1 tablespoon olive oil
4 green onions, finely chopped
1/2 teaspoon minced garlic
3 tablespoons fresh minced parsley
1/4 teaspoon salt
1/8 teaspoon freshly ground black pepper
1 tablespoon lemon juice
1/4 cup nonfat ricotta cheese
1/4 cup fine bread crumbs

1. Preheat oven to 400° F.

2. Wash mushrooms quickly under cold water, and pat them dry on a towel. Carefully remove the stem from the cap. Set the caps aside, and finely chop the stems.

3. In a medium skillet, heat olive oil. Add chopped onions, chopped stems, and garlic. Sauté for 2 minutes. Add parsley, salt, pepper, lemon juice, and cheese to the skillet, and blend until smooth.

4. Stuff the mushroom caps with the cheese mixture, and place on a baking sheet. Dust the top with bread crumbs. Bake for 7 minutes, and serve immediately.

---

48 calories per serving: 2 g. fat, 2 g. protein,
7 g. carbohydrate, 0 cholesterol, 100 mg. sodium.
For exchange diets, count 1 vegetable, 1/2 fat.

EASY FRENCH CREPES

Wrap these versatile pancakes around leftovers or fruit filling.

Preparation time: 10 minutes
Standing time: 20 minutes; Cooking time: 30 minutes
8 servings—2 5-inch crepes each

Crepes:
   2 eggs or 1/2 cup liquid egg substitute
   1 cup skim milk
   1/2 teaspoon salt
   1 cup flour
   2 tablespoons soft margarine, melted

   nonstick cooking spray

Topping:
   cinnamon
   powdered sugar

1. In a blender, combine all ingredients for crepes, and blend until smooth. Let prepared batter stand at least 20 minutes.

2. Spray a 7" skillet or crepe pan with cooking spray, then heat over medium heat until medium hot.

3. Using a ladle, pour in a scant 1/4 cup of batter, then quickly tilt the skillet so the batter spreads evenly over the pan. Cook for 2 to 3 minutes or until the edge of the pancake lifts easily from the pan. Turn it with a spatula, and cook on the second side for 1 to 2 minutes. Place prepared crepes on a warm platter.

4. Dust crepes with cinnamon and powdered sugar, then roll and eat plain or with a fruit filling. Crepes are also good with a meat filling.

....

103 calories per serving: 13 g. fat, 5 g. protein,
14 g. carbohydrate, 1 mg. cholesterol (0 cholesterol
with egg substitute),200 mg. sodium.
For exchange diets, count 1 starch, 1/2 very lean meat.

BRIOCHE

Preparation time: 10 minutes
Bread machine time: 1 hour, 30 minutes
Manual method preparation time: 25 minutes
Rising time: 1 hour; Additional rising time: 30 minutes
Baking time: 15 minutes

18 servings—1 brioche each

1/2 cup water
3 eggs
3 cups white bread flour
3 tablespoons sugar
2 tablespoons nonfat dry milk powder
1 teaspoon salt
1 teaspoon yeast
1 tablespoon soft margarine
nonstick cooking spray
1 egg
1 tablespoon sugar

1. Place first 8 ingredients in order listed in bread machine pan. Select "dough" from menu, and push "start." Wait approximately 1 hour and 30 minutes for the dough to be prepared. Go to number 3.

2. If you prefer making bread from scratch: gently mix hot tap water, sugar, dry milk, yeast, salt, and margarine in a large mixing bowl. Allow mixture to rest 5 minutes. Stir in 3 eggs, one at a time, then gradually add flour, working the mixture to a smooth dough. Knead for 10 minutes. Return dough to a bowl, then cover and allow dough to rise for 1 hour in a warm place.

3. Remove bread from the bread machine or from the bowl. Divide the dough into 4 equal portions. Shape 3 of the portions into 6 balls each, making a total of 18 balls. Set these aside.

4. Shape the remaining portion into 18 balls. Place large balls of dough into fluted brioche pans or muffin tins that have been sprayed with cooking spray. Make an indentation in the middle of each large ball of dough, and press a small ball of dough into each indentation. Dough will look like a snowman. Allow dough to rise 30 minutes.

Brioche (continued)

5. Preheat oven to 375°. Stir together 1 egg and 1 tablespoon sugar. Brush this onto the tops, and bake for 14 to 16 minutes or until they are golden. Cool for 5 minutes, then remove brioche to a cooling rack.

....

153 calories per serving: 5 g. fat, 5 g. protein,
22 g. carbohydrate, 52 mg. cholesterol, 140 mg. sodium.
For exchange diets, count 1 1/2 starch, 1/2 fat.

FRENCH BREAD

Preparation time: 20 minutes
Rising/baking time: 1 hour
40 servings—1 slice each

cornmeal
2 packages dry yeast
1/2 cup warm water
1/2 teaspoon sugar
2 tablespoons sugar
2 tablespoons margarine
2 teaspoons salt
2 cups boiling water
7 1/2 cups flour

1. Dust 2 French bread loaf pans with cornmeal.

2. In a glass measuring cup, dissolve yeast in water; stir in 1/2 teaspoon sugar.

3. Combine 2 tablespoons sugar, margarine, salt, and boiling water in a large mixing bowl. Cool to lukewarm, then stir in yeast. Slowly add flour, processing with a food processor or electric mixer or by hand until dough is smooth and elastic. Cover and allow to rise until double in bulk.

4. Preheat oven to 400°. Form dough into 2 loaves, and place in prepared pans. Place a pan of boiling water in the bottom of the oven. Bake bread for 20 minutes. Remove from oven and cool for 10 minutes, then remove loaves from pan and continue cooling on a rack.

96 calories per serving: 1 g. fat, 2 g. protein,
16 g. carbohydrate, 0 cholesterol, 107 mg. sodium.
For exchange diets, count 1 starch.

ROSEMARY BREAD

Preparation time: 10 minutes
Bread machine time: 4 hours, 10 minutes
Manual method preparation time: 25 minutes
Rising time: 2 hours; Baking time: 25 minutes
Cooling time: 15 minutes
24 servings—1/2 slice each

1 1/8 cups water
3 cups white bread flour
2 teaspoons sugar
3 tablespoons cornmeal
2 tablespoons nonfat dry milk powder
1 teaspoon salt
1/2 teaspoon coarsely ground black pepper
1 teaspoon dried rosemary
1 teaspoon yeast
1 tablespoon soft margarine

1. Place ingredients in bread machine pan in order listed. Push "start."

2. Loaf will be done in 4 hours and 10 minutes using a Hitachi bread machine.

3. If you prefer making bread from scratch: gently mix hot tap water with sugar, cornmeal, dry milk powder, yeast, rosemary, pepper, salt, and margarine in a large mixing bowl. Allow mixture to rest 5 minutes. Gradually add flour, working the mixture to a smooth dough. Knead for 10 minutes. Return dough to the bowl, then cover and allow dough to rise for 1 hour in a warm place. Punch the dough down, form a loaf shape and place in a loaf pan that has been sprayed with nonstick cooking spray. Allow dough to rise again for 1 hour and bake in a preheated 350° oven for 25 minutes or until the top is browned. Cool for 15 minutes, then remove bread to a cooling rack.

4. Serve bread with a slice of Brie cheese.

80 calories per serving: 1 g. fat, 3 g. protein,
14 g. carbohydrate, 1 mg. cholesterol, 73 mg. sodium.
For exchange diets, count 1 starch.

ONION SOUP

For especially sweet onion flavor, use Vidalia or Maui onions.
The extra cost is well worth it for the flavor.

Preparation time: 15 minutes
Cooking time: 45 minutes
8 servings—3/4 cup each

Soup:
- 2 tablespoons reduced-fat margarine
- 3 pounds sliced onions
- 1/2 teaspoon sugar
- 1/8 teaspoon salt
- 2 tablespoons flour
- 4 cups fat-free chicken broth
- 2 tablespoons dry white wine
- 1 1/2 tablespoons brandy
- 1 1/2 teaspoons Dijon mustard
- 1/4 teaspoon black pepper

Garnish:
- 8 slices toasted French bread
- 1/2 cup shredded low-fat Swiss cheese

1. In a large, heavy saucepan, melt margarine over low heat. Add onions, sugar, and salt. Cover pan, and cook until onions are very soft, stirring occasionally, about 20 minutes.

2. Uncover pan, and increase heat to high. Cook onions about 10 minutes more or until golden brown. Add flour; stir 2 minutes. Stir in chicken broth, wine, brandy, and mustard. Bring soup to a boil, stirring frequently. Reduce heat to low, then cover and cook 10 minutes.

3. Season soup with pepper.

4. Preheat broiler. Ladle soup into 8 broilerproof bowls. Top each with 1 slice of toast. Sprinkle 1 tablespoon cheese over each slice of toast. Broil until cheese melts.

---

198 calories per serving: 4 g. fat, 8 g. protein,
31 g. carbohydrate, 0 cholesterol, 577 mg. sodium
(To reduce sodium, use no-added-salt chicken broth.)
For exchange diets, count 1 starch, 3 vegetable, 1/2 skim milk.

ASPARAGUS SOUP

*This soup is puréed, which thickens and enriches
the soup without the addition of cream.*

Preparation time: 10 minutes
Cooking time: 25 minutes
8 servings—1 cup each

---

1 tablespoon reduced-fat margarine
1 cup chopped onion
1 cup chopped leek (discard dark green parts)
6 cups fat-free no-added-salt chicken broth
2 pounds fresh, thin asparagus, ends trimmed, cut into 1-inch
  pieces
1/2 teaspoon salt
1/4 teaspoon white pepper

1. Melt margarine in a large saucepan. Add onions and leeks; cook
about 10 to 15 minutes or until tender.

2. Add chicken broth and asparagus; simmer 10 minutes or until
asparagus is tender.

3. Purée soup in small batches in a blender. Return soup to saucepan.
Season with salt and pepper.

....

51 calories per serving: 1 g. fat, 4 g. protein,
9 g. carbohydrate, 0 cholesterol, 153 mg. sodium.
For exchange diets, count 2 vegetable.

SALAD NIÇOISE

*Niçoise means "as prepared in Nice," a city on the
Riviera known for its black olives and anchovies.*

Preparation time: 15 minutes
8 servings—2 cups each

Salad:
    1/4 teaspoon minced garlic
    6 medium tomatoes, peeled and quartered
    1 large cucumber, peeled and diced
    6 coarsely chopped anchovy fillets
    8 coarsely chopped black olives
    4 cups finely torn Bibb lettuce
    4 cups finely torn romaine lettuce

Dressing:
    1/3 cup lemon juice
    1/4 cup olive oil
    3/4 teaspoon salt
    3/4 teaspoon prepared mustard
    1/4 teaspoon black pepper
    1/4 teaspoon minced garlic

1. Use a wooden salad bowl, if possible. Rub the sides and bottom of
the bowl with garlic. Combine remaining salad ingredients in the
bowl.

2. In a shaker container, combine ingredients for dressing.

3. Pour dressing over the salad. Toss and serve.

106 calories per serving: 6 g. fat, 1 g. protein,
11 g. carbohydrate, 0 cholesterol, 288 mg. sodium.
For exchange diets, count 2 vegetables, 1 fat.

BEEF BURGUNDY

This classic French entrée makes a nice
centerpiece for a winter dinner party.

Preparation time: 20 minutes
Marinating time: 3 to 24 hours; Roasting time: 4 hours
8 servings—4 ounces each

2 pounds boneless beef roast, such as rump, sirloin top,
  or top round
1/2 teaspoon salt
1/4 teaspoon black pepper

Marinade:
3 cups red wine
1 cup water
1 medium onion, sliced
1 large carrot, sliced thin
1/4 teaspoon minced garlic
1 bay leaf
2 teaspoons chopped fresh parsley
1 teaspoon thyme

Braising ingredients:
2 strips bacon, diced
1 fresh tomato
1 bay leaf
3 green onions, chopped
1 cup beef bouillon
1/2 teaspoon salt
2 tablespoons fresh parsley

Thickening:
2 tablespoons flour
1/2 cup beef bouillon
1/2 cup red wine
2 tablespoons brandy

1. Trim all visible fat from the roast, then rub with salt and pepper.

2. In a shallow casserole dish or roasting pan, combine ingredients for marinade. Place roast in the marinade, and turn several times. Cover tightly, and place in the refrigerator for at least 3 hours or up to 24 hours.

3. In a Dutch oven, cook diced bacon until crisp; drain fat. Add all remaining braising ingredients, and simmer for 5 minutes. Place roast on top of the braising ingredients.

4. Cover the Dutch oven, and roast at 325° F. for 4 hours. When meat is done, remove it to a board for slicing.

5. Combine ingredients for thickening in a shaker container. Slowly stir into the braising ingredients over medium heat. Simmer for 2 minutes, then pour over sliced meat.

242 calories per serving: 10 g. fat, 35 g. protein,
3 g. carbohydrate, 98 mg. cholesterol, 276 mg. sodium.
For exchange diets, count 4 lean meat, 1 vegetable.

BOUILLABAISSE

(BOOL-yuh-BAYZ)

Saffron and orange rind set this seafood stew apart from the rest.

Preparation time: 20 minutes
Cooking time: 45 minutes
8 servings—2 cups each

1 tablespoon vegetable oil
2 large onions, chopped
1 teaspoon minced garlic
16 ounces chunky tomatoes
2 cups bottled clam juice
4 cups no-added-salt chicken broth
1/4 teaspoon pepper
1/4 teaspoon saffron
1/2 teaspoon thyme
1 bay leaf
grated rind of 1 orange
1 pound shellfish meat (lobster, scallops, crab, or shrimp)
2 pounds assorted white fish fillets such as cod, flounder, or snapper, cut into chunks

Garnish:

chopped parsley

1. Heat vegetable oil in a large Dutch oven. Sauté onions for several minutes. Add all remaining ingredients except the fish. Simmer for 30 minutes.

2. Add shellfish meat and white fish fillets. Boil for 10 minutes or until white fish is flaky.

3. Ladle into bowls, and garnish generously with parsley.

266 calories per serving: 3 g. fat, 42 g. protein,
15 g. carbohydrate, 108 mg. cholesterol, 410 mg. sodium.
For exchange diets, count 6 very lean meat, 2 vegetable.

BEEF WELLINGTON

Preparation time: 30 minutes
Total roasting time: 1 1/2 hours
16 servings—4 to 6 ounces of meat, vegetable, and pastry each

3 pounds boneless beef roast
1/2 teaspoon salt
1/4 teaspoon black pepper
2 tablespoons vegetable oil
2 pounds fresh mushrooms, sliced thin
2 green onions, finely chopped
2 tablespoons flour
1 tablespoon lemon juice
1/3 cup sherry
1 package pie crust mix
1 egg yolk
2 tablespoons skim milk

1. Preheat oven to 400° F. Trim the roast of all visible fat, and season it with salt and pepper. Place the beef on a roasting rack, and roast for 20 minutes.

2. Meanwhile, heat oil in a large skillet and add mushrooms and green onions. Sauté for 10 minutes. Stir in flour, lemon juice, and sherry; mix well. Spread the mushroom mixture over the top of the browned roast beef.

3. Prepare the pie crust mix according to package directions. Wrap the beef in the crust, completely covering the entire surface and pinching the edges neatly. Place the beef on a baking sheet. Prick the surface of the pastry to allow the steam to escape while it is cooking.

4. Combine the egg yolk and skim milk in a cup. Brush the pastry surface with the egg mixture. Roast the beef for 15 minutes at 400°, then reduce heat to 350° and continue cooking for 30 to 45 minutes or until the beef is cooked to desired doneness. Allow the beef to rest 15 minutes before cutting into slices.

284 calories per serving: 15 g. fat, 27 g. protein,
9 g. carbohydrate, 88 mg. cholesterol, 245 mg. sodium.
For exchange diets, count 3 1/2 lean meat, 2 vegetable, 1 fat.

Coquilles Saint-Jacques

(ko-KEEL sahn-ZHAHK)

This fancy name is French for scallops.

Preparation time: 15 minutes
Cooking time: 10 minutes; Broiling time: 5 minutes
8 servings—5 ounces each

Scallops:
>1 1/2 pounds fresh scallops
>1 cup dry white wine
>1/2 cup water
>1/4 cup fresh parsley
>1/2 teaspoon salt
>1 teaspoon reduced-fat margarine
>2 cups sliced mushrooms
>2 thinly sliced green onions

Sauce:
>2 tablespoons reduced-fat margarine
>2 tablespoons flour
>1/2 cup evaporated skim milk
>1/2 cup low-fat Swiss cheese, divided
>1/2 cup no-fat bread crumbs
>nonstick cooking spray

1. In a large saucepan, place scallops, wine, water, parsley, and salt. Heat to a boil; reduce heat and simmer about 8 minutes or until scallops are tender. Remove scallops with a slotted spoon; reserve liquid.

2. Heat reserved liquid to a boil; boil until reduced to 1 cup. Set aside.

3. Heat 1 teaspoon margarine in saucepan until melted. Add mushrooms and onions, and cook about 5 minutes, stirring frequently. Remove from pan.

4. To make sauce, add 2 tablespoons margarine and flour pan. Cook over low heat, stirring constantly, until bubbly. Remove from heat; add reserved liquid. Cook 1 minute, stirring constantly. Stir in milk, scallops, mushroom mixture, and 1/4 cup Swiss cheese; heat through.

5. Coat a 13" x 9" baking pan or 8 individual broilerproof ramekins with cooking spray. Place scallop mixture in pan. Sprinkle with bread crumbs and remaining cheese. Broil about 5 minutes or until crumbs are toasted.

194 calories per serving: 4 g. fat, 21 g. protein,
14 g. carbohydrate, 36 mg. cholesterol, 577 mg. sodium.
For exchange diets, count 2 vegetable, 1/2 skim, 2 lean meat.

POACHED SALMON WITH DILL SAUCE

This salmon entrée may be served warm or cold.

Preparation time: 10 minutes
Cooking time: 7 minutes
8 servings—4 ounces each

Salmon:

    12 ounces clam juice
    1 1/2 cups dry white wine
    1/4 cup fresh dill
    1/4 cup fresh lemon slices
    8 3-ounce salmon fillets

Dill sauce:

    1/2 cup fat-free sour cream
    1 1/2 tablespoons chopped fresh dill
    1/2 tablespoon lemon juice
    1/4 teaspoon white pepper

1. To poach salmon, combine first four ingredients in a deep skillet over medium heat. Bring mixture to a boil. Add salmon fillets, then reduce heat to simmer for 5 minutes.

2. In a small bowl, stir together all sauce ingredients just until mixed.

3. Remove salmon to a serving platter, and dress with sauce.

204 calories per serving: 8 g. fat, 25 g. protein,
8 g. carbohydrate, 75 mg. cholesterol, 150 mg. sodium.
For exchange diets, count 3 lean meat, 1/2 skim milk.

GLAZED CARROTS

Children love these cooked carrots!

Preparation time: 10 minutes
Cooking time: 16 minutes
6 servings—1/2 cup each

1 1/4 pounds carrots sliced into 1-inch pieces
2 tablespoons water
1 tablespoon reduced-fat margarine
2 tablespoons honey
1/2 teaspoon instant beef bouillon
1/8 teaspoon black pepper
1 tablespoon chopped parsley

1. In a covered microwave dish, cook carrots in water in microwave on high for about 8 minutes or until crisp-tender.

2. Meanwhile, in a large skillet, melt margarine; add honey and beef bouillon. Stir to mix. Add cooked carrots and water to skillet; stir to coat with glaze. Cook over medium-low heat about 8 minutes, stirring frequently.

3. Sprinkle with pepper and parsley.

70 calories per serving: 1 g. fat, 1 g. protein,
15 g. carbohydrate, 0 cholesterol, 52 mg. sodium.
For exchange diets, count 1 starch.

POTATO PANCAKES

Preparation time: 10 minutes
Cooking time: 13 minutes
6 servings—1 pancake each

4 cups grated peeled russet potatoes
1/2 teaspoon salt
1/4 teaspoon black pepper
1 tablespoon reduced-fat margarine
1/2 teaspoon cumin
2 ounces shredded reduced-fat cheddar cheese

1. Season potatoes with salt and pepper; mix well.

2. In a large nonstick skillet, melt margarine over medium-high heat. Place 1/3 cup of potatoes in the skillet, flattening with a spatula to form a pancake. Repeat, forming 3 more pancakes. Cook until golden brown, about 5 minutes.

3. Sprinkle each pancake with 1/8 teaspoon cumin. Cover each with 1/4 ounce cheese. Top each pancake with 1/3 cup potatoes. Press with a spatula to flatten. Turn, and cook the other side about 8 minutes or until potatoes are cooked through.

167 calories per serving: 3 g. fat, 6 g. protein,
31 g. carbohydrate, 5 mg. cholesterol, 47 mg. sodium.
For exchange diets, count 2 starch.

HERBED POTATOES BROILED WITH CHEESE

Preparation time: 10 minutes
Cooking time: 21 minutes
8 servings—1/2 potato each

4 large Idaho potatoes
nonstick cooking spray
1 large yellow onion, diced
1 cup fresh parsley, minced
1 teaspoon ground thyme
2 tablespoons herb vinegar
4 ounces goat cheese
1/2 teaspoon black pepper

1. Boil whole potatoes in their skins for 15 minutes. Remove from water, and slice in half lengthwise. Place potatoes in a shallow baking dish that has been sprayed with cooking spray.

2. Combine diced onion, parsley, thyme, vinegar, chunks of goat cheese, and pepper in a mixing bowl. Spoon herb and cheese mixture over the potatoes.

3. Broil for 6 minutes under low flame until cheese is melted.

116 calories per serving: 4 g. fat, 4 g. protein,
16 g. carbohydrate, 7 mg. cholesterol, 60 mg. sodium.
For exchange diets, count 1 starch, 1 fat.

SAUTÉED MUSHROOMS

Mushrooms are delicious spread over warm slices
of crusty French bread or grilled beef.

Preparation time: 5 minutes
Cooking time: 12 minutes
6 servings—1/3 cup each

8 ounces sliced fresh mushrooms
1/2 teaspoon minced garlic
2 teaspoons reduced-fat margarine
1/3 cup white wine
1 teaspoon Worcestershire sauce

1. In a small skillet, sauté mushrooms and garlic in margarine for 2 minutes, stirring occasionally.

2. Add remaining ingredients, and simmer about 10 minutes.

3. Remove garlic and discard.

25 calories per serving: 0 fat, 0 protein,
2 g. carbohydrate, 0 cholesterol, 21 mg. sodium.
For exchange diets, count 1 vegetable.

CHERRIES JUBILEE

Preparation time: 15 minutes
Cooking time: 11 minutes
12 servings—1/4 cup each

1 pound fresh cherries
1/2 cup water
1 cup sugar
1 tablespoon cornstarch dissolved in 2 tablespoons cold water
1 teaspoon almond extract
1 tablespoon cherry brandy
1/4 cup brandy, warmed

1. Remove stems and pits from the cherries.

2. Combine water and sugar in a saucepan, and cook over medium heat for 5 minutes. Add the cherries, and cook for 5 more minutes.

3. Remove the cherries from the pan with a slotted spoon to a shallow serving bowl. Stir cornstarch and water mixture into the sugar mixture. Continue cooking and stirring over medium heat for 1 minute or until the mixture is thick. Stir in almond extract and cherry brandy.

4. Pour thickened sauce over cherries. Pour warmed brandy over the sauce. Light with a match and serve flaming cherries as a topping for ice cream.

90 calories per serving: 0 fat, 1 g. protein,
22 g. carbohydrate, 0 cholesterol, 2 mg. sodium.
For exchange diets, count 1 1/2 fruit.

STRAWBERRIES WITH RASPBERRY SAUCE

A simple, yet elegant French dessert.

Preparation time: 10 minutes

8 servings—1/2 cup each

2 10-ounce packages thawed frozen raspberries
1 tablespoon raspberry brandy
4 cups whole strawberries, stems removed
3/4 cup reduced-fat whipped topping
chocolate shavings (optional)

1. Purée raspberries in a blender; pour through a sieve to remove seeds. Add brandy, and mix well.

2. Place strawberries in 8 individual dessert dishes. Pour raspberry sauce over strawberries. Garnish each serving with 2 tablespoons whipped topping. Top with chocolate shavings if desired.

161 calories per serving: 4 g. fat, 1 g. protein,
33 g. carbohydrate, 0 cholesterol, 2 mg. sodium.
For exchange diets, count 2 fruit, 1 fat.

Chapter Six

Germany

Suggested German Menus

Caraway Cabbage Salad
Rouladen
Fruited Barley Ring
Mocha Cake With Raspberry Sauce

Cottage Cheese German Style
Sauerbraten
Crockpot Kraut
Black Forest Cherry Cake

Add Fun, Subtract Expense

Open a bag of Birds Eye International Recipe Bavarian-Style Vegetables to add a German touch to an ordinary menu.

Look for "Bavarian-Style Seasoning," a one-shot rub to make any plain roast meat more German.

Try some juniper berries in your favorite stew. They are used in many German dishes such as sauerbraten and stuffed poultry. The berry has long been recognized as a remedy for a hangover.

Add juniper, cloves, or allspice to meat marinades.

Poppy seeds originated in Holland and intensify the sweet flavor in fruit salads or breads.

Add savory leaves to soups, stews, broiled fish, or chicken for a German flavor that was popular during the Roman empire.

Germans consider pepper the most important spice.

Add buttermilk and a dash of nutmeg to mashed potatoes.

Caraway can be added to cabbage, breads, and potatoes to make a Bavarian-style side dish.

To make soup more German, throw in a few dumplings. You can cheat and use a reduced-fat baking mix—just follow the directions for dumplings on the back of the box.

To make Berlin pea soup, dice a large leek into canned pea soup, and simmer at least 10 minutes or until the leek is tender.

For a quick salad, mix shredded carrots with equal parts lemon juice and sugar, then sprinkle with celery seeds. Marinate in the refrigerator at least 30 minutes.

PICKLED HAM

This appetizer is very popular in the Amana Colonies,
a German settlement in Iowa.

Preparation time: 10 minutes
Marinating time: 24 hours
10 servings—1 1/2 ounces each

1 pound lean cooked ham cut into 1-inch cubes
1 cup sliced onion
1 1/2 cups water
1 cup white vinegar
1 teaspoon celery seed
1/2 teaspoon black pepper

1. In a large bowl, combine all ingredients; refrigerate 24 hours.

86 calories per serving: 4 g. fat, 10 g. protein
4 g. carbohydrate, 26 mg. cholesterol, 628 mg. sodium.
For exchange diets, count 1 lean meat, 1 vegetable.

STREUSEL BREAKFAST CAKE

Preparation time: 15 minutes
Rising time: 35 minutes
Baking time: 45 minutes
16 servings—1/16 of pan each

16-ounce package hot roll mix
nonstick cooking spray
2 tablespoons butter-flavored margarine, melted
1 cup flour
1 cup sugar
1 tablespoon cinnamon
1 teaspoon grated orange rind
2 tablespoons margarine

1. Prepare hot roll mix according to package directions. Allow the dough to rise, then knead the dough 5 times on a floured surface. Roll into a large rectangle, 13 by 9 inches.

2. Spray a 13" x 9" pan with cooking spray. Transfer the dough to the prepared pan. Brush the top with melted margarine, then cover and allow to rise 15 minutes.

3. Preheat oven to 350° F. In a medium mixing bowl, combine flour, sugar, cinnamon, and orange rind. Cut in the margarine with a pastry blender.

4. Sprinkle sugar mixture over the surface of the dough, and bake for 40 to 45 minutes or until browned.

204 calories per serving: 4 g. fat, 5 g. protein
37 g. carbohydrate, 0 cholesterol, 234 mg. sodium.
For exchange diets, count 2 starch, 1 fat.

PORRIDGE

*This hot oatmeal is flavored with vanilla and lemon zest
as it would be served in Germany.*

Preparation time: 5 minutes
Cooking time: 5 minutes
8 servings—1/2 cup each

3 1/4 cups water
1/4 teaspoon salt
2 cups quick oats
1 cup skim milk
2 tablespoons brown sugar
1 teaspoon vanilla
1 teaspoon grated lemon zest

1. In a large saucepan, bring water and salt to a boil. Add oats, and cook over medium heat 1 minute, stirring occasionally. Remove from heat; cover pan, and let sit for 2 minutes.

2. Stir in remaining ingredients. Serve with additional milk if desired.

102 calories per serving: 1 g. fat, 5 g. protein
17 g. carbohydrate, 1 mg. cholesterol, 84 mg. sodium.
For exchange diets, count 1 1/2 starch.

CABBAGE SALAD
Preparation time: 15 minutes
6 servings—3/4 cup each

Cabbage salad:
    3 cups shredded cabbage
    2 finely chopped celery stalks
    1 shredded carrot
    2 tablespoons chopped green pepper
Dressing:
    1/4 cup fat-free sour cream
    1/4 cup buttermilk
    2 tablespoons vinegar
    1 tablespoon fat-free mayonnaise
    1/2 teaspoon sugar
    1/2 teaspoon celery seed
    1/2 teaspoon celery salt
    1/4 teaspoon black pepper

1. In a medium bowl, combine all ingredients for cabbage salad.

2. In a small bowl, whisk together all ingredients for dressing. Mix dressing into cabbage salad.

52 calories per serving: 0 fat, 3 g. protein
11 g. carbohydrate, 0 cholesterol, 60 mg. sodium.
For exchange diets, count 2 vegetable.

COTTAGE CHEESE GERMAN STYLE

Green onions add color and extra flavor to this simple salad.

Preparation time: 5 minutes
Chilling time: 20 minutes
4 servings—1/2 cup each

16-ounce carton low-fat cottage cheese
2 green onions, thinly sliced
2 tablespoons buttermilk
1/8 teaspoon pepper

1. Mix all ingredients together, and chill for at least 20 minutes.

83 calories per serving: 1 g. fat, 14 g. protein
3 g. carbohydrate, 5 mg. cholesterol, 462 mg. sodium.
For exchange diets, count 2 very lean meat.

DUTCH LETTUCE

Preparation time: 20 minutes
6 servings—1 1/2 cups each

6 cups lettuce torn into bite-size pieces
3 small sliced cooked potatoes
2 tablespoons chopped onion
1 hard-cooked egg, peeled and chopped (optional)
1/4 cup fat-free vinaigrette, warmed in microwave
2 slices chopped bacon, cooked until crisp

1. In a large bowl, gently toss together lettuce, potatoes, onion, and egg (if desired).

2. Pour warm dressing over salad. Crumble bacon over top.

132 calories per serving: 3 g. fat, 6 g. protein
20 g. carbohydrate, 38 mg. cholesterol, 87 mg. sodium.
For exchange diets, count 1 starch, 1 vegetable, 1/2 fat.

CARAWAY CABBAGE SALAD
Preparation time: 10 minutes
Cooking time: 10 minutes
8 servings—1 cup each

2 cups water
1 teaspoon salt
1 pound bag shredded cabbage
1 teaspoon caraway seed
4 slices bacon, broiled crisp and diced
1 medium onion, finely chopped
1/4 cup vinegar

1. Bring water and salt to a boil. Add cabbage and caraway seed. Return mixture to a boil, and boil for 7 minutes. Drain well.

2. Transfer drained cabbage to a salad bowl. Add bacon and onion. Toss with vinegar, and serve immediately.

51 calories per serving: 2 g. fat, 3 g. protein
8 g. carbohydrate, 2 mg. cholesterol, 324 mg. sodium.
For exchange diets, count: 2 vegetable.

SAUERKRAUT SALAD

Preparation time: 15 minutes
8 servings—3/4 cup each

16-ounce can sauerkraut, drained
2 apples, peeled and chopped
1 large carrot, peeled and grated
1 small onion, chopped fine
1 teaspoon dried dill weed
1 teaspoon dried parsley
2 tablespoons sugar
2 tablespoons lemon juice
2 tablespoons vegetable oil

1. Combine sauerkraut, apples, carrot, onion, dill, parsley, sugar, and lemon juice in a large salad bowl. Mix ingredients well.

2. Heat the oil in a glass measuring cup in the microwave for 30 seconds. Pour the oil over the salad, and toss. Chill until serving time.

79 calories per serving: 4 g. fat, 1 g. protein
8 g. carbohydrate, 0 cholesterol, 434 mg. sodium.
For exchange diets, count 1 fat, 2 vegetable.

CHICKEN AND ASPARAGUS SALAD

Preparation time: 15 minutes
Cooking time: 3 minutes
8 servings—1 1/2 cups each

1 pound fresh asparagus, cleaned, stemmed, and sliced diagonally into 1-inch pieces
1 tablespoon lemon juice
1/2 cup reduced-fat mayonnaise
2 teaspoons cider vinegar
1 tablespoon dried parsley flakes
1/2 teaspoon salt
1 teaspoon sugar
2 10-ounce cans white meat chicken, well drained
20-ounce can pineapple chunks, well drained
2 large tomatoes, seeded and dried

1. Place chopped asparagus in a microwave-safe dish. Sprinkle with lemon juice, cover, and microwave 3 minutes. Carefully remove cover, allowing steam to escape and cooking to stop.

2. In a large salad bowl, combine mayonnaise, vinegar, parsley, salt, and sugar. Add chicken, pineapple, tomatoes, and steamed asparagus. Use two forks to toss the salad ingredients with the dressing, and serve.

221 calories per serving: 5 g. fat, 27 g. protein
17 g. carbohydrate, 65 mg. cholesterol, 558 mg. sodium.
For exchange diets, count 3 very lean meat, 1 fruit, 1 vegetable.

HOLIDAY DUTCH BABY

*This puff pancake is filled with fresh fruit and is
very elegant when served at a Christmas brunch.*

**Preparation time: 15 minutes
Cooking time: 20 minutes
4 servings—1/4 slice each**

1/2 cup all-purpose flour
1/2 cup light eggnog
1/2 cup liquid egg substitute
1/2 teaspoon ground nutmeg
nonstick cooking spray
3 cups sliced fresh fruit
1 tablespoon lemon juice
powdered sugar (optional)

1. Preheat oven to 425° F.

2. In a mixing bowl, beat flour, eggnog, egg substitute, and nutmeg
until smooth.

3. Spray a 9- or 10-inch ovenproof skillet with cooking spray. Heat
over medium heat. Remove from heat, and pour pancake batter into
skillet.

4. Bake uncovered for 15 to 20 minutes or until puffy and golden.

5. Toss fruit with lemon juice. Top pancake with fruit. Sprinkle with
powdered sugar, if desired. Serve immediately.

267 calories per serving: 12 g. fat, 16 g. protein
0 carbohydrate, 76 mg. cholesterol, 110 mg. sodium.
For exchange diets, count 4 lean meat.

Black Forest Venison

This savory stew features cranberries.

Preparation time: 25 minutes
Marinating time: 4 to 24 hours; Cooking time: 1 1/4 hours
8 servings—4 ounces each

Marinade:

1 large onion, chopped
1 carrot, diced
1 large stalk celery, diced
1/4 teaspoon minced garlic
2 whole cloves
1/2 teaspoon rosemary
1/2 teaspoon thyme
1 bay leaf
1/4 cup fresh cranberries
5 peppercorns
1 tablespoon chopped fresh parsley
1/2 teaspoon salt
3 cups dry red wine
1/4 cup red wine vinegar
1 tablespoon vegetable oil

Venison stew:

2 pounds venison stewing meat, cut into 8 4-ounce portions
1/2 tsp. marjoram
1 large onion, diced fine
1/4 cup flour
1 cup no-added-salt beef broth
1/4 teaspoon pepper
1 cup nonfat sour cream

1. Combine all marinade ingredients in a medium saucepan. Bring to a boil, reduce heat, and simmer for 5 minutes.

2. Place venison in a large casserole dish. Pour marinade over the meat. Cover and refrigerate for 4 to 24 hours, stirring several times.

3. Drain meat, and place in a large stockpot. Rub marjoram into the meat, and sprinkle with diced onion.

4. In a shaker container, combine flour, broth, and pepper. Pour over venison and onions.

5. Cover and bring mixture to a boil over medium-high heat. Reduce heat to low, and simmer for 1 hour.

6. Just before serving, remove meat to a casserole dish. Fold sour cream into the broth mixture. Heat through (but don't overcook), and pour over the meat. Serve with rye bread or boiled potatoes.

262 calories per serving: 6 g. fat, 38 g. protein
14 g. carbohydrate, 127 mg. cholesterol, 410 mg. sodium.
For exchange diets, count 5 very lean meat.

VEGETABLES AND KIELBASA DELIGHT

Preparation time: 10 minutes
Cooking time: 15 minutes
8 servings—3/4 cup each

1/4 pound reduced-fat ring sausage, diced fine
1/4 cup beer or water
16 ounces frozen brussels sprouts, cauliflower, and carrot mixture
1/3 cup all-fruit apricot preserves
2 tablespoons brown mustard
1 small red apple, cored and sliced thin

1. In a large skillet, cook diced sausage over medium heat until it is browned.

2. Add beer or water, vegetables, preserves, and mustard. Continue cooking uncovered over medium heat for 6 minutes or until the vegetables are tender.

3. Stir in the apple slices, and cook for 2 more minutes, just until the apples are heated through. Serve hot.

90 calories per serving: 4 g. fat, 2 g. protein
12 g. carbohydrate, 9 mg. cholesterol, 176 mg. sodium.
For exchange diets, count 2 vegetable, 1 fat.

ROULADEN

This is a spicy variation of the traditional recipe.

Preparation time: 25 minutes
Roasting time: 1 1/4 hours
8 servings—1 roll each

1 1/2 pounds lean boneless round steak, trimmed and
   cut 1/2-inch thick
1/2 teaspoon salt
1/2 teaspoon dried oregano
1/2 teaspoon black pepper
4 ounces reduced-fat ham, sliced
2 medium size ripe tomatoes, chopped
4-ounce can mild green chilies, drained and chopped
1 medium onion, chopped fine
1/4 teaspoon minced garlic
1/4 cup dry bread crumbs
2 medium carrots
2 tablespoons vegetable oil
3/4 cup water
1 teaspoon vinegar
1 teaspoon Worcestershire sauce
1 bay leaf

1. Pound trimmed steak with a mallet until it's 1/4-inch thick. Cut
into 8 pieces. Sprinkle with salt, oregano and pepper. Arrange slices
of ham over the beef. Sprinkle with chopped tomatoes, chilies, onion,
garlic, and bread crumbs.

2. Cut the carrot lengthwise into halves, then cut the halves lengthwise into 2 strips. Arrange 2 pieces on the ham. Carefully roll up the
beef slices, and secure the rolls with skewers or a string.

3. Heat vegetable oil in a large Dutch oven. Transfer beef rolls to the
Dutch oven, and brown the rolls on all sides. Add water, vinegar,
Worcestershire sauce, and bay leaf.

Rouladen (continued)

4. Cover the Dutch oven, and roast in a 325° oven for 1 hour and 15 minutes or until beef is tender. Serve beef rolls with noodles or potatoes.

239 calories per serving: 9 g. fat, 30 g. protein
8 g. carbohydrate, 94 mg. cholesterol, 538 mg. sodium.
For exchange diets, count: 4 lean meat, 1 vegetable.

SAUERBRATEN

Marinated beef is one of the most well-known German dishes. Sauerbraten gets its unique flavor from the tangy marinade and the addition of gingersnap cookies.

Preparation time: 20 minutes
Marinating time: 24 hours; Cooking time: 3 hours
12 servings—3 ounces each

3 pound lean boneless chuck roast, well trimmed
1 1/2 cups water
1 cup red wine vinegar
1 sliced medium onion
1 sliced carrot
1 sliced celery stalk
6 whole cloves
1 bay leaf
1/4 teaspoon black pepper
1 tablespoon vegetable oil
2 tablespoons brown sugar
8 crushed gingersnap cookies (about 1/3 cup)

1. Place beef in a large glass bowl. Prick thoroughly with a fork. Add all remaining ingredients except oil, brown sugar, and gingersnaps. Cover and marinate in refrigerator for 24 to 36 hours (for stronger flavor, use longer marinating time).

2. Remove meat from marinade; drain well, reserving marinade. Strain marinade.

3. Heat oil in a large nonstick skillet. Add beef, and brown on all sides. Add 1 1/2 cups reserved marinade. Cover and simmer 2 1/2 to 3 hours or until tender.

4. Place beef on a warm platter. Add brown sugar and gingersnaps to marinade in skillet. Cook until mixture comes to a boil, stirring constantly. Pour over meat.

289 calories per serving: 13 g. fat, 36 g. protein
7 g. carbohydrate, 120 mg. cholesterol, 117 mg. sodium.
For exchange diets, count 4 1/2 lean meat, 1/2 starch.

PORK AND PRUNES

Preparation time: 15 minutes
Roasting time: 1 1/2 hours

8 servings—4 ounces pork and 2 tablespoons fruit each

1 tablespoon flour
2 pounds boneless rolled pork, well trimmed
1/2 cup dried apricots
1/2 cup pitted prunes
1/8 cup brown sugar
1/4 cup dry white wine

1. Preheat oven to 325° F.

2. Select a plastic cooking bag to fit the pork roast. Sprinkle the inside of the bag with flour. Insert meat thermometer. Place meat and fruit in the bag, then sprinkle with sugar and wine.

3. Tie the bag securely, poke 4 small holes in the top of the bag, and roast for 1 1/2 hours or until meat thermometer registers 170° F.

4. Transfer pork roast to a serving platter, and arrange apricots and prunes around the meat.

254 calories per serving: 6 g. fat, 32 g. protein
18 g. carbohydrate, 173 mg. cholesterol, 170 mg. sodium.
For exchange diets, count 5 very lean meat, 1 fruit.

TROUT WITH POTATOES

Preparation time: 10 minutes
Cooking time: 15 minutes
8 servings—4 ounces of trout and 2 potatoes each

2 pounds freshwater trout fillets
1 cup vinegar
4 cups water
1 teaspoon salt
1/4 cup white wine
16 very small potatoes
butter-flavored cooking spray
1 sprig parsley
1 lemon
1 tomato

1. Arrange trout fillets in a shallow bowl. Heat vinegar in the microwave in a glass cup measure for 2 minutes on high. Pour the vinegar over the trout (the trout will turn blue).

2. In a 4-quart saucepan, bring water, salt, and wine to a simmer. Carefully place trout fillets in the water, and simmer for 15 minutes.

3. Meanwhile, place washed unpeeled potatoes in a casserole dish, sprinkle with 2 tablespoons of water, and cover. Cook potatoes in the microwave on 70% power for 15 minutes. Remove cooked potatoes to a serving platter. Spray with cooking spray.

4. Remove trout with a slotted spoon, and place in the center of the platter. Garnish the platter with fresh parsley, lemon, and tomato wedges.

276 calories per serving: 4 g. fat, 30 g. protein
30 g. carbohydrate, 67 mg. cholesterol, 300 mg. sodium.
For exchange diets, count 4 very lean meat, 1 1/2 starch.

SAUERKRAUT

Caraway seeds add intense flavor to this German favorite.

Preparation time: 5 minutes
Cooking time: 15 minutes
4 servings—4 ounces each

16-ounce can sauerkraut
1 teaspoon caraway seeds
1/2 teaspoon margarine

1. Combine all ingredients in a saucepan. Simmer for 15 minutes.

20 calories per serving: 0 fat, 0 protein
4 g. carbohydrate, 0 cholesterol, 1,426 mg. sodium.
For exchange diets, count 1 vegetable.

FRUITED BARLEY RING

This elegant side dish will complement any plain meat entree.

Preparation time: 15 minutes
Cooking time: 30 minutes; Chilling time: 30 minutes
8 servings—1 cup each

---

6 cups water
1 cup dried apricots, diced
1 cup pearl barley, washed
2 tablespoons fresh lemon zest (tiny strips of thin lemon peel)
1 tablespoon cornstarch
2 tablespoons cold water or apple juice
1/2 cup golden raisins
1/4 cup brown sugar

1. Bring 6 cups of water to a boil. Add apricots, barley, and lemon zest. Cook over medium heat for 30 minutes or until barley is tender. Drain away any excess liquid.

2. Pack the barley and apricot mixture into a 4-cup ring mold, and refrigerate at least 30 minutes.

3. Dissolve cornstarch in cold water. In a small saucepan, combine raisins, brown sugar, and cornstarch and water mixture. Bring mixture to a boil, then reduce heat and simmer for 1 to 2 minutes until it is thick and clear. Allow raisins to cool slightly.

4. Unmold barley and apricot combination onto a serving plate, and pour raisin sauce around the top. You may need to ease unmolding by gently dipping pan in very warm tap water to loosen the edges.

206 calories per serving: 0 fat, 5 g. protein
48 g. carbohydrate, 0 cholesterol, 7 mg. sodium.
For exchange diets, count 1 starch, 2 fruit.

HOT GERMAN POTATO SALAD

Leftovers are delicious!

Preparation time: 15 minutes
Cooking time: 30 minutes
16 servings—3/4 cup each

Salad:
    3 slices bacon, diced
    1 medium onion, chopped
    9 medium red potatoes, boiled and sliced 1/2-inch thick (leave
      the skin on)
    2 tablespoons chopped dill pickle

Dressing:
    3/4 cup water
    1/3 cup cider vinegar
    2 tablespoons sugar
    1/2 teaspoon salt
    1/2 teaspoon celery seeds
    1/4 teaspoon dry mustard
    1/8 teaspoon pepper

1. In a heavy skillet, cook diced bacon and onion until crisp. Remove bacon mixture with a slotted spoon, and set aside. Drain off all fat from the pan.

2. Add all dressing ingredients to the skillet, and boil for 1 minute, stirring constantly.

3. In a large bowl, gently stir together the cooked potatoes, chopped pickle, bacon and onion, and cooked dressing, and serve immediately.

135 calories per serving: 1 g. fat, 3 g. protein
31 g. carbohydrate, 2 mg. cholesterol, 109 mg. sodium.
For exchange diets, count 1 starch, 1 fruit.

CROCKPOT KRAUT

Preparation time: 20 minutes
Crockpot cooking time: 2 to 3 hours
8 servings—1 cup each

1 tablespoon vegetable oil
1 large onion, chopped fine
16-ounce can sauerkraut, drained
1 cup reduced-sodium beef broth
2 apples, sliced thin
2 slices bacon, broiled crisp and diced
1 large potato, peeled and grated

1. Heat vegetable oil in a large skillet. Add the onion, and sauté until golden brown.

2. Transfer the onions to a Crockpot or slow cooker. Add remaining ingredients, and stir well.

3. Cook for 2 to 3 hours on high or until apples are tender.

84 calories per serving: 3 g. fat, 6 g. protein
13 g. carbohydrate, 4 mg. cholesterol, 808 mg. sodium.
For exchange diets, count 2 vegetable, 1/2 fat.

CHEESY BRUSSELS SPROUTS

Preparation time: 10 minutes
Microwave time: 10 minutes
Broiling time: 5 minutes
8 servings—1 cup each

2 quarts fresh brussels sprouts, washed and trimmed
1 cup no-added-salt beef broth
4 ounces grated Gouda cheese
dash of nutmeg
1 tablespoon margarine

1. Place cleaned and trimmed brussels sprouts in a microwave-safe casserole dish. Add beef broth, and cover. Cook in the microwave for 8 to 10 minutes or until brussels sprouts are tender crisp.

2. Drain away broth, and sprinkle with cheese and nutmeg. Dot with margarine. Broil for 5 minutes until cheese melts.

151 calories per serving: 6 g. fat, 10 g. protein
20 g. carbohydrate, 16 mg. cholesterol, 177 mg. sodium.
For exchange diets, count 4 vegetable, 1 fat.

MOCHA CAKE WITH RASPBERRY SAUCE

Preparation time: 15 minutes
Baking time: 35 minutes
16 servings—1 slice each

nonstick cooking spray
1 cup flour
1/3 cup cocoa
1 teaspoon instant coffee granules
1 teaspoon baking powder
1 teaspoon baking soda
5 large egg whites, at room temperature
1 1/3 cups brown sugar
1 cup coffee-flavored nonfat yogurt
1 teaspoon vanilla extract
1/2 teaspoon sifted powdered sugar
1/2 cup all-fruit raspberry jam

1. Preheat oven to 350° F. Spray a 9" round cake pan with cooking spray.

2. In a medium mixing bowl, mix flour, cocoa, coffee granules, baking power, and soda with an electric mixer.

3. In another large bowl, beat egg whites, brown sugar, yogurt, and vanilla together until well blended, about 1 minute.

4. Fold dry ingredients into the egg white and sugar mixture. Transfer batter to the prepared pan, and bake for 35 minutes or until the cake tests done.

5. Cool the cake in the pan for 10 minutes, then cut around the edges and turn out onto a serving platter. Dust the top with powdered sugar, and cut into 16 slices. To serve, warm jam in the microwave for 30 seconds. Transfer slices of cake to a dessert plate, and top with warm jam. Consider nonfat vanilla ice milk as a second optional topping.

144 calories per serving: 1 g. fat, 6 g. protein
33 g. carbohydrate, 1 mg. cholesterol, 115 mg. sodium.
For exchange diets, count 1 fruit, 1 starch.

PFEFFERNESSE

(FEHF-uhr-noos)

My uncle Keith Carroll taught me how to dip
these spicy nuggets in coffee.

Preparation time: 20 minutes
Baking time: 20 minutes
30 servings—2 cookies each

6 tablespoons margarine
1/4 cup sugar
1/4 cup brown sugar
1/4 cup cold coffee
3/4 cup maple syrup
3 cups sifted flour
1 teaspoon baking powder
1/8 teaspoon cloves
1/8 teaspoon black pepper
1/8 teaspoon cinnamon
1/8 teaspoon anise seeds
1/4 cup chopped walnuts
nonstick cooking spray

1. Preheat oven to 300° F.

2. In a medium bowl, combine margarine with sugars. Stir in coffee and syrup. In another medium bowl, sift together flour, baking powder, cloves, pepper, and cinnamon. Fold into creamed mixture. Add anise seeds and nuts.

3. Shape dough into small balls, and place on a baking sheet that has been sprayed with cooking spray.

4. Bake for 20 minutes or until golden brown.

107 calories per serving: 3 g. fat, 2 g. protein
19 g. carbohydrate, 0 cholesterol, 38 mg. sodium.
For exchange diets, count: 1 1/2 starch.

BLACK FOREST CHERRY CAKE

Preparation time: 20 minutes
Baking time: 30 minutes
16 servings—1 slice each

nonstick cooking spray
2 1/4 cups flour
1 2/3 cups sugar
2/3 cup cocoa
1 1/4 teaspoon baking soda
1 teaspoon salt
1/4 teaspoon baking powder
1 1/4 cups water
1/4 cup margarine
1/2 cup liquid egg substitute
2 teaspoons vanilla
18-ounce can reduced-sugar cherry pie filling
2 cups reduced-fat frozen whipped topping, thawed

Optional garnish:
2 ounces sweet chocolate, softened to room temperature and
   peeled into curls

1. Preheat oven to 350°. Spray 2 9" round cake pans with cooking spray.

2. In a medium mixing bowl, beat flour, sugar, cocoa, soda, salt, baking powder, water, margarine, egg substitute, and vanilla together on low speed, scraping the bowl constantly. Increase speed to high, and beat for 3 more minutes or until smooth.

3. Pour the batter into the prepared pans, and bake for 30 minutes. Cool for 5 minutes, then remove the cakes from the pans and continue cooling on wire racks.

Black Forest Cherry Cake (continued)

4. Place one cake layer upside down on a serving plate. Spread 1 cup of cherry pie filling on the cake, then top with 1 cup of whipped topping. Place the other layer upside down on the whipped topping. Spread the remaining pie filling on the top, and frost the sides with the remaining whipped topping. Refrigerate until serving. Garnish each slice with a few chocolate curls if desired.

220 calories per serving: 4 g. fat, 5 g. protein
41 g. carbohydrate, 26 mg. cholesterol, 599 mg. sodium.
For exchange diets, count 1 1/2 starch, 1 fruit, 1 fat.

WINE-STEWED PEARS

This recipe is great for fresh baking apples as well.

Preparation time: 15 minutes
Cooking time: 20 minutes
Chilling time: 30 minutes

8 servings—1 pear plus liquid each

1 cup water
1 cup rosé wine
1/3 cup sugar
8 large pears, peeled, cored, and quartered
2 cinnamon sticks
1 teaspoon grated orange rind
Optional garnish:
    chopped walnuts

1. Combine first 3 ingredients in a medium saucepan, and cook until sugar is dissolved. Add pears, and simmer for 15 minutes.

2. Add cinnamon and orange rind; simmer until fruit is tender.

3. Chill for 30 minutes or until ready to serve. Ladle fruit with juice into dessert bowls. Garnish with a sprinkle of chopped walnuts if desired.

195 calories per serving (to reduce calories, discard the juice):
0 fat, 160 g. protein, 47 g. carbohydrate, 0 cholesterol, 4 mg. sodium.
For exchange diets, count 3 fruit.

Chapter Seven

Scandinavia

Suggested Scandinavian Menu

Glögg
Marinated Salmon
Limpa
Swedish Meatballs
Hasselback Potatoes
Fruit Soup

Add Fun, Subtract Expense

The Swedish word for rutabaga is rotabagge. Rutabagas are larger, rounder, denser, and sweeter than their cousins, the turnips. They have a pronounced flavor and lend themselves to baking, boiling, steaming, or stir-frying. They also make a nice raw veggie dipper.

In the winter, eat as the Norwegians do. People from Norway have long regarded food as a fuel to help keep out the cold. Breakfast tends to be substantial with herring, cold meats, and cheese served with crusty bread. Lunch breaks are short and this midday meal often consists of open sandwiches. The hot meal of the day may be eaten as early as 5 o'clock.

The Danes eat more meat than other Scandinavians. Home-produced ham and bacon are favorites, as are hare and pheasant.

Flatbreads and crispbreads originated in Finland, where they accompany stews.

Scandinavians use mainly the sweeter spices, even in their sauces. Try cardamom, poppy seed, cinnamon, nutmeg, or caraway for a Scandinavian touch.

Dill seed is very popular in Scandinavia, and is used to flavor all types of seafood.

GLÖGG

This Swedish tradition, also called Grog, is a warm spicy wine.
Great for coming in out of the snow.

Preparation time: 5 minutes
Cooking time: 5 minutes
6 servings—5 ounces each

1/2 cup water
3 tablespoons sugar
4 crushed cardamom pods
3 whole cloves
2 cinnamon sticks
2 1/4 cups dry red wine
3/4 cup cranberry juice

Garnish:
1/4 cup dried cranberries
1 orange, cut into 6 slices

1. In a medium saucepan, combine water, sugar, cardamom, cloves, and cinnamon. Simmer over medium heat about 3 minutes. Discard cardamom pods.

2. Add wine and cranberry juice. Heat through; do not boil. Pour into cups, and garnish with cranberries and orange slices.

114 calories per serving: 0 fat, 0 protein,
15 g. carbohydrate, 0 cholesterol, 7 mg. sodium.
For exchange diets, count 2 fruit.

MARINATED SALMON

Preparation time: 10 minutes
Marinating time: 30 minutes
16 servings—1 ounce each

1 pound can red salmon, drained well
1 teaspoon salt
2 tablespoons sugar
1 tablespoon freshly ground pepper
1 tablespoon dill weed
1/8 cup cider vinegar

1. Drain salmon well, and place in a shallow dish. Sprinkle remaining ingredients over the top. Cover and refrigerate at least 30 minutes.

2. Use a fork to lightly toss salmon with seasonings. Serve with toasted cocktail rye bread or rye crackers.

39 calories per serving: 1 g. fat, 5 g. protein,
2 g. carbohydrate, 7 mg. cholesterol, 229 mg. sodium.
For exchange diets, count 1 very lean meat.

SWEDISH MEATBALLS

A must for the holidays!
Preparation time: 15 minutes
Baking time: 25 minutes
8 servings—3 ounces each

Meatballs:
1 pound extra-lean ground beef
1/2 pound lean ground turkey
3/4 cup nonfat bread crumbs
1/4 cup skim milk
1/4 cup liquid egg substitute
1/4 cup finely chopped onion
1/2 teaspoon salt
1/2 teaspoon black pepper

Sauce:
2 tablespoons flour
3/4 cup water
1 cup skim milk
1 teaspoon instant beef bouillon
1/4 teaspoon salt
1/4 teaspoon nutmeg

1. Preheat oven to 350° F.

2. In a large bowl, mix together all ingredients for meatballs. Shape into 1-inch balls. Place meatballs in a 15" x 10" x 1" jelly roll pan. Bake for 20 to 25 minutes or until browned.

3. In a saucepan, stir together flour and 2 tablespoons drippings from meatballs. Cook over low heat until mixture is smooth and bubbly. Stir in water, milk, bouillon, and salt. Heat to boiling, stirring constantly. Boil and stir 1 minute.

4. Pour sauce over meatballs. Sprinkle with nutmeg.

256 calories per serving: 12 g. fat, 26 g. protein,
11 g. carbohydrate, 79 mg. cholesterol, 398 mg. sodium.
For exchange diets, count 4 lean meat, 1/2 starch.

LIMPA

Preparation time: 10 minutes
Bread machine time: 4 hours, 10 minutes
Manual method preparation time: 25 minutes
Rising time: 2 hours; Baking time: 25 minutes
Cooling time: 15 minutes
24 servings—1/2 slice each

1 1/8 cups water
2 cups white bread flour
1 cup rye flour
3 tablespoons honey
2 tablespoons nonfat dry milk powder
1 teaspoon salt
2 teaspoons grated orange peel
1/2 teaspoon fennel
1/2 teaspoon caraway seed
1 teaspoon yeast
1 tablespoon soft margarine

1. Place all ingredients in order listed in bread machine pan. Push "start."

2. Loaf will be done in 4 hours and 10 minutes using a Hitachi bread machine.

3. Serve with cold smoked salmon.

4. If you prefer making bread from scratch, gently mix hot tap water with honey, dry milk powder, yeast, orange peel, fennel, caraway seed, salt, and margarine in a large mixing bowl. Allow mixture to rest 5 minutes. Gradually add white flour and rye flour, working the mixture to a smooth dough. Knead for 10 minutes, then cover and allow dough to rise for 1 hour in a warm place. Punch the dough down, form a loaf shape, and place in a loaf pan that has been sprayed with nonstick cooking spray. Allow dough to rise again for an hour. Bake in a preheated 350° oven for 25 minutes or until the top is browned. Cool for 15 minutes, then remove bread to a cooling rack.

75 calories per serving: 1 g. fat, 2 g. protein,
14 g. carbohydrate, 0 cholesterol, 110 mg. sodium.
For exchange diets, count 1 starch.

CRANBERRY BEEF STEW

Preparation time: 15 minutes
Cooking time: 1 3/4 hours
16 servings—2/3 cup each

3 pounds lean beef stew meat, cubed
1 teaspoon salt
1/2 teaspoon pepper
1/4 cup flour
1 tablespoon vegetable oil
2 medium onions, chopped
2 bay leaves
1 pound whole cranberry sauce

1. Place beef cubes in a plastic bag. Sprinkle with salt and pepper. Add flour to the bag, and shake to coat the meat.

2. Heat the oil in a Dutch oven; add meat. Brown for 10 minutes or until meat is no longer pink. Stir in onions, bay leaves, and cranberry sauce. Cover, and cook over medium-low heat for 1 1/2 hours.

254 calories per serving: 10 g. fat, 24 g. protein,
17 g. carbohydrate, 57 mg. cholesterol, 214 mg. sodium.
For exchange diets, count 3 very lean meat, 1 fruit, 1 vegetable.

MARINATED POT ROAST OF BEEF OR VENISON

A tradition of Swedish farmers.

Preparation time: 20 minutes
Marinating time: at least 12 hours; Cooking time: 1 1/2 hours
8 servings—4 ounces each

2 pound beef or venison roast
Marinade:
   2 cups red wine
   1/3 cup red wine vinegar
   2 large onions, sliced thin
   10 allspice berries
   10 peppercorns
   4 bay leaves
   nonstick cooking spray
Sauce:
   2 tablespoons flour
   1/4 cup water
   1/2 cup half and half

1. Place the roast in a shallow pan.

2. Combine the ingredients for the marinade, and pour over the roast. Cover, and marinate in the refrigerator for at least 12 hours or up to 3 days. Turn the meat several times to ensure even marinating.

3. Spray a large Dutch oven with nonstick cooking spray. Remove the meat from the marinade, and brown the meat on all sides. Pour the marinade through a strainer over the meat, and cover. Cook over low heat for 1 1/2 hours. Remove the meat to a warm platter.

4. Combine flour, water, and half and half in a shaker container. Stir the sauce into the meat drippings with a whisk. Bring the sauce to a boil, and boil for 2 minutes. Serve with the roast and boiled potatoes.

280 calories per serving: 11 g. fat, 25 g. protein,
8 g. carbohydrate, 77 mg. cholesterol, 63 mg. sodium.
For exchange diets, count 3 very lean meat, 1 fat, 1 vegetable, 1/2 fruit.

HASSELBACK POTATOES

Preparation time: 15 minutes
Baking time: 45 minutes
8 servings—1 potato each

6 medium baking potatoes
nonstick cooking spray
1/4 teaspoon salt
1/2 teaspoon pepper
1/4 cup Parmesan cheese
2 tablespoons margarine, melted
2 tablespoons dry bread crumbs

1. Preheat oven to 425° F.

2. Cut potatoes crosswise into 1/8-inch slices, cutting only three-fourths of the way through the potato. Place the potatoes, cut side up, in a baking dish that has been sprayed with cooking spray.

3. Sprinkle the potatoes with salt and pepper. Cover, and bake for 25 minutes. Mix cheese, melted margarine, and bread crumbs together in a small bowl; sprinkle over the potatoes. Bake an additional 20 minutes or until tender.

205 calories per serving: 4 g. fat, 2 g. protein,
40 g. carbohydrate, 0 cholesterol, 163 mg. sodium.
For exchange diets, count 2 starch, 1 fat.

MUSHROOMS IN CREAM SAUCE

The forests of Finland yield edible mushrooms for this recipe.

Preparation time: 10 minutes
Cooking time: 10 minutes
8 servings—3/4 cup each

1 1/2 pounds fresh mushrooms
1 tablespoon lemon juice
1 large onion, chopped
1 tablespoon margarine
1 tablespoon flour
1 cup evaporated skim milk
1/4 teaspoon white pepper
1 teaspoon finely chopped parsley
1 tablespoon finely chopped chives
1/2 cup reduced-fat sour cream

1. Clean and slice the mushrooms. Put the slices in a skillet.

2. Sprinkle the mushrooms with lemon juice; add onion and margarine. Cook over medium heat until mushrooms and onion are soft.

3. In a shaker container, combine flour and evaporated milk. Pour over the mushrooms, and continue cooking over medium heat until sauce is thick.

4. Sprinkle with parsley and chives; fold in sour cream. Serve as an accompaniment to any meat dish.

81 calories per serving: 2 g. fat, 5 g. protein,
12 g. carbohydrate, 1 mg. cholesterol, 76 mg. sodium.
For exchange diets, count 2 vegetable, 1/2 fat.

STUFFED ONIONS

This is a popular dish on smorgasbords.

Preparation time: 20 minutes
Baking time: 30 minutes
8 servings—2 stuffed skins each

---

4 large onions
Filling:
   1 large onion, finely chopped
   2 boiled potatoes, mashed
   1/3 cup bread crumbs
   1/4 cup skim milk
   1/4 teaspoon white pepper
   1 teaspoon Worcestershire sauce
Topping:
   1/4 cup bread crumbs
   2 tablespoons margarine, melted
   1/4 cup chopped fresh parsley

1. Peel the onions. Place them in a microwave-safe dish, and sprinkle with 1/4 cup water. Cover and cook for 15 minutes on high power. Remove the cover, and allow them to cool.

2. Meanwhile, prepare the filling by mixing the ingredients together in a mixing bowl.

3. Make a cut from the top of the steamed onion to the bottom, carefully pulling awaw the layers of onion skin. Fill each skin with stuffing, then fold the ends over and lay each stuffed skin, folded ends down in a casserole dish.

4. Preheat oven to 400° F. Combine the ingredients for the topping in a small bowl, and sprinkle over the onions. Bake for 30 minutes.

---

119 calories per serving: 3 g. fat, 3 g. protein,
20 g. carbohydrate, 0 cholesterol, 101 mg. sodium.
For exchange diets, count 1 vegetable, 1 starch.

FRUIT SOUP

Preparation time: 10 minutes
Cooking time: 20 minutes; Chilling time: 2 hours
8 servings—1 cup each

2 12-ounce packages mixed dried fruit
8 cups water
1/4 cup sugar
1 teaspoon ground mace
1/4 cup cornstarch
1/3 cup water

1. Combine fruit and water in a medium saucepan. Bring mixture to a simmer over medium heat; cook for 15 minutes. Stir in sugar and mace.

2. Combine cornstarch with cold water in a small bowl. Gradually add it to the fruit mixture, stirring very gently, but constantly, until mixture is thick.

3. Refrigerate soup. Serve cold as a dessert with a sugar cookie.

128 calories per serving: 1 g. fat, 1 g. protein,
25 g. carbohydrate, 0 cholesterol, 4 mg. sodium.
For exchange diets, count: 2 fruit.

ORANGE CAKE

I prefer whole eggs for their color contribution in this recipe.

Preparation time: 20 minutes
Baking time: 40 minutes; Cooling time: 20 minutes
12 servings—1 slice each

1/2 cup reduced-fat margarine
1 cup sugar
3 whole eggs
1 3/4 cups flour
1 teaspoon soda
1 teaspoon cinnamon
1 teaspoon ginger
1 cup nonfat sour cream
1 teaspoon vanilla
2 teaspoons orange zest (finely grated orange rind)
Non-stick cooking spray

1. Preheat oven to 350° F.

2. In a large mixing bowl, cream the margarine and sugar together with an electric mixer until fluffy. Beat in the eggs one at a time.

3. In another medium bowl, combine flour, soda, cinnamon, and ginger. Add dry ingredients to egg mixture alternately with sour cream, beginning and ending with the dry ingredients.

4. Fold in vanilla and orange zest. Pour batter into a 9" loaf pan that has been sprayed with cooking spray. Bake for 40 minutes or until cake tests done. Allow cake to cool for 20 minutes, then remove to a wire rack. Slice and serve with fruit.

135 calories per serving: 5 g. fat, 3 g. protein,
21 g. carbohydrate, 53 mg. cholesterol, 189 mg. sodium.
For exchange diets, count 1 fat, 1 starch.

Chapter Eight

the
Mediterranean

Suggested Mediterranean Menus

Flaming Kasseri Appetizer
Pasta Salad With Feta
Cocoa Flan

Gazpacho
St. Lucia Buns
Mediterranean Cod
Cottage Cheese Torte

Cucumber Dip
Challah
Citrus Ginger Chicken
Rice and Pepper Salad
Sliced Persian Melon

Add Fun, Subtract Expense

Some commonly used Mediterranean spices are garlic, lemon, oregano, mint, bay leaf, and parsley.

Flavor a reduced-fat yellow cake with anise seed for a simple Mediterranean dessert.

Annatto seed is a must for Spanish cooking. Use it to impart a natural red-yellow color and pungent flavor to rice and seafood.

Greek oregano is sweet and strong and makes any tomato sauce Mediterranean.

Saffron is recognized in many Spanish dishes such as paella. Go ahead and splurge on this expensive spice, which is produced from the stigma of a fall-flowering crocus.

Oil and vinegar can be stored and displayed in lovely Spanish cruets with cork stoppers. These vessels allow for pouring the thinnest stream of salad dressing.

Open a can of mandarin oranges and pretend you are basking in the sun on the Mediterranean coast, where they are grown.

CUCUMBER DIP

This delicious light dip is from Greece. Fresh vegetables, pita bread, or chilled, cooked shrimp can be served with this dip as a first course.

Preparation time: 10 minutes
Chilling time: 1 hour
12 servings—1/3 cup each

1 cup plain low-fat yogurt
2 peeled, seeded, chopped cucumbers
1 minced garlic clove
1 tablespoon lemon juice
2 tablespoons chopped fresh mint leaves (or 1/2 teaspoon dried
    mint flakes)
1 teaspoon dill weed
1/4 teaspoon white pepper

1. Combine all ingredients in a medium bowl; refrigerate for an hour.

18 calories per serving: 0 fat, 1 g. protein,
3 g. carbohydrate, 1 mg. cholesterol, 14 mg. sodium.
For exchange diets, count 1 vegetable.

FLAMING KASSERI APPETIZER

Thank you, Judy and Rick Nugent.

Preparation time: 5 minutes
Broiling time: 6 minutes
6 servings—1 ounce each

1/2 pound Kasseri cheese, cut into wedges
1 tablespoon melted margarine
2 tablespoons brandy
1/2 fresh lemon

1. Preheat oven broiler to low flame.

2. Arrange wedges of cheese in a shallow casserole dish. Brush with melted margarine. Broil until bubbly, about 6 minutes.

3. Meanwhile, heat brandy in a glass cup measure in the microwave for 20 seconds or until warm. At your serving area, pour warm brandy over the cheese, and ignite immediately. When flame goes out, squeeze lemon juice over cheese. Serve with chunks of home-baked French bread or reduced-fat sesame crackers for dipping.

95 calories per serving: 7 g. fat, 6 g. protein,
2 g. carbohydrate, 21 mg. cholesterol, 118 mg. sodium.
For exchange diets, count 1 very lean meat, 1 fat.

TURKISH STUFFED ZUCCHINI

Preparation time: 20 minutes
Cooking time: 20-30 minutes
Baking time: 20 minutes
8 servings—1 zucchini each

8 medium zucchini, 6-8 inches long and
  about 2 inches in diameter
1 large ripe tomato, peeled and cut into chunks
1 teaspoon vegetable oil
1/4 pound ground lamb
1 large onion, finely chopped
1 cup cracked wheat
1/4 cup water
1 tablespoon fresh jalapeño pepper, seeded (note: always wear
  rubber gloves when working with hot peppers)
1 teaspoon tomato paste
pinch of pickling spice
pinch of summer savory
pinch of black pepper
pinch of cinnamon
pinch of nutmeg
pinch of cumin

Garnish:
1 fresh lemon, cut into wedges

1. Preheat oven to 425° F.

2. Wash the zucchini; cut off the ends. Use an apple corer or iced-tea spoon to hollow out the middle of the zucchini, leaving 1/2 inch of flesh next to the peeling (they will resemble hollowed-out logs).

3. In a medium skillet, sauté tomato in olive oil. Add all remaining ingredients. Cover and cook over low heat for 5 minutes.

4. Spoon the stuffing inside the zucchini. Place the zucchini on a baking sheet, and bake for 20 minutes. Serve with a lemon wedge garnish.

84 calories per serving: 4 g. fat, 6 g. protein,
9 g. carbohydrate, 14 mg. cholesterol, 18 mg. sodium.
For exchange diets, count 2 vegetable, 1 fat.

MEDITERRANEAN GAZPACHO

Preparation time: 15 minutes
Chilling time: at least 30 minutes
8 servings—1 1/2 cups each

8 tomatoes, peeled, seeded, and chopped fine
1 cucumber, peeled, seeded, and chopped fine
1 large onion, chopped find
1 green pepper, seeded and chopped fine
1 teaspoon salt
1 teaspoon minced garlic
2 tablespoons olive oil
1/4 cup lemon juice
1/4 teaspoon pepper
dash cayenne
2 cups tomato juice

1. Mix all ingredients in a large salad bowl. Cover with a tight-fitting lid, and refrigerate until ready to serve.

2. This can served as an appetizer with toasted pita bread.

> 92 calories per serving: 4 g. fat, 2 g. protein,
> 14 g. carbohydrate, 0 cholesterol, 339 mg. sodium.
> For exchange diets, count 2 vegetable, 1 fat.

PITA BREAD

Preparation time: 5 minutes
Bread machine time: 1 hour, 30 minutes
Manual method preparation time: 30 minutes
Rising time: 1 hour; Additional rising time: 30 minutes
Baking time: 6 minutes

20 servings—1/2 pita each

---

1 1/4 cups water
3 cups white bread flour
3 tablespoons sugar
2 tablespoons nonfat dry milk powder
1 teaspoon salt
1 teaspoon yeast
1 tablespoon olive oil
nonstick cooking spray

1. Place ingredients in order listed in bread machine pan. Select "dough" from the menu, and push "start." Wait approximately 1 hour and 30 minutes for the dough to be prepared. Go to number 3.

2. To make bread from scratch: gently mix hot tap water, sugar, dry milk powder, yeast, salt, and olive oil in a large mixing bowl. Allow mixture to rest 5 minutes. Gradually add flour, working the mixture to a smooth dough. Knead for 10 minutes, then cover and allow dough to rise for 1 hour in a warm place.

3. Remove bread from the bread machine or from the bowl. Divide dough into 10 portions. Shape each one into a smooth ball, then use a rolling pin to roll each ball into a 6-inch circle on a lightly floured surface. Cover the dough, and allow to rise 30 minutes.

4. Preheat oven to 450° F. Spray a baking sheet with cooking spray. Arrange 2 or 3 rounds on the sheet, and bake for 6 minutes or until the bread is puffed up and top is brown, turning once after 3 minutes. Remove from oven, and cool on a wire rack. Repeat with the remaining dough.

5. To serve, split the pita rounds, and fill with vegetable or meat salad.

88 calories per serving: 3 g. fat, 6 g. protein,
30 g. carbohydrate, 2 mg. cholesterol, 166 mg. sodium.
For exchange diets, count 1 starch.

CHALLAH

Preparation time: 45 minutes
Rising time: 3 hours; Baking time: 25 minutes
48 servings—1 slice each

2 packages dry yeast
1/2 cup lukewarm water
2 cups boiling water
3 tablespoons vegetable oil
1 tablespoon salt
1 tablespoon sugar
2 eggs, well beaten, or 1/2 cup liquid egg substitute
8 cups flour
nonstick cooking spray
1 egg
1 teaspoon cold water

1. Soften yeast in lukewarm water in a glass measuring cup. In a large mixing bowl, combine boiling water, oil, salt, and sugar. Stir until sugar is dissolved. When mixture has cooled to lukewarm, add softened yeast.

2. Add beaten eggs. Stir in 3 cups of flour; beat until smooth. Allow dough to rest for 10 minutes. Add remaining flour. Turn dough out onto a floured board, and knead until dough is smooth and elastic. Allow dough to rise until double in bulk. Knead again until dough is fine grained.

3. Divide dough in half. Cut each half into 3 pieces. Roll each piece into a long roll. Braid three strips together. Place braided dough on a baking sheet that has been sprayed with cooking spray.

4. Allow dough to rise 1 hour. Preheat oven to 350° F. Beat 1 egg with 1 teaspoon cold water. Brush surface of dough with egg and water mixture. Bake for 25 minutes or until golden brown.

148 calories per serving: 1 g. fat, 3 g. protein,
30 g. carbohydrate, 9 mg. cholesterol, 102 mg. sodium.
For exchange diets, count 2 starch.

St. Lucia Buns

Preparation time: 20 minutes
Bread machine time: 1 hour, 30 minutes
Manual method preparation time: 25 minutes
Rising time: 1 hour; Additional rising time: 30 minutes
Baking time: 10 minutes

24 servings—1/2 bun each

---

1 cup water
1 egg
3 cups white bread flour
3 tablespoons brown sugar
2 tablespoons nonfat dry milk powder
1 teaspoon salt
1 teaspoon yeast
2 teaspoons orange peel
1/8 teaspoon ground saffron
1 tablespoon soft margarine
nonstick cooking spray
1 egg, beaten
1 tablespoon water
1/4 cup raisins
3 tablespoons sugar

1. Place the first 10 ingredients in the order listed in bread machine pan. Select "dough" from the menu, and push " start." Wait approximately 1 hour and 30 minutes for the dough to be prepared. Go to number 3.

2. If you prefer making bread from scratch, gently mix hot tap water, egg, brown sugar, dry milk powder, yeast, salt, and margarine in a large mixing bowl. Allow mixture to rest 5 minutes. Stir in orange peel and saffron, then gradually add flour, working the mixture to a smooth dough. Knead for 10 minutes, then cover and allow dough to rise for 1 hour in a warm place.

3. Remove bread from the bread machine or from the bowl. Divide the dough into 24 pieces. On a floured surface, roll each portion into a smooth 10-inch long rope. Form each rope into an "S" shape, and curve both ends in a coil. Cross two of these "S" shaped ropes to form an "X," repeating with remaining "S" shaped ropes. The two "S"

shapes crossed over each other make a cursive "X" shape.

4. Place shapes on a baking sheet that has been sprayed with cooking spray. Cover and let rise in a warm place for 30 minutes. Preheat oven to 375° F.

5. Mix egg and water together in a small bowl, and brush onto the buns. Place a raisin in the center of each coil, then sprinkle with sugar. Bake for 10 minutes or until buns are golden. Cool on a wire rack.

130 calories per serving: 3 g. fat, 4 g. protein,
24 g. carbohydrate, 276 mg. cholesterol, 106 mg. sodium.
For exchange diets, count 1 1/2 starch.

RICE AND PEPPER SALAD

Preparation time: 15 minutes
Cooking time: 3 minutes; Cooling time: 15 minutes
8 servings—3/4 cup each

1 cup instant rice
1 cup no-added-salt beef broth
1 red pepper, seeded and cut into strips
1 yellow pepper, seeded and cut into strips
1 green pepper, seeded and cut into strips
1 red onion, sliced thin
3 ounces feta cheese, crumbled
1 tablespoon olive oil
1/3 cup red wine vinegar
1/2 teaspoon marjoram
1/2 teaspoon seasoned salt

1. In a medium bowl, combine instant rice with beef broth. Cover and cook in the microwave for 3 minutes on high power. Remove cover and fluff rice. Transfer bowl to the refrigerator to speed cooling.

2. In a salad bowl, combine pepper strips, onion, and cheese.

3. In a shaker container, combine oil, vinegar, marjoram, and salt.

4. When rice has cooled to room temperature, mix it with the peppers. Add dressing just before serving, and toss to mix well.

101 calories per serving: 4 g. fat, 3 g. protein,
21 g. carbohydrate, 92 mg. cholesterol, 254 mg. sodium.
For exchange diets, count 1 vegetable, 1 starch.

MELON STUFFED WITH BEEF AND RICE

Preparation time: 20 minutes
Baking time: 30 minutes
8 servings—2 cups each

1 Persian melon (may substitute cantaloupe)
2 cups cooked roast beef or pork, shredded
1 medium onion, chopped
1 tablespoon margarine
1 cup cooked rice
1/3 cup golden raisins
1/4 cup pine nuts, chopped
1/3 cup sweet white wine, such as Reisling or Madeira

1. Cut off the top of the melon and remove the seeds. Scoop out balls of the fruit, but leave at least 1 inch of flesh on the melon rind.

2. Preheat oven to 350° F. In a skillet, lightly sauté the cooked beef and onion in the margarine.

3. Add cooked rice, raisins, pine nuts, and just 1 cup of the melon balls to the skillet. Stir until well blended.

4. Fill the melon shell with the meat mixture. Sprinkle the white wine over the mixture in the melon.

5. Place the melon on a baking sheet, and bake for 30 minutes or until the mixture is steaming. To serve, slice the melon into 8 wedges, and serve on a salad plate. Garnish the plate with leftover melon balls.

152 calories per wedge: 4 g. fat, 17 g. protein,
12 g. carbohydrate, 51 mg. cholesterol, 61 mg. sodium.
For exchange diets, count 1 fruit, 2 lean meat.

PASTA SALAD WITH FETA

For a very colorful dish, use a variety of flavored pastas, including tomato, spinach, and whole wheat. Use Italia™ brand feta cheese with sun-dried tomatoes and basil for extra flavor.

Preparation time: 20 minutes
Pasta cooking time: 8 minutes
12 servings—1 cup each

12-ounce package spinach fettuccini, cooked according
  to package directions
4 peeled, cored, chopped tomatoes
1/2 cup chopped onion
1/2 cup chopped fresh basil
1/4 cup crumbled feta cheese
1/4 cup sliced and pitted black olives
1/4 cup chopped, roasted red bell pepper
2 tablespoons fat-free mayonnaise
1 tablespoon olive oil
1/2 teaspoon salt
1/4 teaspoon black pepper

1. Combine all ingredients in a large bowl. The juice from the tomatoes provides most of the dressing for this salad. If tomatoes are not very juicy, add an additional tablespoon of mayonnaise.

67 calories per serving: 3 g. fat, 2 g. protein,
8 g. carbohydrate, 11 mg. cholesterol, 220 mg. sodium.
For exchange diets, count 2 vegetable, 1/2 fat.

STUFFED PORK LOIN

Preparation time: 15 minutes
Cooking time: 10 minutes
Roasting time: 1 hour, 45 minutes
12 servings—4 ounces each

---

3 pound lean boneless pork loin
1/2 teaspoon salt
1/2 teaspoon pepper
1 tablespoon olive oil
1 onion, finely chopped
1/4 teaspoon minced garlic
3 medium tomatoes, peeled, seeded, and chopped
1 teaspoon chili powder
1/3 cup raisins
1 cup instant rice
1/2 cup no-added-salt chicken broth or water
1/2 cup dry white wine

1. Preheat oven to 350° F.

2. Cut the pork roast almost in half lengthwise to form a pocket for the stuffing. Season the meat with salt and pepper.

3. In a small skillet, sauté the onion and garlic in the olive oil for 2 minutes or until onions soften. Add the tomatoes and chili powder, and simmer for 5 minutes. Add the raisins, rice, broth, and wine. Bring mixture to a boil, then simmer for 2 minutes.

4. Stuff the pocket of the roast with the rice mixture, then fold the pork over the stuffing. Tie the meat with string at 2-inch intervals. Insert the meat thermometer.

5. Roast the meat on a rack for 1 hour and 45 minutes or until the meat thermometer registers 170° F. Allow roast to sit 20 to 30 minutes before carving.

231 calories per serving: 7 g. fat, 34 g. protein,
8 g. carbohydrate, 87 mg. cholesterol, 189 mg. sodium.
For exchange diets, count 4 very lean meat, 1 vegetable.

STEWED CHICKEN WITH POLENTA

Preparation time: 15 minutes
Cooking time: 15 minutes

8 servings—1 chicken breast and 1/2 cup cornmeal each

nonstick cooking spray
8 chicken breast halves, skinned and boned
1 small onion, chopped fine
14-ounce can no-added-salt chunky tomatoes
5 whole cloves
2 bay leaves
3 cups water
3/4 cup cornmeal
4 ounces reduced-fat Swiss cheese, shredded

1. Spray a large skillet with cooking spray. Brown chicken breast halves. Add onion, tomatoes, cloves, and bay leaves. Cook for 10 minutes, uncovered, over medium heat.

2. Meanwhile, bring 3 cups of water to a boil; add cornmeal. Boil for 10 minutes, uncovered, stirring occasionally until mixture becomes thick.

3. Spray a large baking dish with cooking spray. Spoon cornmeal into the baking dish, and sprinkle with cheese. Cook in the microwave on high power for 2 minutes or until the cheese melts.

4. Spoon chicken breast and tomatoes on top of the cornmeal and cheese, and serve.

242 calories per serving: 6 g. fat, 20 g. protein,
27 g. carbohydrate, 49 mg. cholesterol, 142 mg. sodium.
For exchange diets, count 2 very lean meat, 1 starch, 2 vegetable.

CITRUS GINGER CHICKEN

Preparation time: 15 minutes
Cooking time: 12 minutes
8 servings—1 chicken breast each

1/4 cup all-fruit orange marmalade
1 tablespoon prepared mustard
3/4 teaspoon ground ginger
1/8 teaspoon curry powder
8 chicken breast halves, skinned and boned
1 tablespoon margarine
1/2 teaspoon finely grated orange rind
1/4 teaspoon ground ginger

1. Combine first 4 ingredients in a small bowl. Brush the mixture on the chicken breasts.

2. Preheat broiler or grill. Broil or grill chicken breasts for 6 minutes on one side.

3. Meanwhile, combine margarine, orange rind, and ginger in a small dish. Turn chicken breasts over; brush with margarine and orange rind mixture. Grill an additional 6 minutes or until chicken is cooked through.

4. This dish goes nicely with Herbed Rice or Rice and Pepper Salad.

184 calories per serving: 5 g. fat, 27 g. protein,
7 g. carbohydrate, 71 mg. cholesterol, 140 mg. sodium.
For exchange diets, count 3 lean meat, 1/2 fruit.

MARINATED CHICKEN WITH CARROTS

Preparation time: 15 minutes
Marinating time: 30 minutes; Baking time: 45 minutes
8 servings—1 chicken breast and 1 cup carrots each

1/2 teaspoon minced garlic
3 tablespoons lemon juice
1 tablespoon olive oil
1 small onion, finely grated
1 1/4 teaspoons ground cumin
1/2 teaspoon paprika
1/2 teaspoon turmeric
1/8 teaspoon cayenne pepper
1/4 teaspoon cinnamon
8 chicken breast halves, skinned and boned
8 medium carrots, peeled and sliced into 1/2-inch chunks

1. Combine first 10 ingredients in a large zipper-type bag. Zip the bag shut, and shake to coat the chicken. Allow chicken to mix with spices in the refrigerator for at least 30 minutes.

2. Preheat oven to 400° F. Place chicken breasts in a large roasting pan, and sprinkle with carrot chunks. Roast for 45 minutes or until chicken is cooked through.

257 calories per serving: 9 g. fat, 29 g. protein,
15 g. carbohydrate, 78 mg. cholesterol, 108 mg. sodium.
For exchange diets, count 4 lean meat, 2 vegetable.

MEDITERRANEAN COD

Preparation time: 5 minutes
Cooking time: 15 minutes

8 servings—3/4 cup vegetables and 4 ounces cod each

2 pounds frozen broccoli, green bean, onion,
  and red pepper blend
2 14-ounce cans chunky tomatoes
1 teaspoon dried basil
2 pounds cod fillets, cut into serving pieces
1 cup orange juice, divided
1/4 cup flour

1. Combine vegetables, tomatoes, and basil in a large skillet. Bring the mixture to a boil over medium heat.

2. Place cod on top of vegetables, then pour 1/2 cup of orange juice over the fish. Cover the pan, and cook for 7 minutes or until fish is tender and flakes with a fork.

3. Remove cod to a warm platter. In a glass cup measure, blend flour with remaining orange juice. Stir into the vegetables, cooking and stirring until the liquid is thickened and vegetables are coated. Spoon vegetables and sauce over the warm cod, and serve.

215 calories per serving: 3 g. fat, 29 g. protein,
20 g. carbohydrate, 63 mg. cholesterol, 310 mg. sodium.
For exchange diets, count 4 very lean meat, 1/2 starch, 1 vegetable.

BAKED TOMATOES STUFFED WITH RICE AND FISH

Preparation time: 20 minutes
Cooking time: 20 minutes; Baking time: 45 minutes
8 servings—1 stuffed tomato each

2 pounds fillet of sole
2 cups white wine
3 cups water
1 medium carrot, cleaned and cut in half
1 bay leaf
1 whole clove
1/8 teaspoon thyme
5 whole black peppercorns
1 cup instant rice
1 cup no-added-salt chicken broth
1/3 cup canned spinach, squeezed dry and finely chopped
1/4 cup finely chopped parsley
1/2 teaspoon minced garlic
2 tablespoons olive oil
8 large ripe tomatoes
dried basil (optional)

1. Place fish in a medium saucepan. Pour wine and water over the fish. Bring the liquid to a boil over medium-high heat. Add the carrot, bay leaf, clove, thyme, and peppercorns. Allow mixture to simmer for 20 minutes.

2. Meanwhile, combine the rice, chicken broth, spinach, parsley, garlic, and oil in a microwave-safe casserole dish. Cover and cook according to rice package directions.

3. Preheat oven to 350° F. Cut 1/2 inch off the top of each tomato. Use a large serving spoon to carefully scoop out the insides, being careful not to puncture the skin.

4. When fish is done, discard liquid, carrot, and spices. Use a fork to cut fish into flakes. Add flaked fish to cooked rice mixture.

5. Stuff tomatoes with rice and fish mixture. Place tomatoes in a shallow baking dish. Cover and bake for 35 to 45 minutes, until heated through. If desired, sprinkle dried basil on each tomato just before serving.

169 calories per serving: 5 g. fat, 19 g. protein,
12 g. carbohydrate, 35 mg. cholesterol, 145 mg. sodium.
For exchange diets, count 3 very lean meat, 1/2 starch, 1 vegetable.

STUFFED CABBAGE ROLLS

Preparation time: 25 minutes
Baking time: 40 minutes
6 servings—2 rolls each

1 large head green cabbage
3/4 pound lean ground turkey
1/4 cup finely chopped onion
3/4 cup soft bread crumbs
1/2 cup cooked rice
1/4 cup chopped celery
1/4 cup liquid egg substitute
1 tablespoon fresh parsley
1 1/2 teaspoons caraway seeds, divided
3/4 teaspoon salt
1/4 teaspoon black pepper
15-ounce can tomato sauce, divided

1. Discard outer leaves of cabbage. Remove core, and wash cabbage. Dip cabbage in boiling water to loosen leaves. Carefully peel off 12 leaves. Steam leaves in a small amount of water for 3 minutes or until crisp-tender. Drain; cool. Cut hard stem section out of each leaf.

2. Preheat oven to 350° F. In a medium skillet, brown turkey and onion; drain.

3. In a medium bowl, combine bread crumbs, rice, celery, egg, parsley, 1 teaspoon caraway seeds, salt, pepper, 3/4 cup tomato sauce, and turkey mixture.

4. Place 1/4 cup of turkey mixture at the stem end of each cabbage leaf. Roll leaves around turkey mixture. Place seam-side down in a single layer in an 11" x 7" x 2" baking dish. Pour remaining tomato sauce over cabbage rolls. Sprinkle with remaining caraway seeds. Cover.

5. Bake for 40 minutes or until heated through.

253 calories per serving: 5 g. fat, 21 g. protein,
31 g. carbohydrate, 58 mg. cholesterol, 905 mg. sodium
(To reduce sodium, omit salt.)
For exchange diets, count 1 starch, 2 vegetable, 2 lean meat

COCOA FLAN

Preparation time: 20 minutes
Baking time: 20 minutes
12 servings—1 slice each

1/2 cup cocoa powder
1/2 cup boiling water
1/2 cup dark beer
1 1/2 cups sugar
1/2 cup soft reduced-fat margarine
2 eggs, separated
1 teaspoon vanilla
2 cups cake flour, divided
1 teaspoon baking soda
1 teaspoon baking powder
1/2 teaspoon salt
1/2 cup skim milk
fresh raspberries (optional)

1. Preheat oven to 350° F.

2. In a medium mixing bowl, combine cocoa with boiling water; stir well. Stir in beer; set aside to cool.

3. In another mixing bowl, combine sugar with margarine, and mix until smooth. Beat in egg yolks and vanilla. Beat in 1 cup of flour, soda, baking powder, and salt. Add milk. Beat in remaining 1 cup of flour. Fold in cooled cocoa mixture.

4. In a clean bowl, beat egg whites until they are stiff. Fold them into the batter, then pour batter into a flan pan. You may substitute an 8" round cake pan or shallow glass casserole dish for the flan pan.

5. Bake for 20 minutes. Cool and slice. Garnish with fresh raspberries, if desired.

---

229 calories per serving: 5 g. fat, 4 g. protein,
42 g. carbohydrate, 14 mg. cholesterol, 219 mg. sodium.
For exchange diets, count 2 1/2 starch, 1 fat.

COTTAGE CHEESE TORTE

Preparation time: 20 minutes
Baking time: 1 hour; Cooling time: 1 hour
12 servings, 1 slice each

1 prepared reduced-fat graham cracker pie crust

Filling:
1/3 cup skim milk
1 1/2 tablespoons cornstarch
2 1/2 cups nonfat cottage cheese
2/3 cup nonfat sour cream
1 cup sugar
2 large eggs, separated
1/4 cup lemon juice
1 1/2 teaspoons lemon zest
1 tablespoon margarine, melted
1/2 teaspoon cinnamon
1/4 teaspoon nutmeg
2 large egg whites
1 pint fresh strawberries, stemmed and sliced

1. Preheat oven to 325° F.

2. In a small bowl, combine milk and cornstarch; whisk until smooth.

3. In a blender, puree cottage cheese and sour cream until smooth.
Add sugar, egg yolks, lemon juice, lemon zest, margarine, cinnamon,
nutmeg, and milk mixture. Process until smooth.

4. In a large mixing bowl, beat 4 egg whites until stiff, but not dry.
Fold the cottage cheese mixture into the egg whites. Pour into the
prepared crust.

5. Bake for 1 hour, then turn off the oven and leave the torte in the
oven for another hour to cool gradually. Cut into 12 portions, and
top with sliced strawberries.

263 calories per serving: 1 g. fat, 11 g. protein,
48 g. carbohydrate, 10 mg. cholesterol, 255 mg. sodium.
For exchange diets, count 1 1/2 fruit, 1 starch, 1 skim milk.

ORANGE FLAN

*The ingredients sound dull, but you'll discover why
this dessert has endured for ages.*

Preparation time: 10 minutes; Cooking time: 8 minutes
Baking time: 35 minutes; Chilling time: 4 hours
8 servings—1 slice each

1 2/3 cups sugar, divided
nonstick cooking spray
4 cups skim milk
grated rind of 1 orange
1 teaspoon vanilla
4 eggs or 1 cup liquid egg substitute
Garnish:
colorful fresh fruit

1. Melt 2/3 cup of sugar in a small saucepan, and cook over medium heat until it is a rich brown color. Move the pan back and forth constantly, watching so the sugar doesn't burn.

2. Immediately pour the liquid sugar into an 8" round baking dish that has been sprayed with cooking spray.

3. Bring the milk to the simmering point in a large saucepan (bubbles should just be starting to form around the edge of the pan). Add the remaining sugar and orange rind, and simmer for 5 minutes. Remove from heat, and stir in vanilla. Let the milk cool for several minutes.

4. Beat eggs well in a large mixing bowl. Using an electric beater, beat warm milk mixture slowly into the eggs. Pour the egg and milk mixture into the baking dish, and bake for 35 minutes or until the custard is set.

5. Chill for 4 hours in the refrigerator and then unmold custard onto a serving plate. You may need to ease unmolding by gently dipping pan into very warm water to loosen edges. Slice, and serve with fresh fruit for garnish.

231 calories per serving: 1 g. fat, 8 g. protein,
48 g. carbohydrate, 86 mg. cholesterol with eggs
(2 mg. cholesterol with egg substitute), 119 mg. sodium.
For exchange diets, count 1/2 skim milk, 3 fruit.

Chapter Nine

Italy

Suggested Italian Menus

Antipasto
Italian Breadsticks
Classic Lasagna
Lemon Spumante

Minestrone
Green Salad With Italian Dressing
Fettuccine Alfredo
Honey Orange Biscotti

Cucumber Raisin Salad
Queen's Pizza
Sponge Cake With Fruit Sauce

Add Fun, Subtract Expense

Add 1/4 teaspoon each of rosemary, oregano, and thyme to 1 cup of plain tomato sauce for an Italian delight.

Look for a pasta maker that turns out dough for breadsticks and bagels (Pasta Express is about $150).

A 4-inch deep lasagna pan will be a lifetime investment in keeping your oven free from messy boilovers (stainless steel model is about $40).

Grate fresh Parmesan cheese with a hand-held processor. A set of 3 stainless steel disks allows fine to coarse grating and the unit can also shave chocolate (about $15).

For uniform slices of cheese, meat, and bread, consider an Italian slicing knife that allows you to select slices from 3/4-inch thick to paper-thin. It comes with a 10-inch serrated blade (about $25).

Pizza lovers will love a pizza stone for perfect chewy home-baked crusts.

For a super simple way to cook Italian-style without purchasing several spices, buy Italian seasoning, which is a spice blend made especially for Italian dishes. Classic Italian ingredients and seasonings are garlic, thyme, basil, oregano, parsley, and marjoram. Wine and tomatoes are also used liberally in Italian cooking.

CAPPUCCINO

Cappuccino originated in Southern Europe. It is a combination of espresso and steamed milk. Espresso is made from a dark brown roast coffee made in an espresso machine (also called a caffettiera). Hot water is forced under pressure through the finely ground, tightly packed coffee, rather than the traditional brewing process where coffee is steeped in hot water.

Preparation time: 5 minutes
4 servings—1 cup each

2 tablespoons Italian roasted coffee beans, finely ground
2 cups water
2 cups steamed 2% milk

1. Make espresso according to manufacturer's instructions for your espresso machine.

2. Pour equal amounts espresso and steamed milk into 4 large mugs. Sprinkle with ground cinnamon.

61 calories per serving: 2 g. fat, 4 g. protein,
6 g. carbohydrate, 9 mg. cholesterol, 61 mg. sodium.
For exchange diets, count 1/2 skim milk.

ORANGE CAPPUCCINO

If you don't have an espresso machine, substitute strong coffee.

Preparation time: 5 minutes
8 servings—1/2 cup each

2 cups espresso or strong coffee
2 cups 2% milk
1 tablespoon thawed frozen orange juice concentrate
1/4 teaspoon cinnamon
1/2 cup reduced-fat whipped topping
nutmeg
grated orange peel

1. Make espresso according to manufacturer's instructions for your espresso machine.

2. Heat milk in a medium saucepan; add orange juice concentrate and cinnamon. Stir to mix. Remove from heat.

3. Pour equal amounts espresso and steamed milk mixture into small cups. Top each with 1 tablespoon whipped topping. Sprinkle with nutmeg. Garnish with grated orange peel.

72 calories per serving: 4 g. fat, 2 g. protein,
9 g. carbohydrate, 5 mg. cholesterol, 31 mg. sodium.
For exchange diets, count 1/2 fruit, 1 fat.

ANTIPASTO

Enjoy this traditional first course before your next Italian banquet.

Preparation time: 15 minutes
12 servings—1/12 of platter each

Fresh greens
1 large ripe tomato, sliced thin
1/2 pound Italian ham, sliced thin
1/2 pound smoked turkey, sliced thin
2 cooked eggs, cut in half
1 cup radishes, cleaned and stemmed
1/4 cup green olives
16-ounce can artichoke hearts, drained well
1 tablespoon olive oil
1/8 cup red wine vinegar

1. Line a large platter with your favorite fresh greens.

2. Arrange the next 7 ingredients on the greens.

3. Sprinkle the olive oil and vinegar over the platter. Serve with Italian breadsticks.

99 calories per serving: 4 g. fat, 11 g. protein,
4 g. carbohydrate, 58 mg. cholesterol, 388 mg. sodium.
For exchange diets, count 1 1/2 lean meat, 1 vegetable.

LEMON ASTI SPUMANTE

Asti Spumante, a slightly sweet sparkling wine, originated in Italy.
If you prefer dry wine, you may substitute champagne.

Preparation time: 10 minutes
Freezing time: 1 hour

8 servings—5 ounces each

1 pint softened lemon sherbet
1 cup reduced-fat whipped topping
2 tablespoons lemon juice
1 teaspoon grated lemon peel
12 ounces chilled Asti Spumante
6 strawberries

1. In a medium bowl, combine sherbet, whipped topping, lemon juice, and lemon peel. Spoon mixture into champagne glasses until 3/4 full. Cover with plastic wrap, and freeze at least 1 hour.

2. Remove from freezer 10 minutes before serving. Garnish each with a strawberry. Pour 2 ounces Asti Spumante over each. Add more, if desired, to fill glass.

141 calories per serving: 1 g. fat, 1 g. protein,
32 g. carbohydrate, 4 mg. cholesterol, 41 mg. sodium.
For exchange diets, count 2 1/2 fruit.

CAPONATA

Serve this Italian eggplant specialty as a dip
or as part of an antipasto tray.

Preparation time: 15 minutes
Cooking time: 13 minutes; Chilling time: 2 hours
24 servings—2 tablespoons each

---

2 teaspoons olive oil
1/2 cup chopped onion
2 minced garlic cloves
7 cups chopped, peeled eggplant
1 chopped tomato
2 tablespoons chopped fresh basil
1 teaspoon chopped fresh parsley
1/2 teaspoon oregano
2 tablespoons balsamic vinegar
1/2 teaspoon salt
1/4 teaspoon black pepper

1. Heat olive oil in a large skillet. Cook onion and garlic over medium heat about 2 minutes or until tender. Stir in eggplant and tomato. Cook 10 minutes, stirring frequently. Stir in remaining ingredients.

2. Refrigerate at least 2 hours.

14 calories per serving: 0 fat, 0 protein,
2 g. carbohydrate, 0 cholesterol, 46 mg. sodium.
For exchange diets, count as a free food.

CUCUMBER SANDWICHES

These popular American appetizers originated in Italy.

Preparation time: 10 minutes
8 servings—1/2 bagel each

4 split toasted bagels
4 tablespoons fat-free cream cheese
1 large sliced cucumber
2 teaspoons dill weed

1. Spread each bagel half with 1/2 tablespoon cream cheese. Top each with sliced cucumber. Sprinkle with dill weed.

2. Serve open-faced.

108 calories per serving: 0 fat, 5 g. protein,
21 g. carbohydrate, 0 cholesterol, 190 mg. sodium.
For exchange diets, count 1/2 skim milk, 1 starch.

QUEEN'S PIZZA

*The story behind this pizza suggests the garlic was left out
to suit Queen Margaret of Savoy.*

Preparation time: 20 minutes
Baking time: 14 minutes
8 servings—1 slice each

---

1 pound frozen bread dough, thawed
1 tablespoon olive oil
1/2 cup tomato sauce
2 ounces part-skim mozzarella cheese, sliced 1/2-inch thick
1/4 teaspoon salt
1/4 teaspoon black pepper
1/2 cup loosely packed fresh basil leaves
1/4 cup freshly grated Parmesan cheese

1. Place an inverted baking sheet on the bottom rack of a cold oven, then preheat oven to 500° F. for 15 minutes.

2. Place thawed bread dough on a lightly floured source, and pat into a round form about 1/4-inch thick. Transfer dough to the preheated baking sheet.

3. Brush the dough with olive oil, spread with tomato sauce, and arrange mozzarella slices over the sauce.

4. Season with salt and pepper. Sprinkle with basil leaves and Parmesan cheese. Bake for 14 minutes or until the top is bubbly.

128 calories per serving: 4 g. fat, 5 g. protein,
18 g. carbohydrate, 6 mg. cholesterol, 297 mg. sodium.
For exchange diets, count 1 starch, 1 lean meat.

FOCACCIA

Preparation time: 10 minutes
Bread machine time: 1 hour, 30 minutes
Manual method preparation time: 20 minutes
Rising time: 1 hour; Additional rising time: 30 minutes
Baking time: 30 minutes

24 servings—1 slice each

1 cup water
3 cups white bread flour
3 tablespoons sugar
2 tablespoons nonfat dry milk powder
1 teaspoon salt
1 teaspoon yeast
2 teaspoons dried oregano
1 tablespoon soft margarine
nonstick cooking spray
3 tablespoons olive oil
1/2 teaspoon minced garlic
1/2 cup grated Parmesan cheese
1/4 cup fresh snipped parsley

1. Place first 8 ingredients in order listed in bread machine pan.
Select "dough" from menu, and push "start." Wait approximately 1
hour and 30 minutes for the dough to be prepared. Go to number 3.

2. If you prefer making bread from scratch, gently mix hot tap water,
sugar, dry milk powder, yeast, salt, and margarine in a large mixing
bowl. Allow mixture to rest 5 minutes. Gradually add flour and
oregano, working the mixture to a smooth dough. Knead for 10 minutes, then cover and allow dough to rise for 1 hour in a warm place.

3. Spray a 12" round pizza pan with cooking spray. Remove bread
from the bread machine or from the bowl. Gently press the dough in
the pizza pan. Cover and let rise 30 minutes.

Focaccia (continued)

4. Preheat oven to 400° F. With three fingers, poke holes all over the dough. In a small cup, stir together olive oil and garlic. Drizzle over the dough. Sprinkle with cheese and parsley, then bake for 30 minutes. Serve warm.

101 calories per serving: 4 g. fat, 3 g. protein,
13 g. carbohydrate, 2 mg. cholesterol, 112 mg. sodium.
For exchange diets, count 1 starch, 1/2 fat.

PANETTONE

Use a coffee can to bake this cylindrical bread from Milan.

Preparation time: 10 minutes
Bread machine time: 4 hours, 10 minutes
Manual method preparation time: 30 minutes
Rising time: 2 hours; Baking time: 25 minutes
Cooling time: 15 minutes

24 servings—1/2 slice each

1 cup water
1/4 cup cream sherry
1 egg
3 cups white bread flour
3 tablespoons sugar
2 tablespoons nonfat dry milk powder
1 teaspoon salt
1/4 teaspoon cloves
1 teaspoon crushed anise
1 teaspoon yeast
1 tablespoon soft margarine
1/4 cup raisins
1/4 cup diced citron
1/4 cup chopped walnuts

1. Place first 11 ingredients in order listed in bread machine pan. Select "add bread" from menu, and push "start." Wait approximately 25 minutes for the beeper, then add raisins, citron, and walnuts.

2. Loaf will be done in 4 hours and 10 minutes using a Hitachi bread machine.

3. If you prefer making bread from scratch, gently mix hot tap water with sherry, sugar, dry milk powder, yeast, salt, and margarine in a large mixing bowl. Allow mixture to rest 5 minutes. Stir in egg, cloves, and anise; then gradually add flour, working the mixture to a smooth dough. Fold in raisins, citron, and walnuts. Knead for 10 minutes, then cover and allow dough to rise for 1 hour in a warm place. Punch the dough down, form a cylinder shape, and place in a 3-pound coffee can that has been sprayed with nonstick cooking spray.

Pannetone (continued)

Allow dough to rise again for 1 hour, and bake in a preheated 350° oven for 25 minutes or until the top is browned. Cool for 15 minutes, then remove bread to a cooling rack.

4. Serve this bread with a bowl of minestrone.

130 calories per serving: 3 g. fat, 4 g. protein,
22 g. carbohydrate, 14 mg. cholesterol, 90 mg. sodium.
For exchange diets, count 1 starch, 1/2 fat.

MINESTRONE

This classic Italian soup is chock-full of vegetables, beans, and pasta.

Preparation time: 20 minutes
Cooking time: 40 minutes
6 servings—1 1/2 cups each

1 3/4 cups water
14 1/2-ounce can fat-free chicken broth
16-ounce can low-sodium tomatoes, cut up
1 cup chopped onion
1 cup shredded cabbage
3/4 cup tomato juice
1/2 cup shredded carrot
1/2 cup chopped celery
1 teaspoon crushed basil
1/4 teaspoon garlic powder
15-ounce can rinsed and drained kidney beans
1 cup chopped zucchini
1 cup fresh or frozen green beans
1/2 cup elbow macaroni
2 tablespoons Parmesan cheese

1. In a large saucepan, combine water, chicken broth, undrained tomatoes, onion, cabbage, tomato juice, carrot, celery, basil, and garlic powder; bring to a boil. Reduce heat; cover and simmer for 20 minutes.

2. Stir in remaining ingredients except Parmesan cheese. Return to a boil; reduce heat, cover, and simmer 10 to 15 minutes or until vegetables are tender.

178 calories per serving: 1 g. fat, 9 g. protein,
36 g. carbohydrate, 1 mg. cholesterol, 375 mg. sodium.
For exchange diets, count 1 starch, 2 vegetable, 1 very lean meat.

ITALIAN PASTA SALAD

A make-ahead Italian salad.
Preparation time: 20 minutes
8 servings—1 cup each

2 cups cooked tricolor pasta spirals
1 cup thinly sliced zucchini
1/2 cup shredded carrot
1/4 cup chopped green pepper
1/4 cup sliced green onions
1/4 cup chopped, seeded tomato
2 tablespoons sliced black olives
1/2 cup fat-free Italian dressing
4 ounces cubed smoked mozzarella cheese
1 tablespoon chopped fresh parsley

1. In a large bowl, combine pasta, zucchini, carrot, pepper, onion, tomato, and olives. Pour dressing over salad; refrigerate 2 hours.

2. Just before serving, add cheese and parsley.

108 calories per serving: 2 g. fat, 5 g. protein,
18 g. carbohydrate, 23 mg. cholesterol, 82 mg. sodium.
For exchange diets, count 1 starch, 1 vegetable.

ITALIAN DRESSING
FOR RED BEANS

This keeps well in the refrigerator for up to a month. Mix with drained kidney beans as a salad or use as a dressing for your favorite green salad.

Preparation time: 10 minutes
Marinating time: overnight
20 servings—2 tablespoons each

16-ounce bottle fat-free Italian dressing
1 chopped medium onion
1 chopped green pepper
1 chopped tomato
2 tablespoons chopped fresh parsley

1. Combine all ingredients in a medium bowl; marinate overnight.

4 calories per serving: 0 fat, 0 protein,
1 g. carbohydrate, 1 mg. cholesterol, 90 mg. sodium.
For exchange diets, count as a free food.

CUCUMBER AND RAISIN SALAD

Preparation time: 15 minutes
8 servings—3/4 cup each

2 large cucumbers, peeled and grated
1 medium onion, finely chopped
1 cup golden raisins

Dressing:

1 cup nonfat plain yogurt
1/2 teaspoon salt
1/4 teaspoon freshly ground pepper
1/2 teaspoon dried mint or 3 tablespoons chopped fresh mint
1/2 teaspoon dried basil or 1 tablespoon chopped fresh basil

1. Combine cucumber, onion, and raisins in a large salad bowl.

2. In a small mixing bowl, combine ingredients for the dressing. Pour dressing over salad ingredients, and toss to mix. Serve on the side with any traditional Italian dish.

95 calories per serving: 1 g. fat, 3 g. protein,
22 g. carbohydrate, 1 mg. cholesterol, 159 mg. sodium.
For exchange diets, count 1 fruit, 1 vegetable.

MARINATED RICE SALAD WITH HAM AND OLIVES

Preparation time: 20 minutes
Chilling time: 30 minutes
8 servings—2 cups each

4 cups instant rice
4 cups no-added-salt chicken broth
8 ounces lean ham, cut into slivers
8 ounces reduced-fat mozzarella cheese, shredded
2 ripe tomatoes, chopped
2 tablespoons sliced pitted black olives
1/2 cup reduced-fat Italian dressing
1 large green pepper, cut into thin 1-inch strips
4 green onions, diced

1. Mix rice with chicken broth in a microwave-safe container. Cook according to package directions.

2. Combine cooked rice with all remaining ingredients in a large salad bowl. Chill at least 30 minutes or up to overnight.

220 calories per serving: 12 g. fat, 15 g. protein,
13 g. carbohydrate, 38 mg. cholesterol, 613 mg. sodium.
For exchange diets, count 1 starch, 2 lean meat, 1 fat.

BRUSCHETTA

This Italian treat is tasty without the oil
and butter found on garlic bread.

Preparation time: 10 minutes
8 servings—2 slices each

---

1 loaf fresh French bread, sliced lengthwise
1/2 cup fat-free Italian dressing
1 large chopped tomato
1/4 cup chopped green pepper
1/4 cup chopped onion
2 tablespoons chopped fresh basil
1/8 teaspoon black pepper
1/4 cup Parmesan cheese (optional)

1. Preheat broiler. Toast bread about 2 minutes or just until lightly browned. Watch carefully so bread doesn't burn.

2. In a medium bowl, combine remaining ingredients except Parmesan. Spread on both halves of bread. Top with Parmesan if desired. Cut each half loaf into 8 slices.

103 calories per serving: 3 g. fat, 4 g. protein,
16 g. carbohydrate, 3 mg. cholesterol, 309 mg. sodium.
For exchange diets, count 1 starch, 1/2 fat.

SIMPLE ITALIAN TOMATO SAUCE

Preparation time: 15 minutes
Cooking time: 1 hour
8 servings—3/4 cup each

1 slice Canadian bacon, diced fine
1 sprig of parsley, minced
1 medium onion, quartered
1 celery rib, cut into chunks
1 large carrot, cut into chunks
1 tablespoon olive oil
2 16-ounce cans no-added-salt chunky tomatoes
1/8 cup dry white wine

1. In a food processor, combine Canadian bacon, parsley, onion, celery, and carrot; process until almost pureed.

2. Heat oil in a Dutch oven. Add pureed vegetables; cook and stir until they're browned. Add tomatoes and wine; simmer uncovered for an hour. Serve over your favorite pasta.

74 calories per serving: 2 g. fat, 3 g. protein,
11 g. carbohydrate, 3 mg. cholesterol, 387 mg. sodium.
For exchange diets, count 2 vegetables, 1/2 fat.

FETTUCCINE ALFREDO

The Italians serve this delicate dish as a first course.

Preparation time: 5 minutes
Cooking time: 10 minutes
8 servings—1 cup each

8 ounces fettuccine noodles
1 tablespoon margarine, melted
1 cup evaporated skimmed milk, warmed
4 ounces Parmesan cheese, grated
1/4 teaspoon salt
1/4 teaspoon pepper

1. In a large kettle, cook noodles in boiling water for 8 minutes.

2. Drain noodles, and put them in a large bowl. Quickly add remaining ingredients. Toss briskly to coat the noodles, and serve at once.

165 calories per serving: 4 g. fat, 8 g. protein,
24 g. carbohydrate, 4 mg. cholesterol, 209 mg. sodium.
For exchange diets, count 4 lean meat, 1 skim milk, 1 starch.

MANICOTTI

Preparation time: 15 minutes
Cooking time: 15 minutes
Baking time: 30 minutes
4 servings—2 manicotti each

8 manicotti
1/2 ounce lean ground pork or beef
1 medium onion, chopped fine
1/2 teaspoon minced garlic
2 ounces Parmesan cheese, freshly grated
3 eggs or 3/4 cup liquid egg substitute
10-ounce package frozen spinach, thawed, drained and chopped
1/4 teaspoon black pepper
2 cups Simple Italian Tomato Sauce (see recipe on page 241)
  or 2 cups of your favorite prepared tomato sauce
minced oregano or parsley

1. Preheat oven to 375° F.

2. In a large kettle, cook manicotti shells in boiling water for 6 minutes; drain and rinse with cold water. Allow shells to continue to drain.

3. In a large skillet, brown pork or beef with onion and garlic. When meat is no longer pink, drain mixture well. Return meat to the skillet, and mix with cheese, eggs, spinach, and pepper.

4. Stuff the cooked manicotti with the meat mixture. Place in an 11" x 7" baking dish. Spoon tomato sauce on top.

5. Cover with foil, and bake for 30 minutes. Garnish manicotti with minced oregano or basil before serving.

183 calories per serving: 4 g. fat, 15 g. protein,
24 g. carbohydrate, 20 mg. cholesterol, 528 mg. sodium.
For exchange diets, count 1 lean meat, 1 starch, 2 vegetable.

EASY MOSTACCIOLI BAKE

*Fix this supper fast. When it's in the oven take some time
to read the kids a story.*

Preparation time: 15 minutes
Baking time: 30 minutes
8 servings—1 1/2 cups each

---

2 cups mostaccioli, cooked according to package directions
  (4 cups cooked)
3/4 pound browned lean ground beef
16-ounce jar reduced-fat spaghetti sauce
8 ounces shredded reduced-fat mozzarella cheese
1/4 cup grated Parmesan cheese

1. Preheat oven to 350° F.

2. In a 13" x 9" pan, stir together mostaccioli, ground beef, and
spaghetti sauce. Top with mozzarella cheese, then sprinkle Parmesan
cheese on top.

3. Bake 20 to 30 minutes or until heated through and cheese is melted.

254 calories per serving: 10 g. fat, 24 g. protein,
17 g. carbohydrate, 60 mg. cholesterol, 295 mg. sodium.
For exchange diets, count 1 starch, 3 lean meat.

STRAW AND HAY

The name for this recipe comes from the blend of spinach and egg noodles.

Preparation time: 15 minutes
Cooking time: 15 minutes
8 servings—1 1/2 cups each

nonstick cooking spray
1/4 teaspoon minced garlic
1 large yellow onion, diced
8 ounces fresh mushrooms, sliced thin
10-ounce package frozen peas
8 ounces lean cooked ham, cut in thin slivers
1/2 teaspoon dried basil
1/8 teaspoon nutmeg
8 ounces white egg noodles
8 ounces spinach noodles
1 1/2 cups evaporated skim milk
1/4 teaspoon salt
1/2 teaspoon white pepper
1/4 cup grated Parmesan cheese

1. Spray a large skillet with cooking spray. Add garlic and onion, and cook slowly until soft. Add mushrooms, and sauté quickly.

2. Add peas and ham, and heat through. Season with basil and nutmeg.

3. Meanwhile, cook green and white pasta according to package directions. Do not overcook. Drain and toss in skillet.

4. Add evaporated milk, salt, pepper, and cheese. Heat through, and serve.

181 calories per serving: 3 g. fat, 15 g. protein,
23 g. carbohydrate, 32 mg. cholesterol, 537 mg. sodium.
For exchange diets, count 1 vegetable, 1 starch, 1 1/2 lean meat

EILEEN'S OVERNIGHT LASAGNA

Eileen Egloff, an excellent cook, is a friend of the family who loves to experiment with recipes.

Preparation time: 20 minutes; Cooking time: 20 minutes
Chilling time: 8 hours to 3 days; Baking time: 1 1/2 hours
12 servings—1 square each

Meat sauce:
- 1 pound ground turkey
- 3/4 cup chopped onion
- 2 cloves minced garlic
- 2 1/2 cups water
- 1 cup tomato juice
- 8-ounce can tomato sauce
- 6-ounce can tomato paste
- 1 teaspoon Italian seasoning
- 1 teaspoon basil
- 1 teaspoon oregano
- 1 teaspoon salt

Cheese sauce:
- 2 cups 1% cottage cheese
- 1/4 cup grated Parmesan cheese
- 2 tablespoons chopped fresh parsley
- 1/4 teaspoon black pepper

Lasagna:
- 8 ounces uncooked lasagna noodles
- 8 ounces reduced-fat mozzarella cheese
- 1/4 cup Parmesan cheese

1. In a large skillet, brown turkey, onion, and garlic; drain well. Add remaining meat sauce ingredients; simmer 10 minutes. Mixture will be thin.

2. In a medium bowl, stir together cheese sauce ingredients.

3. Spread 1 1/2 cups sauce evenly in a 13" x 9" pan. Place a layer of uncooked noodles over the sauce. Top with a third of the cottage cheese sauce. Repeat layers 2 more times.

4. Top with mozzarella cheese. Sprinkle Parmesan over mozzarella. Cover pan with foil. Refrigerate overnight.

5. Preheat oven to 350° F. Bake lasagna covered with foil for 1 1/2 hours. Remove from oven; let stand 10 minutes before cutting.

282 calories per serving: 11 g. fat, 25 g. protein,
22 g. carbohydrate, 54 mg. cholesterol, 633 mg. sodium.
For exchange diets, count 1 vegetable, 3 lean meat, 1 starch.

CLASSIC LASAGNA

The carrots and chunky tomatoes give this lasagna an old-world appeal.

Preparation time: 20 minutes
Cooking time: 25 minutes; Baking time: 1 1/4 hours
12 servings—1/12 pan each

---

1 teaspoon olive oil
1 medium onion, chopped fine
1 carrot, peeled and chopped
3/4 teaspoon minced garlic
1 pound lean ground beef
24-ounce can chopped tomatoes
1 teaspoon oregano
1 tablespoon basil
1/2 teaspoon salt
1/2 teaspoon pepper
1 pound lasagna noodles, uncooked
8 ounces part-skim mozzarella cheese, shredded
2 cups nonfat ricotta cheese
2 ounces Parmesan cheese, grated

1. Preheat oven to 375° F.

2. Heat oil in a medium skillet. Add the onion, carrot, and garlic. Cook and stir until onion is soft. Add the beef, and cook until brown. Drain the fat. Add tomatoes, oregano, basil, salt, and pepper. Simmer, uncovered, for 10 minutes.

3. Spread the tomato and meat sauce over the bottom of a lasagna baking pan. Then add a layer of noodles, sprinkle with half of the mozzarella cheese, and spread on half of the ricotta cheese. Make another layer of sauce, noodles, mozzarella, and ricotta. Finish with noodles and sauce.

4. Sprinkle Parmesan cheese evenly over the top. Cover and bake for an hour and 15 minutes. Remove cover the last 15 minutes.

---

238 calories per serving: 11 g. fat, 22 g. protein,
13 g. carbohydrate, 57 mg. cholesterol, 347 mg. sodium.
For exchange diets, count 1 starch, 3 lean meat.

EGGPLANT PARMESAN

Preparation time: 15 minutes
Cooking time: 5 minutes; Baking time: 20 minutes
12 servings—2 to 3 slices each

2 large eggplant
1/4 cup flour
1 egg, slightly beaten, or 1/4 cup liquid egg substitute
1/4 cup skim milk
1 cup seasoned bread crumbs
2 tablespoons vegetable oil
nonstick cooking spray
2 8-ounce cans tomato sauce
1/2 teaspoon dried oregano
1/8 teaspoon black pepper
1/4 pound part-skim mozzarella cheese
1/2 cup freshly grated Parmesan cheese

1. Preheat oven to 400° F.

2. Peel eggplant, and cut into 1/2-inch slices. Place eggplant slices in a plastic bag with the flour, and shake to coat. Combine the egg and milk in a shallow bowl. Dip the eggplant into the egg mixture and then into the bread crumbs.

3. Heat oil in a large skillet. Brown eggplant on one side, then the other. Place eggplant in a large baking dish that has been sprayed with cooking spray.

4. In a small bowl, combine tomato sauce, oregano, and pepper. Pour sauce over the eggplant. Sprinkle with cheeses, then bake for 20 minutes or until bubbly.

143 calories per serving: 6 g. fat, 7 g. protein,
15 g. carbohydrate, 25 mg. cholesterol with egg
(11 mg. with egg substitute), 592 mg. sodium.
For exchange diets, count 1 lean meat, 3 vegetable, 1/2 fat.

SPINACH TORTE

This torte is delicious as a snack or side dish.

Preparation time: 10 minutes
Baking time: 1 hour
16 servings—1/16 of the pan each

---

1 1/2 cups long grain rice, cooked according to
  package directions
2 (10-ounce) packages frozen spinach, cooked and drained
3/4 cup liquid egg substitute
3-ounce package reduced-fat cream cheese
1/4 cup sliced green onion
3 tablespoons chopped fresh parsley
1 tablespoon reduced-fat margarine
1 tablespoon finely chopped green pepper
2 teaspoons Parmesan cheese
1 minced garlic clove
1/2 teaspoon crushed basil
1/4 teaspoon black pepper

1. Preheat oven to 350° F.

2. Mix all ingredients in a large bowl.

3. Spray a 13" x 9" pan with nonstick cooking spray. Fill pan with spinach mixture. Bake for about an hour or until just beginning to brown and knife inserted into the center comes out clean.

....

48 calories per serving: 0 fat, 4 g. protein,
7 g. carbohydrate, 0 cholesterol, 62 mg. sodium.
For exchange diets, count 2 vegetable.

MICROWAVE RATATOUILLE

This dish is chock-full of vegetables and has no fat!

Preparation time: 15 minutes
Cooking time: 10 minutes
8 servings—1 cup each

1 large eggplant, cubed
1 large onion, coarsely chopped
1 small zucchini, sliced
1 green pepper, sliced
2 tablespoons fresh parsley
1 tablespoon water
3 cloves crushed garlic
1 teaspoon crushed rosemary
1 teaspoon crushed basil
1/2 teaspoon salt
1/4 teaspoon black pepper
2 cups fresh tomato wedges

1. In a 2-quart microwaveable casserole dish, combine all ingredients except tomatoes. Cover, and cook on high 5 minutes.

2. Add tomatoes, and stir mixture. Cover and cook an additional 4 to 5 minutes in the microwave or until vegetables are tender.

26 calories per serving: 0 fat, 1 g. protein,
6 g. carbohydrate, 0 cholesterol, 74 mg. sodium.
For exchange diets, count 1 vegetable.

ITALIAN GRILLED POTATOES
Preparation time: 5 minutes; Microwave time: 10 minutes
Marinating time: 30 minutes; Grilling time: 16 minutes
6 servings—3/4 cup each

4 medium potatoes
2 tablespoons water
1/2 cup fat-free Italian dressing
1/2 teaspoon salt
1/4 teaspoon pepper

1. Cut potatoes, with skins on, into 1/2-inch slices into a shallow microwave-safe baking dish. Add 2 tablespoons of water, cover and cook in the microwave for 10 minutes on high power. Remove cover, and drain water off the potatoes. Pour dressing over potatoes.

2. Let stand at least 30 minutes, turning slices over once.

3. Preheat barbecue. Cook potatoes over hot coals for about 8 minutes on each side or until golden brown. Season with salt and pepper.

85 calories per serving: 0 fat, 2 g. protein,
20 g. carbohydrate, 0 cholesterol, 281 mg. sodium.
For exchange diets, count 1 starch.

HONEY ORANGE BISCOTTI

Preparation time: 15 minutes
Baking time: 35 minutes
Cooling time: 20 minutes
24 servings—1 biscotti each

1/2 cup chopped dates
3 tablespoons orange-flavored liqueur, such as Grand Marnier, or
   1 tablespoon orange extract
2 1/4 cups flour
3/4 cup sugar
3/4 teaspoon baking soda
1/4 teaspoon salt
1/3 cup orange juice
1/4 cup honey
1 tablespoon grated orange zest
1/2 teaspoon vanilla
1/4 cup chopped almonds

1. In a small bowl, combine the dates and orange liqueur; allow to soak for at least 10 minutes.

2. Preheat oven to 375°.

3. In a medium mixing bowl, blend flour, sugar, baking soda, and salt together. In a glass measure, whisk together the orange juice, honey, zest, and vanilla. Add this to the flour and sugar mixture. Drain the dates, saving the liqueur. Add the drained liqueur to the flour and sugar mixture.

4. Beat until a dough is formed. Stir in the chopped dates and almonds. Knead the dough on a floured surface several times, then cut the dough in half.

5. Roll each half into a log approximately 12 inches long. Flatten the log to about 2 inches wide.

6. Place the logs at least 3 inches apart on a greased baking sheet. Bake for 25 minutes. Remove from the oven, and let biscotti cool for 10 minutes. Cut the logs diagonally into 1/2-inch thick strips. Reduce oven temperature to 325°.

Honey Orange Biscotti (continued)

7. Place the slices cut side down on the baking sheet, and bake for 10 minutes. Remove from the oven, and cool again. The biscotti will be very hard, and will keep indefinitely in an airtight container.

97 calories per serving: 1 g. fat, 2 g. protein,
20 g. carbohydrate, 0 cholesterol, 63 mg. sodium.
For exchange diets, count 1 starch

Chapter Ten

Eastern Europe

Suggested Eastern European Menus

Potato Caraway Bread
Marinated Lamb Kabobs
Snowy Potatoes
Raspberries With Lemon Cream

Cucumbers With Fennel
Goulash
Dilled Zucchini
Prune Dumplings

Add Fun, Subtract Expense

There is no substitute for the flavor of fresh herbs in old world cooking. Easy to grow, top quality herb plants can be found in floral shops, produce sections of large markets, or by mail order from kitchen equipment and supply businesses.

Marjoram is probably in your cupboard and is used in many Polish meat dishes. Add marjoram near the end of cooking, as its delicate flavor can be simmered away.

Stuffed peppers become Hungarian when they are flavored with sweet paprika.

To turn an ordinary meal into Eastern European fare, add some caraway to breads or stuffing.

Thyme, marjoram, basil, and bay leaf added to your meats, stews, and sauces are typical of Eastern Europe. Don't forget to remove the bay leaf before serving. Other spices for desserts or beverages include mace and mint.

A Bulgarian garlic pot holds 5 to 6 heads of garlic and is a fragrant, pretty decoration in any kitchen (about $18).

Eastern Europeans would love the Krups Espresso Novo Compact, designed for small kitchens (about $150).

Try a Russian Bear:
Stir 1 ounce vodka, 1/2 ounce creme de cacao, and 1/2 ounce sweet cream with cracked ice. Strain into a 3-ounce cocktail glass.

Try a Russian Cocktail:
Shake 3/4 ounce creme de cacao, 3/4 ounce dry gin, and 3/4 ounce vodka with cracked ice; strain into a 3-ounce cocktail glass.

Taste a Black Russian:
Pour 1 1/2 ounces vodka and 3/4 ounces kahlua on ice cubes in an old-fashioned cocktail glass.

FLAT BREAD

Preparation time: 10 minutes
Bread machine time: 1 hour, 30 minutes
Manual method preparation time: 25 minutes
Rising time: 1 hour; Baking time: 12 minutes
24 servings—1/8 round each

---

1 1/4 cups water
3 cups white bread flour
3 tablespoons sugar
2 tablespoons nonfat dry milk powder
1 teaspoon salt
1 teaspoon yeast
1 tablespoon olive oil
nonstick cooking spray
1 tablespoon sesame seed

1. Place first 7 ingredients in order listed in bread machine pan. Select "dough" from menu, and push "start." Wait approximately 1 hour and 30 minutes for the dough to be prepared. Go to number 3.

2. If you prefer making bread from scratch, gently mix hot tap water, sugar, dry milk powder, yeast, salt, and olive oil in a large mixing bowl. Allow mixture to rest 5 minutes. Gradually add flour, and work the mixture to a smooth dough. Knead for 10 minutes, then cover and allow dough to rise for 1 hour in a warm place.

3. Preheat oven to 400° F. Remove dough from the bread machine or from the bowl. Divide dough into 3 parts. On a floured surface, roll each portion into a 14-inch circle. Transfer the dough to baking sheets that have been sprayed with cooking spray. Use a fork to prick the surface of each many times. Sprinkle with sesame seeds.

4. Bake for 12 minutes or until browned. Cool on a wire rack.

---

88 calories per serving: 2 g. fat, 3 g. protein,
14 g. carbohydrate, 1 mg. cholesterol, 76 mg. sodium.
For exchange diets, count 1 starch.

RUSSIAN RYE BREAD

Preparation time: 10 minutes
Bread machine time: 4 hours, 10 minutes
Manual method preparation time: 30 minutes
Rising time: 2 hours; Baking time: 25 minutes
24 servings—1/2 slice each

1 1/8 cups water
2 cups white bread flour
1 cup rye flour
3 tablespoons molasses
2 tablespoons nonfat dry milk powder
1 teaspoon salt
1 tablespoon cocoa powder
1/2 teaspoon fennel
1/2 teaspoon caraway seed
1 teaspoon yeast
1 tablespoon soft margarine

1. Place ingredients in order listed in bread machine pan. Push "start."

2. Loaf will be done in 4 hours and 10 minutes using a Hitachi bread machine.

3. If you prefer making bread from scratch, gently mix hot tap water with molasses, dry milk powder, yeast, cocoa, fennel, caraway seed, salt, and margarine in a large mixing bowl. Allow mixture to rest 5 minutes. Gradually add white flour and rye flour, working the mixture to a smooth dough. Knead for 10 minutes, then cover and allow dough to rise for 1 hour in a warm place. Punch the dough down, form a loaf shape, and place in a loaf pan that has been sprayed with nonstick cooking spray. Allow dough to rise again for 1 hour. Bake in a preheated 350° oven for 25 minutes or until the top is browned. Cool for 15 minutes, then remove bread to a cooling rack.

4. Serve this bread with lean ham.

75 calories per serving: 1 g. fat, 2 g. protein,
14 g. carbohydrate, 0 cholesterol, 110 mg. sodium.
For exchange diets, count 1 starch.

POTATO CARAWAY BREAD IN THE MACHINE

This recipe makes a large loaf.
Preparation time: 10 minutes
Bread machine time: 4 hours, 10 minutes
24 servings—1/2 slice each

1 medium potato, peeled and shredded
1 cup water
3 cups bread flour
1 1/2 teaspoons salt
3 tablespoons sugar
2 tablespoons nonfat dry milk
1 1/2 teaspoons dry yeast
1 tablespoon margarine
1 tablespoon caraway seeds

1. Place first 8 ingredients in bread machine pan in order listed (recipe tested with a Hitachi). If your machine calls for dry ingredients first, then invert the order of ingredients.

2. Program your machine for the setting which allows ingredients to be folded into the dough. Push "start," then wait about 40 minutes or until the beeper sounds. Add the caraway seeds. Remove the bread from the pan when done, approximately 3 1/2 hours later.

120 calories per serving: 0 fat, 3 g. protein,
27 g. carbohydrate, 0 cholesterol, 150 mg. sodium.
For exchange diets, count 1 1/2 starch.

KULICH

This bread machine delight is frosted to resemble the dome on Russian churches. It makes a large (3 cups of flour) loaf.

Preparation time: 15 minutes
Bread machine time: 4 hours, 10 minutes
16 servings—1 slice each

3/4 cup milk
2 eggs or 1/2 cup liquid egg substitute
3 cups bread flour
1 teaspoon salt
1/4 cup sugar
1 teaspoon nutmeg
1 1/2 teaspoons vanilla
1 teaspoon lemon extract
1 1/2 teaspoons bread machine yeast
1 tablespoon margarine
1/4 cup raisins
2 tablespoons chopped almonds

Frosting:
1/4 cup powdered sugar
fresh lemon juice to thin

1. Place first 10 ingredients in the order given in the bread machine pan. Push "start."

2. Program your machine for the setting which allows ingredients to be folded into the dough. About 40 minutes into the cycle or when beeper sounds, add raisins and almonds.

3. When bread is cooled, combine the powdered sugar with lemon juice in a small bowl. Spread over the top of the loaf.

133 calories per serving: 4 g. fat, 2 g. protein,
24 g. carbohydrate, 26 mg. cholesterol with egg
(0 with egg substitute), 142 mg. sodium.
For exchange diets, count 1 starch, 1 fruit.

VEGETABLE SOUP HUNGARIAN

Hungarian paprika sets this vegetable soup apart.

Preparation time: 15 minutes
Cooking time: 20 minutes
12 servings—1 1/2 cups each

1 lb. boneless beef sirloin, well-trimmed and cubed
2 medium onions, chopped fine
1/2 teaspoon minced garlic
2 teaspoons Hungarian sweet paprika
dash of cayenne pepper
3 cups beef broth
2 cups water
1/2 teaspoon caraway seed
1/2 teaspoon marjoram
1-pound can chunky tomatoes
2 fresh potatoes, washed and diced
2 medium carrots, cut into coins
2 red peppers, cleaned and chopped

1. In a large Dutch oven or soup pot, brown beef, onions, and garlic over medium heat until meat is no longer pink.

2. Add all remaining ingredients, and bring to a boil. Reduce heat to a simmer. Simmer for 15 minutes or until potatoes are tender.

142 calories per serving: 2 g. fat, 6 g. protein,
18 g. carbohydrate, 0 cholesterol, 437 mg. sodium
(To reduce sodium, use no-added-salt tomatoes and beef broth.)
For exchange diets, count 3 vegetable, 1 lean meat.

HUNGARIAN CUCUMBER SALAD

Preparation time: 10 minutes
8 servings—3/4 cup each

1 large tomato, thinly sliced
2 large cucumbers, peeled and thinly sliced
1 small Bermuda onion, thinly sliced
2 ounces feta cheese, crumbled
Dressing:
2 tablespoons olive oil
1/4 cup wine vinegar
1/2 teaspoon marjoram
1/2 teaspoon seasoned salt

1. In a small salad bowl, combine tomato, cucumber, onion, and cheese.

2. In a shaker container, combine the ingredients for dressing; shake well.

3. Pour dressing over vegetables and cheese; cover and refrigerate
until serving time.

58 calories per serving: 5 g. fat, 1 g. protein,
3 g. carbohydrate, 0 cholesterol, 214 mg. sodium.
For exchange diets, count 1 vegetable, 1 fat.

CUCUMBERS WITH FENNEL DRESSING

Fennel is that minty seed you sometimes see on pizza.

Preparation time: 20 minutes
Chilling time: 30 minutes
8 servings—1 cup each

Dressing:

1/4 cup olive oil
3/4 cup red wine vinegar
1/4 cup water
1/2 cup white vinegar
1 teaspoon sugar
1 tablespoon dry mustard
1 teaspoon fennel
2 tablespoons lemon juice
2 tablespoons parsley, minced
1/4 teaspoon white pepper
1/2 teaspoon salt
8 medium cucumbers

1. In a shaker container, combine ingredients for dressing.

2. Slice cucumbers into a salad bowl. Pour prepared dressing over cucumbers; cover and refrigerate for at least 30 minutes.

75 calories per serving: 7 g. fat, 1 g. protein,
3 g. carbohydrate, 0 cholesterol, 139 mg. sodium.
For exchange diets, count 1 vegetable, 1 fat.

GOULASH

Preparation time: 10 minutes
Cooking time: 20 minutes
8 servings—1 1/2 cups each

1 pound extra-lean ground beef
1 cup chopped onion
1/2 cup chopped green pepper
1/2 cup sliced mushrooms
2 cloves minced garlic
2 cups uncooked elbow macaroni
4 cups tomato juice
14-ounce can stewed tomatoes
1 teaspoon thyme
1/2 teaspoon salt
1/4 teaspoon black pepper

1. In a large deep skillet, brown ground beef, onion, green pepper, mushrooms, and garlic. Drain well, and return to the skillet.

2. Meanwhile, cook elbow macaroni for 8 minutes or according to package directions; do not overcook. Drain well.

3. Stir macaroni and all remaining ingredients together with the beef; simmer 10 minutes.

4. Add a little more tomato juice when reheating, if necessary.

258 calories per serving: 6 g. fat, 20 g. protein,
31 g. carbohydrate, 47 mg. cholesterol, 684 mg. sodium
(To reduce sodium, use no-added-salt stewed tomatoes.)
For exchange diets, count 2 lean meat, 1 vegetable, 1 1/2 starch.

MARINATED LAMB KABOBS

Preparation time: 15 minutes
Marinating time: 30 minutes to 24 hours
Grilling time: 20 minutes

8 servings—4 ounces meat and 1 cup vegetables each

2 pounds lean lamb, cut into 1 1/2-inch chunks
Marinade:
    1 medium yellow onion, chopped fine
    1/4 teaspoon minced garlic
    1 tablespoon vegetable oil
    1 1/2 tablespoons red wine vinegar
    1/2 teaspoon dried marjoram
    1/4 teaspoon salt
    1/4 teaspoon pepper
    1 green pepper, cleaned and cut into 1-inch chunks
    1 red pepper, cleaned and cut into 1-inch chunks
    1 large onion, cut into wedges
    8 ounces fresh mushrooms, cleaned and stems removed

1. Place cubed meat in a casserole dish.

2. In a small bowl, combine ingredients for the marinade. Pour the marinade over the meat.

3. Cover meat, and refrigerate for at least 30 minutes or up to 24 hours.

4. Drain meat, and thread meat and vegetables alternately on 8 skewers.

5. Grill kabobs for 10 minutes on each side over medium-hot coals, about 4 inches from the flame.

206 calories per serving: 8 g. fat, 25 g. protein,
9 g. carbohydrate, 72 mg. cholesterol, 75 mg. sodium.
For exchange diets, count 2 vegetable, 3 lean meat.

SNOWY POTATOES

Preparation time: 15 minutes
Cooking time: 10 minutes; Baking time: 20 minutes
8 servings—3/4 cup each

8 small potatoes, washed, peeled and diced
1/2 teaspoon salt
1/4 cup water
1/2 teaspoon garlic salt
1/4 teaspoon white pepper
1 4-ounce package nonfat cream cheese
2 tablespoons chopped chives
1 tablespoon margarine

Garnish:

paprika

1. Place diced potatoes in a microwave-safe casserole dish that's at least 3 inches deep. Sprinkle with salt and water. Cover with plastic wrap, and microwave on 80% power for 10 minutes, stopping at least twice to stir.

2. Preheat oven to 350° F.

3. Drain potatoes, and add all remaining ingredients to the casserole. Use a hand masher or electric mixer to mash potatoes with the seasonings.

4. When potatoes are mixed to desired consistency, smooth out the top and use a paper towel to wipe the inside edge of the casserole dish. Garnish the potatoes with paprika, and bake for 20 minutes.

146 calories per serving: 2 g. fat, 5 g. protein,
27 g. carbohydrate, 0 cholesterol, 358 mg. sodium.
For exchange diets, count 2 starch.

DILLED ZUCCHINI

This side dish is from Hungary.

Preparation time: 10 minutes
Cooking time: 8 minutes
8 servings—3/4 cup each

---

8 small zucchini, cut into slices
1/4 teaspoon minced garlic
1 tablespoon olive oil
1 medium onion, sliced and separated into rings
1/2 teaspoon seasoned salt
1/4 teaspoon pepper
1/2 cup nonfat plain yogurt
1 teaspoon dried dill weed

1. In a medium skillet, cook sliced zucchini and garlic in oil until zucchini is light brown, about 5 minutes. Stir in onion, salt, and pepper; remove from heat.

2. In a serving bowl, combine yogurt and dill weed. Fold in zucchini mixture. Serve warm.

33 calories per serving: 2 g. fat, 2 g. protein,
4 g. carbohydrate, 0 cholesterol, 122 mg. sodium.
For exchange diets, count 1 vegetable.

RASPBERRIES WITH LEMON CREAM

Preparation time: 10 minutes
Cooking time: 10 minutes
8 servings—3/4 cup each

1 quart fresh raspberries or 1 pound whole frozen raspberries
3 large eggs or 3/4 cup liquid egg substitute
6 tablespoons sugar
1 pinch salt
1 tablespoon lemon juice
1 teaspoon grated lemon rind
3/4 cup sweet white wine, such as Rhine

1. Place raspberries in 8 dessert dishes.

2. In a small saucepan, beat eggs until frothy. Beat in sugar and salt. Slowly add lemon juice, lemon rind, and wine, beating until foamy.

3. Place saucepan over very low heat or on the top of a double boiler. Beat constantly with a wire whip until the mixture becomes thick and hot.

4. Pour hot lemon cream over the raspberries in dessert dishes. Serve at once.

110 calories per serving: 1 g. fat, 4 g. protein,
18 g. carbohydrate, 64 mg. cholesterol with eggs
(0 with egg substitute), 58 mg. sodium.
For exchange diets, count 1/2 skim milk, 1 fruit.

APRICOT PUDDING

Preparation time: 5 minutes
Cooking time: 25 minutes; Chilling time: 1 hour
8 servings—1/2 cup each

2 cups water
8 ounces dried apricots
1/4 cup sugar
1 teaspoon cinnamon
3 tablespoons cornstarch

Garnish:
vanilla yogurt and whole almonds

1. In a medium saucepan, combine water and apricots. Bring mixture to a boil, then reduce heat to a simmer for 20 minutes.

2. Place apricots and 1/2 cup of the cooking liquid in a blender. Process until smooth.

3. In a small mixing bowl, combine sugar, cinnamon, and cornstarch. Return pureed apricots to the saucepan, and stir in sugar mixture. Bring mixture to a boil, stirring constantly. Boil for 3 minutes or until mixture is clear.

4. Chill pudding at least one hour or until serving time. To serve, divide among 8 small dessert dishes. Garnish, if desired, with a dollop of vanilla yogurt and a few whole almonds.

72 calories per serving: 0 fat, 0 protein,
18 g. carbohydrate, 0 cholesterol, 2 mg. sodium.
For exchange diets, count 1 fruit.

PRUNE DUMPLINGS

This is an old Czech recipe.

Preparation time: 20 minutes
Cooking time: 20 minutes
12 servings—2 dumplings each

2 cups flour
1/2 cup liquid egg substitute
1/2 cup skim milk
1 teaspoon salt
24 pitted prunes

1. In a large bowl, mix together all ingredients except prunes. If dough is sticky, add additional flour.

2. Form dough into 1-inch balls. Flatten each on a floured board into a circle large enough to cover one prune. Form dough around prunes, sealing tightly.

3. Cook dumplings in boiling salted water 15 to 20 minutes, or until they are firm and hold their shape well.

4. To serve, cut dumplings in half. If desired, dumplings may be spread with margarine and sprinkled with cinnamon-sugar.

200 calories per serving: 0 fat, 5 g. protein,
46 g. carbohydrate, 0 cholesterol, 26 mg. sodium.
For exchange diets, count 2 1/2 starch.

Chapter Eleven

Africa

Suggested African Menu

African Drunken Chicken
Couscous
Cucumber Sambal
Grape Soup

Add Fun, Subtract Expense

Africa is a big continent with many countries, so African food encompasses a wide variety of foods. Favorite foods range from sweet potatoes in Kenya to couscous in Nigeria.

Very spicy dishes evolved from the need to preserve food in the intense heat. It's also said that spicy foods help you keep cool because they make you perspire.

Think of Madagascar when you purchase a vanilla bean (about two dollars). This island off the southeastern coast of Africa produces the prime vanilla flavor preferred around the world. Vanilla beans are commonly used in desserts that have a lot of liquid, such as ice cream and pudding. Split the bean down the middle, peel back the skin and chop into large hunks for cooking.

For African sweet potatoes, bake them with a sprinkle of coconut, cardamom, and brown sugar.

For an African curried fish entree, season white fish fillets with a sprinkle of vinegar, turmeric, chili powder, cumin, and garlic. Add some tomato chunks before baking.

CUCUMBER SAMBAL

Preparation time: 10 minutes
Marinating time: 30 minutes
4 servings—2/3 cup each

2 large cucumbers
1 teaspoon apple cider vinegar
1/2 teaspoon salt
1 green onion, diced
1 teaspoon chili peppers, finely chopped
3 tablespoons fresh lemon juice
2 teaspoons soy sauce
dash of cayenne pepper

1. Peel cucumbers, and slice in half lengthwise. Scoop out the seeds and grate cucumbers coarsely into a salad bowl.

2. Sprinkle cucumbers with vinegar and salt; allow to marinate for at least 30 minutes. Transfer the cucumbers to a colander and squeeze them to remove excess liquid.

3. In the salad bowl, stir together all remaining ingredients. Add drained cucumbers. Cover and refrigerate until ready to serve.

29 calories per serving: 1 g. fat, 2 g. protein,
7 g. carbohydrate, 0 cholesterol, 436 mg. sodium.
For exchange diets, count 1 vegetable.

AFRICAN DRUNKEN CHICKEN

*A hodgepodge of unique ingredients makes this entrée
an interesting change from the usual fare.*

Preparation time: 25 minutes
Cooking time: 1 hour, 45 minutes
12 servings—1 1/2 cups each

2 pounds boneless skinless chicken
1 1/2 cups dry white wine
1/3 cup all-purpose flour
1/2 teaspoon salt
1/2 teaspoon black pepper
2 tablespoons olive oil
4 chopped and peeled ripe tomatoes
1 cup chopped onion
1 teaspoon crushed basil
1/2 teaspoon thyme
1/4 teaspoon cayenne pepper
4 diced bananas
2 diced potatoes
1 1/2 cups peeled and sliced carrots
1 cup whole pitted prunes
1/2 cup sliced stuffed green olives
3/4 teaspoon sugar
2 minced garlic cloves

1. Marinate chicken in wine in refrigerator overnight; drain and
reserve wine.

2. Combine flour, salt, and pepper on a plate. Coat chicken with flour
mixture.

3. In a large skillet, sauté chicken in olive oil just until browned. Add
tomatoes, onion, basil, thyme, pepper, and reserved wine. Cover; simmer 30 minutes.

4. Add bananas, potatoes, carrots, prunes, olives, and sugar; simmer
1 hour.

5. Add garlic; simmer 10 minutes.

African Drunken Chicken (continued)

....

287 calories per serving: 6 g. fat, 20 g. protein,
35 g. carbohydrate, 47 mg. cholesterol, 267 mg. sodium.
For exchange diets, count 1 starch, 1 fruit, 1 vegetable, 2 lean meat.

DATE CHUTNEY

Preparation time: 10 minutes
Roasting time: 35 minutes
24 servings—2 tablespoons each

1 large onion, peeled and cut crosswise into 1/4-inch thick slices
1 cup red wine vinegar
2 dried hot chili peppers, crumbled
1 tablespoon fresh ginger, coarsely chopped
2 teaspoons minced garlic
1 teaspoon salt
1 pound pitted dates, chopped

1. Preheat oven to 325° F. Arrange onion slices on a large baking sheet. Roast onion slices for 35 minutes.

2. Transfer roasted onions to the blender, and add vinegar, chilies, ginger, garlic, and salt. Process for 30 seconds on high speed. Scrape down the sides, and then blend again.

3. Add dates, a small amount at a time, continuing to blend and scrape until mixture is smooth. Refrigerate chutney in a covered container. Use as a condiment.

64 calories per serving: 0 fat, 2 g. protein,
14 g. carbohydrate, 0 cholesterol, 89 mg. sodium.
For exchange diets, count 1 fruit.

VEGETABLE COUSCOUS

Couscous is a very fine grain made from semolina flour. This side dish is believed to have originated in North Africa; however, it may have originated farther east. This dish has been around for a thousand years.

Preparation time: 15 minutes
Cooking time: 20 minutes
8 servings—1 1/4 cups each

Vegetables:
>   1 tablespoon olive oil
>   1/2 cup finely chopped celery
>   1/2 cup finely chopped onion
>   1/2 cup finely chopped carrot
>   2 minced cloves garlic
>   1 teaspoon cumin
>   1/2 teaspoon paprika
>   1/4 teaspoon dry mustard
>   1/4 teaspoon ginger
>   1/8 teaspoon cayenne pepper
>   1 cup fat-free chicken broth
>   1 cup shredded potato
>   1 cup chopped tomato

Couscous:
>   2 1/4 cups water
>   1/2 teaspoon salt
>   10-ounce package couscous
>   1/4 teaspoon cinnamon

1. Heat oil in a large skillet. Add celery, onion, and carrot; cook over medium heat about 5 minutes. Add garlic, cumin, paprika, mustard, ginger, and pepper; cook 30 seconds.

2. Add chicken broth and potato; bring to a boil. Reduce heat to low, and simmer 15 minutes. Stir in tomato; cover and simmer on low while cooking couscous.

3. In a medium saucepan, bring water and salt just to a boil; stir in couscous. Cover, remove from heat, and let stand 5 minutes. Add cinnamon; fluff with a fork.

4. Stir couscous into vegetables. Serve immediately.

....

166 calories per serving: 2 g. fat, 5 g. protein,
32 g. carbohydrate, 0 cholesterol, 93 mg. sodium.
For exchange diets, count 1 1/2 starch, 2 vegetable.

GRAPE SOUP

Preparation time: 5 minutes
Cooking time: 5 minutes
Chilling time: at least 30 minutes
8 servings—3/4 cup each

1/2 cup sugar
2 cups apple juice
1/2 cup Concord grape wine
4 cups fresh purple grapes, stemmed and seeded

Garnish:

sliced almonds

1. In a medium saucepan, bring sugar and apple juice to a boil. Add wine; remove mixture from the heat.

2. Stir in grapes; cover and refrigerate. When soup has cooled, transfer it to a serving bowl. Serve in deep soup bowls garnished with almonds, if desired.

98 calories per serving: 0 fat, 0 protein,
21 g. carbohydrate, 0 cholesterol, 2 mg. sodium.
For exchange diets, count 1 1/2 fruit.

Chapter Twelve

the Middle East

Suggested Middle Eastern Menus

Dolmas
Lamb and Apricot Stew
Zucchini and Couscous in the Microwave
Date Cake

Hummus
Roasted Chicken With Turmeric
Green Herb Rice
Chunky Moroccan Vegetables
Orange Custard

Add Fun, Subtract Expense

Take home a Persian melon from your favorite produce market. They look like overgrown cantaloupes, but have a firmer flesh with a buttery texture. Choose melons weighing 5 pounds or more with a background color turning from gray-green to bronze.

The Middle Eastern "mezze" is an array of appetizers similar to the Spanish tapas and the Italian antipasto. Savor a sliced tomato, quartered cucumber, and hummus served with pita bread.

There are more than 600 varieties of figs grown in the Middle East. You'll discover a few of them, fresh or dried, in your market.

Most Middle Eastern food is extremely healthful, made of whole grains, dried beans, yogurt, vegetables, herbs, garlic, onions, and seasonings.

In Lebanon, cooks create their own individual seasoning combinations to flavor grains and vegetables. For example, 1 part hot pepper to 2 parts sweet paprika and 2 parts cinnamon is a combination that is used with zucchini and green beans. They also combine cumin and crushed coriander in stews.

Grow your own mint for a Middle Eastern flair in salads, tabbouleh, and marinated vegetables.

To spice up Middle Eastern style, splurge on yogurt, garlic, tahini, mint, lemon juice, cinnamon, nutmeg, cumin, and fenugreek. Start with a small amount and go from there.

HUMMUS

Preparation time: 15 minutes
20 servings—2 tablespoons each

16-ounce can garbanzo beans
1/3 cup tahini (sesame paste)
1/3 cup lemon juice
1/2 teaspoon minced garlic
1/4 cup chopped fresh parsley

1. Place beans, tahini, lemon juice, and garlic in a blender. Process until smooth. Pour into a serving bowl, and garnish the top with parsley. Serve as a dip with triangles of toasted pita bread or sesame breadsticks.

52 calories per serving: 2 g. fat, 2 g. protein,
6 g. carbohydrate, 0 cholesterol, 90 mg. sodium.
For exchange diets, count 1/2 starch.

DOLMAS

Dolmas are stuffed grapevine leaves. Look for grapevine leaves in the specialty section of large supermarkets.

Preparation time: 20 minutes
Cooking time: 55 minutes
8 servings—1 dolma each

9-ounce jar grape leaves
2 cups finely chopped onion
2 teaspoons olive oil
1 pound ground lamb or beef
2/3 cup uncooked long-grain rice
1 teaspoon crushed dried mint flakes
1/2 teaspoon salt
1/4 teaspoon pepper
1/8 teaspoon cinnamon
1 1/2 cups water
fresh lemon juice

1. Wash and drain grape leaves.

2. In a medium skillet, cook onions in oil about 5 minutes or until soft. In a large bowl, mix 1/2 the cooked onions, lamb, rice, mint, salt, pepper, and cinnamon.

3. Place a rounded tablespoon of the lamb mixture in the center of a double layer of grape leaves. Fold the stem end over the filling, then fold in the sides. Roll up tightly, and place in a large skillet, seam side down. Repeat with remaining grape leaves.

4. Add water and remaining cooked onions to the skillet. Heat to a boil; reduce heat. Cover and simmer about 50 minutes or until tender.

5. Squeeze lemon juice over dolmas.

184 calories per serving: 9 g. fat, 15 g. protein,
9 g. carbohydrate, 55 mg. cholesterol, 181 mg. sodium.
For exchange diets, count 2 lean meat, 1 fat, 1/2 starch.

GREEK GREEN SALAD

This salad will accompany any Middle Eastern meal.

Preparation time: 15 minutes
8 servings—2 cups each

1 bunch romaine lettuce, torn into bite-size pieces
1 head leaf lettuce, torn into bite-size pieces
1 medium sliced cucumber
3/4 cup sliced radishes
1/2 cup sliced green onion
1/2 cup Greek or black olives
1 teaspoon crushed oregano
1/2 cup fat-free vinaigrette
1/4 cup crumbled feta cheese
2-ounce can drained rolled anchovies with capers (optional)

1. In a large salad bowl, toss together romaine and leaf lettuce. Add cucumber, radishes, onion, olives, and oregano; toss. Refrigerate until serving time.

2. Add vinaigrette to salad. Top with feta cheese and anchovies.

66 calories per serving: 4 g. fat, 4 g. protein,
5 g. carbohydrate, 6 mg. cholesterol, 468 mg. sodium.
For exchange diets, count 1 vegetable, 1 fat.

TABBOULEH

Tabbouleh is a bulgur, parsley, and tomato salad.
Many Middle Eastern countries serve it as a meatless
main dish. Bulgur is also known as wheat pilaf.

Preparation time: 15 minutes
Soaking time: 30 minutes; Chilling time: 1 hour
8 servings—3/4 cup each

Salad:
　3/4 cup bulgur
　cold water
　1 bunch snipped fresh parsley
　2 cups chopped tomatoes
　1/2 cup chopped seeded cucumber
　1/4 cup chopped green onions
　2 teaspoons crushed dried mint flakes
Dressing:
　1/4 cup lemon juice
　2 tablespoons olive oil
　1 minced garlic clove
　1/2 teaspoon salt
　1/4 teaspoon pepper

1. Cover bulgur with cold water in a medium bowl. Let stand 30 minutes. Drain; press out as much water as possible.

2. Combine bulgur, parsley, tomatoes, cucumber, onion, and mint.

3. In a small bowl, whisk together dressing ingredients. Pour over bulgur mixture. Mix well. Cover and refrigerate at least 1 hour.

116 calories per serving: 4 g. fat, 3 g. protein,
20 g. carbohydrate, 0 cholesterol, 142 mg. sodium.
For exchange diets, count 1 1/2 starch.

LAMB AND APRICOT STEW

Preparation time: 15 minutes
Cooking time: 1 3/4 hours
8 servings—4 ounces meat and 1/4 cup apricot mixture each

2 pounds lean lamb, cut into 1-inch cubes
2 medium yellow onions, chopped fine
1 teaspoon ground coriander
1 teaspoon cumin
1 teaspoon ground cinnamon
1/4 teaspoon ginger
1/4 teaspoon black pepper
3 cups water
1/2 pound dried apricots, diced
2 teaspoons almonds
1/4 teaspoon saffron

1. Place lamb cubes in a Dutch oven, and cover with onions. Add coriander, cumin, cinnamon, ginger, and pepper. Sauté over medium heat until lamb is browned.

2. Add 3 cups water, diced apricots, almonds, and saffron. Cook uncovered on low heat for 1 1/2 hours or until lamb is very tender.

221 calories per serving: 8 g. fat, 25 g. protein,
12 g. carbohydrate, 72 mg. cholesterol, 74 mg. sodium.
For exchange diets, count 3 lean meat, 1 fruit.

LEBANESE CHICKEN

Preparation time: 15 minutes
Cooking time: 12 minutes

8 servings—1 chicken breast and 1/2 cup couscous each

8 chicken breast halves, skinned and boned
1 small yellow onion, chopped fine
1/4 teaspoon minced garlic
1 tablespoon olive oil
2 teaspoons finely grated orange peel
1/2 cup orange juice
1/2 teaspoon salt
1/4 teaspoon cinnamon
1/8 teaspoon allspice
2 tablespoons honey
1 1/3 cups couscous
2 cups no-added-salt chicken broth

1. In a large skillet, sauté chicken, onion, and garlic in olive oil. Cook over medium heat for 6 minutes, then turn chicken and cook another 6 minutes.

2. In a small mixing bowl, combine orange peel, orange juice, salt, cinnamon, allspice, and honey. Pour orange juice mixture over the chicken during the last 3 minutes of cooking.

3. In a medium saucepan, cook couscous in chicken broth according to package directions. Serve chicken over couscous.

287 calories per serving: 5 g. fat, 30 g. protein,
29 g. carbohydrate, 73 mg. cholesterol, 145 mg. sodium.
For exchange diets, count 4 very lean meat, 2 starch.

ROASTED CHICKEN WITH TURMERIC AND FENNEL

Preparation time: 15 minutes; Roasting time: 1 1/2 hours

**4 servings—4 ounces chicken and
1/2 cup vegetables and broth each**

1 large roasting chicken
1/2 teaspoon black pepper
1/2 cup lemon juice
1 tablespoon olive oil
1 1/2 teaspoons minced garlic
1 tablespoon ground cumin
1/2 teaspoon cayenne pepper
1/2 teaspoon turmeric
1 tablespoon fennel
1 large onion, diced
1 carrot, peeled and sliced thin
1 rib celery, sliced thin
1 cup no-added-salt chicken broth

1. Preheat oven to 450° F.

2. Sprinkle the cavity of the chicken with pepper.

3. In a blender, combine lemon juice, oil, garlic, cumin, cayenne, and turmeric. Process until smooth, then rub this mixture generously all over the surface of the chicken.

4. Place the chicken on a rack in a roasting pan. Wrap fennel, onion, carrots, and celery in a packet of aluminum foil, and place the packet next to the chicken in the roasting pan.

5. Roast for 1 1/2 hours or until the chicken is fork tender. Remove chicken from the oven, let stand for 10 minutes, then carve and serve.

6. Meanwhile, cook chicken broth for 3 minutes in a microwave-safe serving bowl. Transfer roasted fennel and vegetables to the broth. Serve vegetables and broth over roasted chicken.

230 calories per serving: 6 g. fat, 3 g. protein,
12 g. carbohydrate, 101 mg. cholesterol, 131 mg. sodium.
For exchange diets, count 4 very lean meat, 3 vegetable.

ZUCCHINI AND COUSCOUS IN THE SKILLET

Preparation time: 15 minutes
Cooking time: 6 minutes; Standing time: 5 minutes
8 servings—1 1/2 cups each

1 tablespoon olive oil
1 medium zucchini, peeled and diced
4 ounces fresh mushrooms, cleaned and sliced thin
2 green onions, finely chopped
2 ribs celery, sliced thin
3/4 teaspoon minced garlic
10-ounce package couscous
14-ounce can no-added-salt chicken broth, boiling
1 tablespoon margarine
1/4 teaspoon salt
1/2 teaspoon black pepper

1. Heat vegetable oil in a medium Dutch oven or large skillet. Add zucchini, mushrooms, onion, celery, and garlic; cook for 4 minutes or until vegetables are soft. Add couscous, and cook for 1 minute, stirring constantly.

2. Remove pan from the heat, and stir in hot chicken broth, margarine, salt, and pepper. Let stand for 5 minutes.

158 calories per serving: 4 g. fat, 5 g. protein,
26 g. carbohydrate, 4 mg. cholesterol, 110 mg. sodium.
For exchange diets, count 1 starch, 2 vegetable, 1/2 fat.

GREEN HERB RICE

Fresh herbs make this both fragrant and delicious.

Preparation time: 10 minutes
Cooking time: 25 minutes; Standing time: 5 minutes
4 servings—1 cup each

2 1/4 cups water
1/2 teaspoon salt
1 cup long-grain rice
1/4 cup sliced green onions (tops only)
1/4 cup chopped fresh dill weed
1/4 cup chopped fresh parsley
1/4 cup chopped fresh cilantro
2 teaspoons reduced-fat margarine

1. In a large saucepan, bring water and salt to a boil; stir in remaining ingredients. Reduce heat, cover and simmer for 20 minutes.

2. Remove from heat. Let stand covered 5 minutes or until water is absorbed. Fluff with a fork.

149 calories per 4 ounce serving: 1 g. fat, 1 g. protein,
34 g. carbohydrate, 70 mg. cholesterol, 287 mg. sodium.
For exchange diets, count 2 starch.

PERSIAN RICE

Iranian women soak Persian rice overnight in salted water; however, this is not necessary with American long-grain rice.

Preparation time: 10 minutes
Cooking time: 45 minutes
4 servings—1 cup each

water
1 1/2 cups long-grain rice
1 teaspoon salt
1 tablespoon reduced-fat margarine
1 1/2 teaspoons nonfat plain yogurt

1. Fill a large saucepan with water; bring to a boil.

2. Add rice and salt; boil hard for 10 minutes. Drain in a large colander; rinse well with cold water, and drain again.

3. Melt margarine in a saucepan over medium heat. Add rice and yogurt. Place a dish towel over the inside of the lid, bringing overlapping ends over the top of the lid. Cover the pan with the wrapped lid.

4. Steam over medium-low heat for about 30 minutes or until a cloud of steam emerges from the pan when lifting the lid.

91 calories per serving: 2 g. fat, 2 g. protein,
17 g. carbohydrate, 0 cholesterol, 560 mg. sodium.
For exchange diets, count 1 starch.

CHUNKY MOROCCAN VEGETABLES

Serve these vegetables in a pretty roasting pan.

Preparation time: 15 minutes
Cooking time: 35 minutes
8 servings—1 cup each

1 teaspoon olive oil
1 yellow onion, diced
1/2 teaspoon minced garlic
1 teaspoon paprika
1/2 teaspoon cayenne pepper
1 teaspoon ground ginger
1/4 teaspoon salt
1/2 teaspoon black pepper
1 cup no-added-salt chicken broth
6 carrots, peeled and cut into 2 1/2-inch pieces
1 head cauliflower, cut into florets
2 large white potatoes, peeled and cut into 1 1/2-inch cubes
Garnish:
3 tablespoons chopped fresh mint

1. Preheat oven to 375° F.

2. Heat olive oil in a skillet. Add onion and garlic, and sauté for 3 minutes. Add all the spices and broth, and bring to a boil.

3. Place the vegetables in a roasting pan. Pour broth mixture over the vegetables, and cover.

4. Roast for 30 minutes or until potatoes are fork-tender. Garnish the vegetables with chopped fresh mint before serving.

67 calories per serving: 1 g. fat, 2 g. protein,
14 g. carbohydrate, 0 cholesterol, 97 mg. sodium.
For exchange diets, count 1 starch.

ORANGE CUSTARD

Prepare this when fresh oranges are at their best.

Preparation time: 15 minutes
Baking time: 50 minutes
8 servings—1 slice each

nonstick cooking spray
1/2 cup brown sugar
1 tablespoon hot water
2 large oranges, peeled and sectioned with membrane removed
6 eggs or 1 1/2 cups liquid egg substitute
1/3 cup white sugar
3 cups hot skim milk
1/2 teaspoon salt

Garnish:
grated orange rind

1. Preheat oven to 350° F.

2. Spray a casserole or soufflé dish with cooking spray. In a small saucepan, combine the brown sugar and water. Cook over medium heat for two minutes. Place the orange sections in the casserole dish; pour the brown sugar over them.

3. In a medium bowl, beat the eggs well. Add white sugar. Gradually stir in hot milk and salt.

4. Pour milk and egg mixture over the oranges. Place the casserole in a pan of hot water, and bake for 50 minutes or until a knife inserted in the center comes out clean. Allow to cool, then cut into 8 slices. Garnish the slices with finely grated orange rind.

172 calories per serving: 2 g. fat, 9 g. protein,
31 g. carbohydrate, 129 mg. cholesterol with eggs
(6 mg. with egg substitute), 269 mg. sodium.
For exchange diets, count 1 skim milk, 1 1/2 fruit.

DATE CAKE

The nutmeg elegantly complements an ordinary date cake.

Preparation time: 15 minutes
Baking time: 1 hour; Cooling time: 20 minutes
24 servings—1 slice each

3 cups flour
4 tablespoons baking powder
1/2 cup sugar
1 teaspoon salt
1 teaspoon nutmeg
1 cup chopped dates
1/4 cup chopped pecans
1 beaten egg or 1/4 cup liquid egg substitute
1 1/2 cups skim milk
2 tablespoons melted margarine
nonstick cooking spray

Garnish:
powdered sugar

1. Preheat oven to 350° F.

2. In a medium bowl, combine flour, baking powder, sugar, salt, and nutmeg. Stir in dates and pecans. In a small bowl, combine beaten egg or egg substitute, milk, and melted margarine. Gradually add to the dry ingredients.

3. Stir until the mixture is smooth, then transfer the batter to two loaf pans that have been sprayed with cooking spray.

4. Bake for 1 hour or until the date cake tests done. Cool for 20 minutes, then remove from pan and sprinkle with powdered sugar.

133 calories per serving: 3 g. fat, 3 g. protein,
25 g. carbohydrate, 3 mg. cholesterol with egg
(0 cholesterol with egg substitute), 114 mg. sodium.
For exchange diets, count 1 starch, 1 fruit.

Chapter Thirteen

India

Suggested Indian Menus

Red Lentil Soup
Grilled Chicken Tandoori Style
Indian Spiced Rice
Cucumber Raita
Creamy Apricot Pudding

Indian Mulligatawny
Naan
Pork Kabobs
Stuffed Figs in Yogurt

Add Fun, Subtract Expense

What goes with hot curry? A general rule is that the hotter the food, the sweeter the drink. Sparkling fruit juices or sweet wines go especially well with spicy foods because they counter the heat as they cool and soothe the palate.

Ajwain seed is a traditional addition to many Indian and Pakistani dishes and can be purchased at a spice shop. (If you don't have a favorite outlet for spices, I recommend Penzeys, Ltd., of Waukesha, Wisconsin at 414-574-0277 for mail order.) Shaped like a celery seed, ajwain has a flavor like thyme and is useful in flavoring ordinary lentil and bean dishes. Folklore has it that ajwain seed also tempers the gaseous effects of a legume-based diet.

Sweet curry powder has great flavor and very little heat. Use this seasoning on baked chicken or fish for a rich flavor; or add it to tuna salad or chicken soup.

To make any menu taste Indian, add curry. Curry goes well with meats, rice, grains, sauces, soups, and stews. Turmeric and saffron can be used interchangeably for Indian flavor as well as a bright, appealing yellow color. Saffron has a more desirable, subtle flavor, however many use turmeric because it is much cheaper and more readily available. Other spices to use are cardamom, cinnamon, coriander, cloves, and fenugreek.

Taste a Bombay Cocktail:
Stir 1/2 ounce dry vermouth, 1/2 ounce sweet vermouth, 1 ounce brandy, 1/4 teaspoon absinthe substitute, and 1/2 teaspoon curacao with cracked ice. Strain into a 3-ounce cocktail glass.

NAAN

Preparation time: 20 minutes; Standing time: 45 minutes
Rising time: 1 hour; Cooking time: 15 minutes
12 servings—1 naan each

---

1 tablespoon flour
1 teaspoon sugar
1/2 cup warm water
1 teaspoon yeast
3 cups flour
1 tablespoon salt
1 teaspoon baking power
nonstick cooking spray

1. In a shaker container, combine 1 tablespoon flour, sugar, and warm water. Add yeast. Shake, then let stand for 45 minutes.

2. In a large bowl, combine 3 cups flour, salt, and baking powder. Make a well in the center of the flour mixture, and pour in yeast mixture. Stir to make an elastic dough.

3. Put the dough on a floured surface, and knead for 7 minutes or until smooth. Shape the dough into a ball, return the dough to the bowl, and cover. Allow dough to rise for 1 hour.

4. Preheat oven broiler and heat a griddle. Divide the dough into 12 portions. Roll each portion into a 6-inch round on a floured surface.

5. Spray the griddle with cooking spray. Bake the rounds on a hot griddle, top side down, for 30 seconds or until bubbles appear on the top and the underside is mottled.

6. Lift with a spatula, and place on a baking sheet, uncooked side up. Broil for 30 seconds or until the bread puffs up.

---

112 calories per serving: 0 fat, 3 g. protein,
23 g. carbohydrate, 0 cholesterol, 85 mg. sodium.
For exchange diets, count 1 1/2 starch.

CURRY DIP

Serve this quick and easy dip with pita rounds or fresh vegetable dippers.

Preparation time: 5 minutes
8 servings—2 tablespoons each

1 cup fat-free mayonnaise
1 tablespoon minced onion
1 teaspoon curry powder
1 teaspoon horseradish
1 teaspoon tarragon vinegar
1/2 teaspoon garlic salt

1. Combine all ingredients in a small bowl.

23 calories per serving: 0 fat, 0 protein,
6 g. carbohydrate, 0 cholesterol, 359 mg. sodium.
For exchange diets, count 1 vegetable.

RED LENTIL SOUP

Preparation time: 15 minutes
Cooking time: 1 hour
8 servings—1 1/2 cups each

1 1/4 cups split red lentils
1 tablespoon vegetable oil
1 large white onion, chopped fine
2 ribs celery, chopped fine
12 whole peppercorns
1 tablespoon flour
2 large carrots, cut into thin coins
16-ounce can chunky tomatoes, undrained
1 1/4 teaspoons ground turmeric
1/2 teaspoon salt
1 teaspoon sugar
6 cups water

1. Wash lentils, and drain.

2. In a large Dutch oven or soup pot, heat vegetable oil over medium heat. Add onions, celery, and peppercorns. Cook until the vegetables are soft.

3. Sprinkle the flour over the onions, and cook for 2 minutes. Remove the peppercorns.

4. Add all remaining ingredients. Bring the mixture to a boil, then reduce heat to a simmer. Cook uncovered for 40 minutes or until lentils are soft.

150 calories per serving: 2 g. fat, 9 g. protein,
24 g. carbohydrate, 0 cholesterol, 154 mg. sodium.
For exchange diets, count 1 starch, 1 vegetable, 1 very lean meat.

INDIAN MULLIGATAWNY

Preparation time: 15 minutes
Cooking time: 30 minutes
8 servings—2 cups each

1/2 pound chicken breast, diced
1 1/2 teaspoons salt
1 teaspoon curry powder
4 cups water
1 teaspoon lemon juice
1/8 teaspoon ground cloves
1/8 teaspoon ground mace
1 medium onion, chopped fine
1 tablespoon margarine
1 medium carrot, thinly sliced
1 apple, peeled and chopped
1 green pepper, chopped
1-pound can chunky tomatoes

Garnish:
fresh parsley

1. In a large Dutch oven or soup pot, brown diced chicken with salt and curry powder until meat is no longer pink. Add all remaining ingredients, and bring soup to a boil. Reduce heat to a simmer, and cook at least 15 minutes or until carrots are tender.

2. Ladle into bowls, and garnish with fresh parsley.

94 calories per serving: 3 g. fat, 10 g. protein,
8 g. carbohydrate, 28 mg. cholesterol, 443 mg. sodium
(To reduce sodium, omit salt or use no-added-salt tomatoes.)
For exchange diets, count 1 lean meat, 2 vegetable.

CHICKPEA STEW

Preparation time: 15 minutes
Cooking time: 30 minutes
8 servings—1 1/2 cups each

2 tablespoons vegetable oil
1 bay leaf
3 large yellow onions, chopped fine
1 tablespoon minced garlic
1 teaspoon ginger
1 teaspoon turmeric
1 tablespoon cumin
1 tablespoon ground coriander
3-ounce can chopped green chilies
3 large ripe tomatoes, peeled and chopped
1/2 teaspoon salt
2 15-ounce cans garbanzo beans, drained
diced green onions (optional)

1. Heat oil in a large Dutch oven. Add bay leaf and onion, and sauté until onion is soft. Add the next 6 ingredients, and continue to cook over medium heat for 3 minutes.

2. Add tomatoes, salt, and garbanzo beans. Stir and cook uncovered for 15 minutes.

3. Garnish with green onions, if desired.

245 calories per serving: 5 g. fat, 8 g. protein,
42 g. carbohydrate, 3 mg. cholesterol, 543 mg. sodium.
For exchange diets, count 1 very lean meat, 2 starch, 2 vegetable.

CUCUMBER RAITA

Preparation time: 15 minutes
8 servings—3/4 cup each

1/4 cup fresh cilantro
1 green chili pepper, seeded and stemmed
1/2 teaspoon minced garlic
2 cups nonfat yogurt
1/2 teaspoon freshly ground black pepper
2 large cucumbers, peeled and finely chopped
1/2 teaspoon ground cumin
1/2 teaspoon paprika

1. In a blender container, process cilantro, chili pepper, and garlic to a smooth paste.

2. In a medium salad bowl, combine yogurt with cilantro mixture. Fold in black pepper and cucumber. Cover and chill until serving time.

3. Garnish the salad with cumin and paprika.

40 calories per serving: 0 fat, 4 g. protein,
6 g. carbohydrate, 0 cholesterol, 45 mg. sodium.
For exchange diets, count 2 vegetable.

PORK KABOBS

Preparation time: 15 minutes
Marinating time: 30 minutes; Grilling time: 16 minutes
6 servings—1 kabob each

Marinade:
>   1/4 cup lemon juice
>   2 tablespoons reduced-fat peanut butter
>   2 minced garlic cloves
>   1 tablespoon vegetable oil
>   1 teaspoon crushed coriander seed
>   1 teaspoon garam masala (optional)—see recipe on next page

Kabobs:
>   1 pound cubed pork tenderloin
>   2 green peppers, cut into 1-inch squares
>   1 cup peeled pearl onions or onion wedges
>   1 cup cherry tomatoes or tomato wedges

1. Combine all marinade ingredients in a large bowl. Add pork cubes. Marinate in the refrigerator for at least 30 minutes.

2. Drain meat. Alternate pork, pepper, onion, and tomato on skewers.

3. Grill over medium-hot coals for 6 to 8 minutes on each side.

....

201 calories per serving: 9 g. fat, 24 g. protein,
7 g. carbohydrate, 70 mg. cholesterol, 81 mg. sodium.
For exchange diets, count 3 lean meat, 2 vegetable.

GARAM MASALA

Garam Masala is a sweet spice mixture used to flavor Indian dishes.
This recipe can be made at home since it's hard to find in the supermarket.

Preparation time: 10 minutes
Baking time: 15 minutes
Yield: 2 cups of spice mix

---

6 tablespoons coriander seeds
1/4 cup black peppercorns
1/4 cup cumin seeds
3 cinnamon sticks
2 tablespoons whole cloves
2 tablespoons cardamom seeds, removed from their pods
1/2 nutmeg, grated

1. Preheat oven to 200° F.

2. Spread coriander seeds, peppercorns, and cumin seeds on a baking sheet. Toast for about 15 minutes or until aromatic. Place in a spice grinder or blender, and grind to a fine powder. Place powder in a container with a lid.

3. Place remaining spices in grinder, and grind to a fine powder.

4. Combine the two spice mixtures in the container; shake well to blend.

5. Store in an air-tight container in the refrigerator. Will keep for 2 to 3 months.

Negligible nutrient value.

GRILLED CHICKEN TANDOORI STYLE

The tandoor is a clay oven used in India to cook most meats. The secret to the flavor of this Indian-style chicken is the yogurt marinade.

Preparation time: 20 minutes
Marinating time: 3 hours
Grilling time: 10 minutes
6 servings—1 chicken breast half each

Chicken:
> 6 boneless, skinless chicken breast halves
> 2 tablespoons fresh lemon juice
> 1/2 teaspoon salt

Marinade:
> 1 cup plain nonfat yogurt
> 2 tablespoons chopped fresh ginger
> 2 minced garlic cloves
> 1 minced, seeded jalapeno pepper
> 1/2 teaspoon cumin
> 1/2 teaspoon ground coriander
> 1/4 teaspoon turmeric
> 1/4 teaspoon black pepper

1. Place chicken breasts in a large dish. Sprinkle with lemon juice and salt.

2. Combine marinade ingredients in a medium bowl; pour over chicken. Turn chicken to coat. Cover chicken, and refrigerate at least 3 hours.

3. Cook chicken on the barbecue over medium-hot coals. Grill about 5 minutes on each side or just until cooked through.

108 calories per serving: 2 g. fat, 19 g. protein,
3 g. carbohydrate, 45 mg. cholesterol, 243 mg. sodium.
For exchange diets, count 3 very lean meat.

SPICY CHICKEN CURRY

Preparation time: 15 minutes
Marinating time: 30 minutes; Cooking time: 20 minutes
8 servings—3/4 cup each

3 whole chicken breasts, skinned, boned, and cubed
Marinade:
   3 tablespoons soy sauce
   1/2 teaspoon minced garlic
   1 cup pineapple juice
   2 cups tomato juice
   1 red pepper, seeded and cut into thin strips
   1 green pepper, seeded and cut into thin strips
   2 large yellow onions, chopped fine
   2 teaspoons sweet curry powder
   1/2 teaspoon hot curry powder (more or less, depending on your
      preference for hot)
   2 teaspoons garam masala (see p. 309)
   2 teaspoons paprika
   1/2 cup water
Thickening:
   1/4 cup water
   2 tablespoons cornstarch

saffron rice (recipe follows)

1. In a shallow dish, marinate cubed chicken in soy sauce, garlic, and pineapple juice for at least 30 minutes.

2. Remove chicken from the marinade, and brown in a Dutch oven that has been sprayed with nonstick cooking spray.

3. Add tomato juice, peppers, onions, spices, and water. Bring to a boil and simmer for 3 minutes.

Spicy Chicken Curry (continued)

4. In a glass measure, combine water and cornstarch until smooth. Whisk into the chicken and vegetables, and stir continually until mixture is thickened. Serve chicken curry over saffron rice.

160 calories per serving: 2 g. fat, 17 g. protein, 18 g. carbohydrate, 18 mg. cholesterol, 387 mg. sodium. For exchange diets, count 2 very lean meat, 1/2 starch, 2 vegetable.

SAFFRON RICE

Preparation time: 10 minutes
Cooking time: 15 minutes
8 servings—3/4 cup each

4 cups water
2 cups dry basmati rice
3/4 teaspoon salt
1/4 cup water
1/8 teaspoon yellow food coloring
1 pinch saffron
1 tablespoon margarine
2 1-inch sticks cinnamon
3 whole cardamom
4 whole cloves

1. Bring water to a boil in a large saucepan.

2. Meanwhile, wash the rice, and drain it well. Add the rice to the boiling water.

3. Add salt, bring the rice to a rolling boil, then reduce heat to low. Cover and cook for 8 minutes.

4. In a glass measure, mix together 1/4 cup water, food color, and saffron. Stir into the cooked rice.

5. In a small skillet, sauté cinnamon, cardamom, and cloves in margarine until browned. Stir whole spices into the rice; toss and serve. Invite diners to move the spices to the side of their plate when eating.

166 calories per serving: 1 g. fat, 3 g. protein,
34 g. carbohydrate, 0 cholesterol, 366 mg. sodium.
For exchange diets, count 2 starch.

INDIAN SPICED RICE

Use homemade garam masala to make this an authentic Indian dish.

Preparation time: 10 minutes
Cooking time: 20 minutes; Standing time: 5 minutes
6 servings—3/4 cup each

1 tablespoon reduced-fat margarine
1 1/2 cups long-grain rice
3 1/3 cups water
2/3 cup chopped mixed dried fruit
1 1/2 teaspoons garam masala (see recipe on p. 309)
3/4 teaspoon salt
2 whole cloves
1 cinnamon stick

1. Melt margarine in a medium saucepan. Add rice, and stir for 2 minutes.

2. Add all remaining ingredients. Bring just to a boil; reduce heat to low. Cover and cook for about 18 minutes.

3. Remove from heat, and let stand, covered, about 5 minutes or until water is absorbed. Discard cloves and cinnamon stick. Fluff rice with a fork.

145 calories per serving: 3 g. fat, 1 g. protein,
31 g. carbohydrate, 0 cholesterol, 385 mg. sodium.
For exchange diets, count 2 starch.

INDIAN VEGETABLE CURRY

Preparation time: 5 minutes
Cooking time: 15 minutes
8 servings—1 1/4 cups each

2 teaspoons curry powder
16-ounce can sliced potatoes, drained
1 pound bag frozen broccoli, cauliflower, and carrot blend
15-ounce can chickpeas, drained
14-ounce can chunky tomatoes
13-ounce can no-added-salt chicken broth
2 tablespoons cornstarch

1. Stir curry powder for 1 minute in a large skillet over high heat.

2. Stir in potatoes, vegetables, chick-peas, and tomatoes. Bring mixture to a boil, then reduce heat to medium. Cover and cook for 8 minutes.

3. Blend chicken broth with the cornstarch. Stir into the vegetables during the last 2 minutes of cooking, stirring until mixture is thickened. Serve over rice.

147 calories per serving: 2 g. fat, 5 g. protein,
30 g. carbohydrate, 0 cholesterol, 286 mg. sodium.
For exchange diets, count 3 vegetable, 1 starch.

VEGETABLE PANCAKES

This vegetarian main course is filled with lots of colorful vegetables. Serve with plain nonfat yogurt and chutney.

Preparation time: 20 minutes
Chilling time: 1 hour; Cooking time: 20 minutes
12 servings—1 pancake each

1 1/4 cups corn (thaw if frozen)
1/2 cup grated peeled potato
1/2 cup grated carrot
1/2 cup shredded fresh spinach
1/2 cup finely chopped onion
6 tablespoons all-purpose flour
1/4 cup thawed frozen peas
1/4 cup finely chopped fresh cilantro
1 tablespoon minced, seeded jalapeño pepper (note: always wear rubber gloves when working with hot peppers)
1 minced garlic clove
1 teaspoon minced fresh ginger
1 teaspoon ground cumin
1/2 teaspoon salt
1/4 teaspoon pepper
1/4 cup liquid egg substitute
1 tablespoon vegetable oil

1. In a large bowl, mix together all ingredients except egg substitute and oil. Stir in egg substitute. Form 12 pancakes on a large baking sheet, using about 3 tablespoons of mixture for each. Refrigerate at least an hour or until firm.

2. Heat oil in a large nonstick skillet over medium heat. Cook pancakes about 4 minutes each side.

74 calories per serving: 2 g. fat, 3 g. protein,
13 g. carbohydrate, 0 cholesterol, 112 mg. sodium.
For exchange diets, count 1/2 starch, 1 vegetable.

STUFFED FIGS IN YOGURT

Preparation time: 15 minutes
Marinating time: 30 minutes
8 servings—2 figs each

16 canned figs
1/2 cup chopped almonds
1 cup brandy or red wine
2 cups nonfat yogurt
1 tablespoon honey
1/2 teaspoon almond extract

1. Open each fig, and sprinkle with 1 1/2 teaspoons of chopped almonds. Place figs in a shallow dish, and pour wine over the fruit. Allow figs to marinate in the refrigerator for at least 30 minutes or up to 3 hours.

2. Remove figs. At serving time, combine 1/4 cup of marinade liquid with yogurt, honey, and almond extract. Pour 1/3 cup of the yogurt mixture into 8 shallow dishes; place two figs in each dish.

111 calories per serving: 4 g. fat, 16 g. protein,
14 g. carbohydrate, 2 mg. cholesterol, 45 mg. sodium.
For exchange diets, count 1 fruit, 1 fat.

CREAMY APRICOT PUDDING

Preparation time: 10 minutes
Cooking time: 10 minutes
Chilling time: 2 hours
8 servings—1/2 cup each

24 ounces apricots in juice, undrained
1/4 cup all-fruit apricot preserves
1 teaspoon grated lemon peel
1/2 teaspoon grated orange peel
1 cup nonfat vanilla yogurt
2 tablespoons chopped pecans

1. Combine apricots and juice, preserves, lemon peel, and orange peel in a saucepan. Bring the mixture to a boil. Boil uncovered for 10 minutes, reducing liquid to none.

2. Transfer mixture to a food processor or blender. Process until smooth.

3. Pour into pudding dishes, and chill for 2 hours.

4. Garnish pudding with yogurt and pecans.

70 calories per serving: 0 fat, 1 g. protein,
15 g. carbohydrate, 1 mg. cholesterol, 37 mg. sodium.
For exchange diets, count 1 fruit.

Chapter Fourteen

the Orient

Suggested Oriental Menus

Egg Drop Soup
Bean Sprout Salad
Broccoli Beef
Pineapple Coconut Bread Pudding
Green Tea

Hot and Sour Shrimp Salad
Thai Chicken Curry
Thai Noodles With Peanut Sauce
Fortune Cookies
Ginger Tea

Add Fun, Subtract Expense

Pick up some millet the next time you're in the Chinese foods section of the market. Prepared like rice, millet has a bland flavor that lends itself as a background to other seasonings.

Yes, it is possible to eat a hurried meal using chopsticks (if you hold a rice bowl under your chin and shovel in the food). But the leisurely use of chopsticks allows you to mix rice and accompanying foods so that the flavor is subtly different in each bite. Chopsticks can slow the eating process—a clever weight management trick.

To use chopsticks: Tuck the bottom chopstick in the crook of the thumb and control the tip by resting the end on the tip of the ring finger. Hold the top chopstick like a dart between the thumb and first two fingers. Tap chopsticks on the table to even their points. Open and close the tips to grasp even the smallest grain of rice.

Use short-grain rice like the Chinese do to yield a more glutinous, clumping rice than long-grain; it's perfect for eating with chopsticks.

Thai jasmine rice is available in most Oriental grocery stores; it smells like jasmine flowers when cooked and has just a hint of stickiness. To cook, combine 2 cups of jasmine rice with 2 3/4 cups of water. Bring to a boil, then reduce heat to a very low simmer for 15 minutes.

Dried chili pods are added to Indonesian curries and soups to impart hot flavor.

Cloves are native to Southeast Asia and can be added to rice or fruit for a touch of sweetness.

Cassia cinnamon from China is stronger and spicier than Indonesian cinnamon and is now available in spice shops.

A cast-iron wok doubles as a soup and stew pot or omelet maker (about $40).

You'll find persimmons in your produce market in the fall. These fruits that are native to China and Japan should be fully ripe before using them in fruit desserts.

You'll find lychees, another fruit native to China, fresh, bottled, canned, and dried.

Asian pears are available nearly all year round and taste like a cross between a crunchy apple and a sweet pear.

Try a Shanghai Cocktail:
Shake the juice of 1/4 lemon, 1 teaspoon anisette, 1 ounce rum, and 1/2 teaspoon grenadine with cracked ice. Strain into a 3-ounce cocktail glass.

Mix a Singapore Sling:
Shake the juice of 1/2 lemon, 1 teaspoon powdered sugar, 2 ounces dry gin, and 1/2 ounce cherry brandy with cracked ice. Strain into a 12-ounce collins glass. Add ice cubes, and fill with carbonated water. Stir. Garnish with fresh fruits.

Oriental cooking varies from country to country. To cook Chinese, add ginger, garlic, sesame seeds and/or oil, hot peppers, green onion, mustard, and soy sauce. Japanese cooking uses teriyaki, ginger, garlic, mustard, green onion, and green horseradish, also known as wasabi. To try a little Thai flavor, use red curry paste or powder, coconut milk, basil, cilantro, mint, and red pepper.

GINGER TEA

Hot ginger tea is a soothing refresher as an after-dinner beverage.

Preparation time: 10 minutes
Cooking time: 30 minutes
8 servings—4 ounces each

1 quart water
1/3 pound fresh gingerroot, peeled, sliced, and crushed
1 cup dark brown sugar
1/8 teaspoon salt
fresh peppermint leaves (optional)

1. Combine all ingredients in a medium saucepan.

2. Simmer, partially covered, over low heat for 30 minutes.

3. Strain, and serve hot.

117 calories per serving: 0 fat, 30 g. protein,
0 carbohydrate, 0 cholesterol, 60 mg. sodium.
For exchange diets, count 2 fruit.

GREEN TEA

This is the tea served in most oriental restaurants.

Preparation time: 5 minutes
Steeping time: 5 minutes
6 servings—5 ounces each

---

4 teaspoons green tea
4 cups cold water

1. Place tea leaves in a warmed teapot (warm pot by rinsing with boiling water).

2. Pour boiling water over tea leaves. Cover; steep 5 minutes.

3. Stir briskly; strain into cups.

Negligible nutrient value.

VIETNAMESE PICKLED VEGETABLES

Pickled vegetables are excellent in salads or as a snack.

Preparation time: 20 minutes
Cooking time: 5 minutes; Marinating time: overnight
12 servings—1/4 cup each

---

2 cups rice vinegar or white vinegar
1 cup water
1 1/2 cups sugar
2 cups peeled carrots cut into matchsticks
1 cup thinly sliced cauliflower
1/2 cup peeled daikon (a Japanese radish) cut into very thin matchsticks
1/4 cup green bell pepper cut into matchsticks
1/4 cup red bell pepper cut into matchsticks

1. In a medium saucepan, combine vinegar, water, and sugar. Cook over medium heat until hot and sugar is dissolved. Remove from heat; cool completely.

2. Pour mixture into a large clean glass jar. Add vegetables. Cover jar with a tight-fitting lid. Refrigerate overnight.

122 calories per serving: 0 fat, 1 g. protein,
32 g. carbohydrate, 0 cholesterol, 20 mg. sodium.
For exchange diets, count 2 fruit.

EGG DROP SOUP

This simple first course takes only minutes to prepare.

Preparation time: 5 minutes
Cooking time: 5 minutes
6 servings—3/4 cup each

5 cups water
1 tablespoon instant chicken bouillon
3 tablespoons cold water
1 1/2 tablespoons cornstarch
1 egg, slightly beaten
2 thinly sliced green onions

1. In a large saucepan, heat water and bouillon to boiling.

2. Combine cold water and cornstarch in a small bowl; stir gradually into broth. Boil and stir 1 minute.

3. Slowly pour egg into broth, stirring constantly with a fork to form shreds. Remove from heat.

4. Garnish with green onion.

35 calories per serving: 1 g. fat, 2 g. protein,
5 g. carbohydrate, 36 mg. cholesterol, 26 mg. sodium.
For exchange diets, count 1 vegetable.

JAPANESE CHICKEN SALAD

A perfectly satisfying one-dish meal—just add tea!
Preparation time: 20 minutes
Chilling time: 12 hours
8 servings—2 cups each

Chicken breast rub:
> 2 cups cooked, boneless, skinless chicken breast, cut into chunks
> 1/2 cup thinly sliced green onions
> 1/4 cup poppy seeds

Salad:
> 1 large head lettuce, torn into pieces
> 1 cup sliced fresh mushrooms
> 8-ounce can chopped and drained water chestnuts
> 1/2 cup pineapple chunks (drain, if canned)
> 1/2 cup drained Mandarin oranges
> 1/4 cup chow mein noodles
> 1/4 cup slivered almonds
> 1/4 cup your favorite low-fat salad dressing

1. In a medium bowl, combine all ingredients for chicken breast rub; refrigerate overnight.

2. Toss all salad ingredients in a large salad bowl.

3. Toss chicken mixture into salad.

4. Add your favorite dressing, and toss again.

186 calories per serving: 7 g. fat, 21 g. protein,
9 g. carbohydrate, 42 mg. cholesterol, 46 mg. sodium.
For exchange diets, count 3 very lean meat, 1 fat, 2 vegetable.

ORIENTAL COLESLAW

The Chinese cabbage makes this authentic.

Preparation time: 15 minutes
4 servings—3/4 cup each

Coleslaw:

2 cups shredded Chinese cabbage
1/4 cup thinly sliced green onion
1/4 cup shredded carrot
1/4 cup chopped red bell pepper

Dressing:

3 tablespoons rice vinegar or white wine vinegar
2 teaspoons sugar
2 teaspoons toasted sesame seeds
2 teaspoons reduced-sodium soy sauce
1 teaspoon sesame oil
1/8 teaspoon crushed red pepper

1. Combine vegetables for coleslaw in a large bowl.

2. Combine all dressing ingredients in a shaker container. Shake vigorously.

3. Toss dressing with vegetables.

82 calories per serving: 3 g. fat, 4 g. protein,
13 g. carbohydrate, 0 cholesterol, 212 mg. sodium.
For exchange diets, count 2 vegetable, 1/2 fat.

BEAN SPROUT SALAD

Preparation time: 10 minutes
Cooking time: 2 minutes
4 servings—1 1/4 cups each

Salad:
  2 cups fresh bean sprouts
  1 cup fresh pea pods
  2 cups cucumber cut into matchsticks

Dressing:
  1/4 cup reduced-sodium soy sauce
  2 tablespoons rice vinegar or white vinegar
  2 teaspoons sesame oil
  1 teaspoon sugar
  1 teaspoon minced pickled ginger (found in jars in the Oriental section of the supermarket or at Oriental specialty stores)
  1/8 teaspoon dry mustard
  1/8 teaspoon hot pepper sauce

Garnish:
  1 tablespoon toasted sesame seeds*

1. Cook bean sprouts and pea pods in boiling water for 2 minutes; drain.

2. Combine the sprouts, pea pods, and cucumber in a large bowl.

3. Combine all dressing ingredients in a shaker container. Shake vigorously.

4. Pour dressing over vegetables. Garnish with sesame seeds if desired.

*To toast sesame seeds, spread them in a shallow pan. Spray with nonstick cooking spray, and bake in a 250° F. oven for about 10 minutes, stirring frequently.

89 calories per serving: 3 g. fat, 5 g. protein,
15 g. carbohydrate, 0 cholesterol, 855 mg. sodium
(To reduce sodium, use less soy sauce.)
For exchange diets, count 2 vegetable, 1/2 fat.

SINGAPORE SALAD

Preparation time: 20 minutes
8 servings—3/4 cup each

Dressing:

    3 tablespoons chopped peanuts

    2 tablespoons vinegar

    3/4 cup hot water

    1/2 small ripe banana

    1/2 teaspoon minced garlic

    1 green onion, chopped fine

    1 green chili, seeded and chopped

    2 tablespoons soy sauce

    2 tablespoons molasses

    1 tablespoon brown sugar

    1 tablespoon lime juice

Salad:

    1 cup bean sprouts

    20-ounce can pineapple tidbits in juice, drained

    1 large cucumber, peeled and diced

    1 cup jicama or fresh apple

    1 Asian pear, diced

1. Place all dressing ingredients in a blender; process until smooth.

2. In a large salad bowl, combine ingredients for the salad. Pour dressing over the salad; toss and serve.

117 calories per serving: 3 g. fat, 3 g. protein,
22 g. carbohydrate, 0 cholesterol, 301 mg. sodium.
For exchange diets, count 1 1/2 fruit, 1/2 fat.

INDONESIAN CHICKEN VEGETABLE SALAD

Preparation time: 15 minutes
4 servings—2 cups each

3/4 cup instant rice
3/4 cup no-added-salt chicken broth
1 red bell pepper, diced
1 yellow bell pepper, diced
10 stalks fresh asparagus, diced
11-ounce can white meat chicken
2 green onions, chopped

Dressing:

1/4 cup orange juice
2 teaspoons reduced-sodium soy sauce
1 tablespoon red wine vinegar

1. Combine rice and chicken broth in a microwave-safe casserole dish. Cook rice according to package directions.

2. Meanwhile in a salad bowl, combine diced peppers, asparagus, chicken, and onions. Add cooked rice to the mixture, and toss.

3. In a shaker container, combine orange juice, soy sauce, and vinegar. Pour over salad; mix and serve.

148 calories per serving: 5 g. fat, 12 g. protein,
14 g. carbohydrate, 72 mg. cholesterol, 687 mg. sodium
(To reduce sodium, use less soy sauce.)
For exchange diets, count 1/2 starch, 1 vegetable, 1 1/2 lean meat.

HOT AND SOUR SHRIMP SALAD

Preparation time: 20 minutes
8 servings—2 cups each

1 large head lettuce, washed and broken into large leaves
1 cucumber, sliced thin
1/4 cup lemon juice
2 teaspoons chili powder
2 tablespoons chicken broth
1 teaspoon dried coriander
1 teaspoon sugar
3 tablespoons oyster sauce
1 pound cooked shrimp
1 pound cooked crab meat
1 red onion, sliced thin

1. Line 8 salad plates with lettuce and slices of cucumber.

2. In a skillet, combine lemon juice, chili powder, broth, coriander, sugar, and oyster sauce. Bring this mixture to a boil. Add the shrimp and crab. Remove from heat, and add sliced onions. Mix well.

3. Portion the hot fish salad onto prepared salad plates. Serve with fried rice as a side dish.

187 calories per serving: 8 g. fat, 22 g. protein,
5 g. carbohydrate, 143 mg. cholesterol, 603 mg. sodium
(To reduce sodium, use less oyster sauce.)
For exchange diets, count 3 lean meat, 1 vegetable.

BROCCOLI BEEF

*Savor this entrée with saké, a Japanese wine
usually served at room temperature.*

Preparation time: 20 minutes
Marinating time: 2 hours; Cooking time: 10 minutes
8 servings—1 cup each

Beef and Marinade:
   3/4 pound lean flank steak, cut into thin strips
   2 tablespoons cornstarch
   2 tablespoons reduced-sodium soy sauce
   2 crushed garlic cloves

Sauce:
   1 tablespoon cornstarch
   1 tablespoon reduced-sodium soy sauce
   2 tablespoons oyster sauce
   1/2 cup water

Broccoli stir-fry:
   2 tablespoons vegetable oil, divided
   6 cups broccoli florets
   1/4 cup water
   1 tablespoon minced gingerroot
   1/4 teaspoon black pepper

1. Combine beef and marinade ingredients. Cover and refrigerate for
at least 2 hours or up to 24 hours.

2. In a small bowl, combine all sauce ingredients; set aside.

3. Heat 1 tablespoon of oil in wok or large skillet. Add broccoli, and
stirfry 30 seconds. Add 1/4 cup water; cover and steam about 5 minutes. Remove broccoli from wok and set aside.

4. Add remaining tablespoon oil to wok. Add gingerroot, and stir-fry
for 20 seconds. Then add beef and marinade to hot wok; stir-fry 2
minutes or just until browned. Add sauce mixture; stir into beef until
thickened.

Broccoli Beef (continued)

5. Add broccoli to beef; cover and cook 1 minute. Season with black pepper.

183 calories per serving: 7 g. fat, 17 g. protein,
13 g. carbohydrate, 29 mg. cholesterol, 332 mg. sodium.
For exchange diets, count 2 lean meat, 3 vegetable.

MANDARIN BEEF AND BROCCOLI

Preparation time: 15 minutes
Marinating time: 30 minutes; Cooking time: 7 minutes
8 servings—2 cups each

Marinade:
1 medium white onion, chopped
1 teaspoon minced garlic
1/4 cup soy sauce
1 tablespoon vegetable oil
1 tablespoon sesame seeds
1 tablespoon sugar
2 tablespoons crushed black pepper
3 tablespoons sherry

2 pounds lean sirloin steak, sliced across the grain into thin slices
nonstick cooking spray
1 large bunch broccoli florets, cleaned, stemmed, and coarsely
   chopped
Hot cooked rice

1. In a shallow dish, combine ingredients for the marinade. Place sliced beef in the marinade, and refrigerate at least 30 minutes or up to 8 hours (the longer the better).

2. Spray a wok or large skillet with cooking spray. Add beef and marinade; sear over high heat, stirring frequently, about 4 minutes. When meat is done, add broccoli, and cook 2 to 3 minutes until broccoli turns bright green and is tender crisp.

3. Serve beef and broccoli over hot rice.

270 calories per serving: 12 g. fat, 35 g. protein,
8 g. carbohydrate, 101 mg. cholesterol, 734 mg. sodium
(To reduce sodium, use reduced-sodium soy sauce or use less soy sauce.)
For exchange diets, count 4 lean meat, 2 vegetable.

MARINATED PORK ON A SKEWER

Preparation time: 15 minutes
Marinating time: 30 minutes; Cooking time: 6 minutes
8 servings—3 ounces each

Marinade:
>1/2 teaspoon minced garlic
>1 teaspoon dried coriander
>4 tablespoons oyster sauce
>1 tablespoon reduced-sodium soy sauce
>1/4 cup thick coconut cream
>2 tablespoons vegetable oil
>1 tablespoon sugar
>1/2 teaspoon white pepper
>1 1/2 pounds lean pork, trimmed and cubed

Sauce:
>1 tablespoon oyster sauce
>2 tablespoons lemon juice
>1 tablespoon reduced-sodium soy sauce
>1 teaspoon chili powder
>1 tablespoon sugar

>Hot cooked rice

1. Combine all the marinade ingredients in a shallow pan; mix well. Add the pork; cover and refrigerate for at least 30 minutes.

2. While the pork is marinating, combine all the ingredients for the sauce in a small serving bowl.

3. Preheat the grill or broiler. Thread 8 skewers with the pork. Broil 3 inches from the heat source for 3 minutes on each side or until the meat is thoroughly cooked and no longer pink.

4. Serve over hot rice with the sauce on the side.

187 calories per serving: 8 g. fat, 22 g. protein,
5 g. carbohydrate, 143 mg. cholesterol, 603 mg. sodium.
For exchange diets, count 3 lean meat, 1/2 fruit.

ORIENTAL FIVE-SPICE

Preparation time: 5 minutes
Yield—3 tablespoons spice powder

1 tablespoon Szechuan peppercorns or black peppercorns
1 crushed cinnamon stick
3 whole star anise or 3 teaspoons aniseed
1 tablespoon fennel seeds
4 whole cloves

1. In a spice grinder or blender, pulverize all ingredients to a fine powder. Store in an air-tight container.

Negligible nutrient value.

STIR-FRIED PORK

Preparation time: 20 minutes
Marinating time: 15 minutes; Cooking time: 15 minutes
8 servings—1 1/2 cups each

Pork and marinade:
  3/4 pound thinly sliced boneless pork
  2 tablespoons reduced-sodium soy sauce
  1/4 teaspoon five-spice powder*
Stir-fry:
  1/4 cup reduced-sodium, fat-free chicken broth
  2 teaspoons cornstarch
  1 tablespoon vegetable oil
  1 minced garlic clove
  1 teaspoon grated gingerroot
  5 cups torn fresh spinach leaves
  2 cups chopped Chinese cabbage
  1 cup chopped green onions
  2 cups sliced fresh asparagus

1. Combine pork, soy sauce, and spice. Marinate at least 15 minutes.

2. Combine chicken broth and cornstarch; set aside.

3. Preheat wok or large skillet over high heat; add oil. Stir-fry garlic and gingerroot in oil for 20 seconds. Add spinach and cabbage; stir-fry 2 minutes. Add onions and asparagus; stir-fry 1 minute. Remove vegetables.

4. Add additional oil to wok if necessary. Add half of the pork and marinade to the **hot** wok; stir-fry 2 to 3 minutes or until browned. Remove from wok. Stir-fry remaining pork and marinade 2 to 3 minutes. Return all pork to the wok. Stir chicken broth mixture, and stir into the pork. Cook and stir until thickened.

5. Add vegetables to pork mixture in wok; cover and cook 1 minute.

*Five-spice powder can be purchased in the spice section of your local grocer. You may also make your own blend at home. See recipe on previous page.

152 calories per serving: 7 g. fat, 15 g. protein,
10 g. carbohydrate, 25 mg. cholesterol, 332 mg. sodium.
For exchange diets, count 2 lean meat, 2 vegetable.

ALMOND CHICKEN

Toasted almonds give a unique flavor and crunch to this popular dish.

Preparation time: 20 minutes
Cooking time: 12 minutes
8 servings—1 3/4 cups each

Chicken and marinade:
    2 teaspoons reduced-sodium soy sauce
    1 teaspoon cooking sherry
    1 teaspoon grated gingerroot
    1/4 teaspoon sugar
    1 pound boneless, skinless chicken breast, cut into 1-inch pieces
    2 1/2 tablespoons cornstarch
Stir-fry:
    2 tablespoons vegetable oil, divided
    1 cup diagonally sliced celery
    1 cup fresh snow peas
    1 cup sliced mushrooms
    8-ounce can drained and chopped bamboo shoots
    8-ounce can drained and chopped water chestnuts
    1/2 cup sliced green onions
    1/4 cup toasted slivered almonds
    6 cups cooked rice

1. Combine soy sauce, sherry, gingerroot, and sugar; add chicken, and stir to coat. Sprinkle cornstarch over chicken; mix well. Set aside.

2. Preheat a wok or large skillet over high heat; add 1 tablespoon oil. Stir-fry celery for 2 minutes. Add pea pods; stir-fry 2 minutes. Add mushrooms, bamboo shoots, and water chestnuts; stir-fry 2 minutes. Remove vegetables from wok; set aside.

3. Add remaining tablespoon of oil to wok; add chicken mixture to **hot** wok. Stir-fry 3 to 4 minutes until chicken is lightly browned.

4. Add vegetable mixture, green onions, and almonds; stir-fry 1 to 2 minutes or until heated through.

Almond Chicken *(continued)*

5. Serve over rice.

....

337 calories per serving: 6 g. fat, 20 g. protein,
49 g. carbohydrate, 35 mg. cholesterol, 147 mg. sodium.
For exchange diets, count 2 starch, 3 vegetable, 2 lean meat.

SUKIYAKI

Sukiyaki is a Japanese favorite.

Preparation time: 20 minutes
Cooking time: 8 minutes
6 servings—1 cup each

Sauce:

   1/4 cup boiling water
   1/2 teaspoon instant beef bouillon
   3 tablespoons reduced-sodium soy sauce
   1 tablespoon honey

Sukiyaki:

   2 teaspoons vegetable oil
   3 cups thinly sliced bok choy
   1 cup green onions
   1/2 cup sliced celery
   8 ounces cubed fresh tofu
   1 cup bean sprouts (drain if using canned)
   1/2 cup bamboo shoots (drain if using canned)
   1/2 cup sliced mushrooms
   1/2 cup drained, sliced water chestnuts
   1/2 pound thinly sliced beef top round steak

1. Stir together all ingredients for sauce until bouillon is dissolved. Set aside.

2. Preheat a wok or large skillet over high heat; add oil. Add bok choy, onions, and celery; stir-fry 2 minutes. Remove vegetables.

3. Add tofu, bean sprouts, bamboo shoots, mushrooms, and water chestnuts to wok; stir-fry 1 minute. Remove vegetables.

4. Add additional oil to wok if necessary. Add beef to **hot** wok; stir-fry 2 minutes or just until browned. Add sauce mixture; cook and stir until bubbly. Stir in vegetables. Cover and cook for 1 minute. Serve at once.

191 calories per serving: 7 g. fat, 20 g. protein,
16 g. carbohydrate, 25 mg. cholesterol, 520 mg. sodium.
For exchange diets, count 2 lean meat, 3 vegetable.

CHICKEN CHOW MEIN

This Chinese mainstay may also be prepared with boneless pork.

Preparation time: 20 minutes
Cooking time: 15 minutes
8 servings—1 1/4 cups each

Sauce:
> 1/2 cup fat-free chicken broth
> 1 tablespoon cornstarch
> 3 tablespoons reduced-sodium soy sauce

Chow mein:
> 2 tablespoons vegetable oil, divided
> 1 teaspoon grated gingerroot
> 3 cups cooked fine eggless egg noodles
> 1 tablespoon fat-free chicken broth
> 2/3 cup sliced green onions
> 3 cups chopped Chinese cabbage
> 1 cup sliced mushrooms
> 1 pound boneless, skinless chicken breast, cut into 1-inch pieces

1. In a small bowl, combine chicken broth and cornstarch. Stir in soy sauce; set aside.

2. Preheat a wok or large skillet over high heat; add 1 tablespoon oil. Stir-fry ginger for 20 seconds. Add noodles and 1 tablespoon chicken broth; stir-fry about 5 minutes. Remove noodles; keep warm.

3. Add remaining tablespoon oil to wok; stir-fry green onions 1 minute. Remove onions.

4. Add cabbage and mushrooms to wok; stir-fry 2 minutes. Remove from wok.

5. Add additional oil to wok if necessary. Add chicken to hot wok. Stir-fry 2 minutes or until chicken is no longer pink. Do not over-cook. Stir sauce mixture, and add to wok. Cook and stir until thickened and bubbly.

6. Stir in cooked vegetables; cover and cook 1 minute. Serve with noodles.

....

210 calories per serving: 8 g. fat, 18 g. protein,
16 g. carbohydrate, 39 mg. cholesterol, 454 mg. sodium.
For exchange diets, count 2 lean meat, 3 vegetable, 1/2 fat.

THAI CHICKEN CURRY

This spicy dish is one of the most popular curries in Thailand.

Preparation time: 20 minutes
Cooking time: 6 minutes
4 servings—2 cups each

1/2 pound skinless, boneless chicken, cut into strips
2 teaspoons cornstarch
2 teaspoons vegetable oil
1/2 cup chopped onion
1 minced garlic clove
1 teaspoon curry powder
1 teaspoon minced fresh ginger
1/2 cup coconut milk
1 cup chopped zucchini
1/2 cup sliced mushrooms
1/2 teaspoon Thai fish sauce (optional)
2 tablespoons chopped fresh basil
crushed red pepper to taste
4 cups cooked rice

1. Coat chicken with cornstarch; set aside.

2. Preheat a large skillet or wok over high heat; add vegetable oil. Stir-fry onion and garlic for 1 minute.

3. Add chicken, curry powder, and ginger; stir-fry 2 minutes.

4. Add remaining ingredients. Simmer for 3 minutes; do not boil.

5. Serve with rice.

....

383 calories per serving: 11 g. fat, 20 g. protein,
51 g. carbohydrate, 154 mg. cholesterol, 41 mg. sodium.
For exchange diets, count 2 starch, 1 fruit, 1 vegetable,
1 fat, 2 very lean meat.

PRINCESS CHICKEN

This Szechuan dish is hot and spicy.

Preparation time: 20 minutes
Marinating time: 30 minutes
Cooking time: 8 minutes
6 servings—4 ounces each

Chicken and marinade:
    2 tablespoons cornstarch
    1 tablespoon reduced-sodium soy sauce
    1 pound boneless, skinless chicken breasts, cut into 1-inch pieces
Sauce:
    1 tablespoon cooking sherry
    2 tablespoons reduced-sodium soy sauce
    1 tablespoon sugar
    1 teaspoon cornstarch
    1 teaspoon sesame oil
Stir-fry:
    2 teaspoons vegetable oil
    10 1-inch dried hot red peppers, stems removed
    1 teaspoon Szechuan peppercorns or black peppercorns
    1 teaspoon minced fresh gingerroot
    1/2 cup chopped roasted peanuts

1. In a large bowl, combine cornstarch and soy sauce. Add chicken; mix well. Let stand 30 minutes.

2. In a small bowl, combine all ingredients for sauce; set aside.

3. Preheat a wok or large skillet over high heat; add oil. Stir-fry chicken pieces about 2 minutes, until very lightly browned. Add additional oil only if necessary. Remove chicken from wok.

4. Heat oil remaining in wok over medium heat. Stir-fry red peppers and peppercorns until red peppers turn dark brown. Add gingerroot and cooked chicken; stir-fry 1 minute.

Princess Chicken (continued)

5. Add sauce to wok; stir well, and cook until sauce thickens. Remove wok from heat. Stir in peanuts.

....

214 calories per serving: 9 g. fat, 22 g. protein,
11 g. carbohydrate, 51 mg. cholesterol, 493 mg. sodium.
For exchange diets, count 1 vegetable, 1/2 fruit, 2 1/2 lean meat.

RICE PILAF WITH CURRY AND CHICKEN

Preparation time: 20 minutes; Cooking time: 30 minutes
8 servings—1 1/2 cups each

1 large onion, sliced thin
1 tablespoon vegetable oil
1 1/2 teaspoons curry powder
1 1/2 cups basmati rice
3 cups no-added-salt chicken broth
1 red pepper, chopped
1 large carrot, peeled and grated
1 1/2 pounds skinless, boneless chicken breast, cut into 1-inch
  chunks
1 cup frozen peas
4 green onions, diced

Garnish:
1/4 cup fresh cilantro

Lemon sauce:
1 cup plain nonfat yogurt
1 tablespoon fresh lemon juice
1 teaspoon grated lime rind

1. In a large skillet, sauté onion in vegetable oil for 3 minutes or until onion softens. Stir in curry powder and rice. Add broth, and bring mixture to a boil.

2. Reduce heat to a simmer; cover and cook for 10 minutes. Stir in red pepper, carrot, and chicken. Continue cooking for 5 more minutes.

3. Stir in peas and green onion. Cover and reduce heat to low, and cook for 10 more minutes.

4. Turn out into a serving dish, and garnish with cilantro. Combine ingredients for the sauce in a small serving bowl, and pass with the dish.

255 calories per serving: 8 g. fat, 24 g. protein,
18 g. carbohydrate, 63 mg. cholesterol, 336 mg. sodium.
For exchange diets, count 1 vegetable, 1 starch, 3 lean meat.

ASIAN CHICKEN WITH PASTA

Preparation time: 20 minutes
Marinating time: 10 minutes; Cooking time: 20 minutes
8 servings—1 1/2 cups each

Marinade:

4 tablespoons reduced-sodium soy sauce
2 tablespoons honey
2 tablespoons lime juice
3 teaspoons brown mustard

1 1/2 pounds boneless skinless chicken breasts, cut into cubes
4 cups no-added-salt chicken broth
1 pound bow-tie pasta, uncooked
2 red peppers, sliced thin
6 green onions, sliced thin
1/4 teaspoon ground black pepper
1/4 cup chopped fresh parsley

1. In a shallow dish, combine soy sauce, honey, lime juice, and mustard. Add chicken, and marinate for at least 10 minutes.

2. Meanwhile, bring chicken broth to a boil. Cook pasta in the broth for 8 minutes, then drain well.

3. In a large skillet, cook chicken and marinade over high heat, uncovered, for 10 minutes. Add red peppers, onions, black pepper, and parsley during last 2 minutes of cooking. Stir in cooked noodles, toss, and serve.

247 calories per serving: 4 g. fat, 31 g. protein,
21 g. carbohydrate, 91 mg. cholesterol, 689 mg. sodium.
For exchange diets, count 3 lean meat, 1 starch.

BLACK PEPPER SHRIMP

Preparation time: 20 minutes
Cooking time: 5 minutes
8 servings—1 1/2 cups each

Sauce:

1/4 cup no-added-salt chicken broth
2 tablespoons oyster sauce
2 tablespoons soy sauce
2 tablespoons white wine
1 tablespoon sugar
2 teaspoons cornstarch

1 1/2 tablespoons vegetable oil
3/4 teaspoon minced garlic
1 teaspoon ground ginger
1 chili pepper, seeded and chopped
2 green onions, chopped
2 teaspoons coarsely ground black pepper
1 red pepper, seeded and diced
1 yellow pepper, seeded and diced
1/2 pound snow peas
2 pounds shrimp, peeled and deveined

1. Combine the ingredients for the sauce in a small bowl, and stir to mix. Set aside.

2. Heat a large skillet or wok to a very high temperature. Swirl in the oil. Add garlic, ginger, chili pepper, green onions, and black pepper, and heat for 1 minute.

3. Add red and yellow pepper and snow peas, and stir-fry for 1 minute. Add the shrimp, and stir-fry for 1 more minute.

4. Stir the ingredients for the sauce again, and gradually add them to the shrimp and vegetables. Cook for 1 more minute. Serve at once.

221 calories per serving: 5 g. fat, 27 g. protein,
16 g. carbohydrate, 174 mg. cholesterol, 433 mg. sodium.
For exchange diets, count 4 very lean meat, 3 vegetable.

SHRIMP STIR-FRY

*A melange of colors and flavors make this
a shrimp lover's garden delight.*

Preparation time: 20 minutes; Cooking time: 15 minutes
6 servings—1 1/2 cups each

Sauce:
>1/2 cup no-added-salt chicken broth
>1 tablespoon cornstarch
>1/4 cup reduced-sodium soy sauce

Shrimp stir-fry:
>1 tablespoon vegetable oil
>1 minced clove garlic
>1 teaspoon grated gingerroot
>2 cups peeled and thinly sliced carrots
>1 cup thinly sliced cauliflower
>2 cups chopped bok choy
>1 cup sliced mushrooms
>1 cup fresh snow peas
>1 cup fresh bean sprouts
>1 pound shelled and deveined shrimp, cut in half (thaw, if frozen)

1. In a small bowl, combine chicken broth and cornstarch; stir in soy sauce. Set aside.

2. Preheat a wok or large skillet over high heat; add oil. Stir-fry garlic and ginger for 20 seconds. Add carrots and cauliflower; stir-fry 3 minutes. Add bok choy, mushrooms, snow peas, and bean sprouts; stir-fry 2 minutes or until the vegetables are crisp-tender. Remove vegetables.

3. Add additional oil to wok if necessary. Add shrimp to HOT wok. Stir-fry 7 minutes or until shrimp turn pink and begin to curl. Push shrimp away from center of wok.

4. Stir chicken broth mixture; pour into center of wok. Cook and stir until thickened and bubbly. Stir in vegetables; cover and cook 1 minute.

167 calories per serving: 4 g. fat, 20 g. protein,
14 g. carbohydrate, 114 mg. cholesterol, 523 mg. sodium
(To reduce sodium, use less soy sauce.)
For exchange diets, count 2 lean meat, 2 vegetable.

VEGETARIAN RED CURRY

This zesty Thai curry is full of vegetables.

Preparation time: 15 minutes
Cooking time: 15 minutes
6 servings—1 1/3 cups each

13-ounce can coconut milk
3 tablespoons red curry paste
1/2 cup fat-free chicken broth
2 tablespoons Thai fish sauce
2 tablespoons brown sugar
1/2 cup fresh sweet basil
2 cups sliced mushrooms
2 cups thinly sliced zucchini
1/3 cup sliced bamboo shoots (drain, if canned)
1/4 cup sliced green onions
1 medium seeded and chopped jalapeño pepper (always wear
   rubber gloves when working with hot peppers)

1. In a wok or large skillet, combine coconut milk, curry paste, broth, fish sauce, brown sugar, and basil. Cover and simmer 10 minutes. **Do not boil.**

2. Add remaining ingredients; simmer 5 minutes.

180 calories per serving: 9 g. fat, 5 g. protein,
15 g. carbohydrate, 0 cholesterol, 343 mg. sodium.
For exchange diets, count 3 vegetable, 2 fat.

VEGETABLE STIR-FRY

Preparation time: 20 minutes
Cooking time: 12 minutes
8 servings—1 cup each

Sauce:

2 tablespoons cold water
1 1/2 teaspoons cornstarch
2 tablespoons reduced-sodium soy sauce
1 tablespoon cooking sherry
2 teaspoons sugar
1/8 teaspoon black pepper

Vegetable stir-fry:

1/2 cup water
2 cups carrots cut into matchsticks
2 cups green beans diagonally sliced into 1-inch slices
2 cups sliced cauliflower
1 tablespoon vegetable oil
1 cup sliced onion
1 cup sliced zucchini
1 cup whole baby corn

1. In a small bowl, combine water and cornstarch; stir in remaining sauce ingredients. Set aside.

2. Heat water in a wok or large saucepan until boiling. Add carrots and green beans; cover and cook for 3 minutes. Add cauliflower; cover and cook an additional 2 minutes. Remove vegetables, and drain.

3. Preheat a wok or large skillet over high heat; add oil. Stir-fry onion for 1 minute. Add vegetable mixture, zucchini, and corn; stir-fry 2 minutes or until vegetables are crisp-tender. Stir sauce mixture again, then stir the mixture into the vegetables.

4. Cook and stir 3 minutes or until thickened.

121 calories per serving: 2 g. fat, 4 g. protein,
23 g. carbohydrate, 0 cholesterol, 207 mg. sodium.
For exchange diets, count 1 starch, 2 vegetable.

FRIED RICE

Fried rice complements any Oriental dish. Vary this dish by adding any leftover vegetables and meats you have on hand.

Preparation time: 15 minutes
Cooking time: 10 minutes
6 servings—1 cup each

nonstick cooking spray
1 beaten egg
1 tablespoon peanut oil or vegetable oil
1/4 cup chopped mushrooms
1/4 cup finely sliced green onion
3 tablespoons low-sodium soy sauce
2 tablespoons cooking sherry or fat-free chicken broth
4 cups cold cooked rice
1/2 cup frozen mixed vegetables

1. Spray a wok or 10-inch skillet with cooking spray. Add egg, and cook until set. Remove egg, and cut into short, narrow strips. Set aside.

2. Heat oil in the wok or skillet. Stir in mushrooms, onions, soy sauce, and sherry. Cook, stirring constantly, about 3 minutes or until tender.

3. Add rice, vegetables, and egg; heat through.

4. Serve with additional soy sauce, if desired.

184 calories per serving: 4 g. fat, 5 g. protein,
33 g. carbohydrate, 35 mg. cholesterol, 378 mg. sodium.
For exchange diets, count 2 starch, 1 vegetable.

TURMERIC RICE

Preparation time: 10 minutes
Cooking time: 20 minutes; Standing time: 10 minutes
8 servings—1/2 cup each

4 green onions
1 tablespoon margarine
1 1/2 cups white rice
3 cups water
1 teaspoon instant beef bouillon
1 tablespoon lemon juice
1/4 teaspoon turmeric
1/2 cup golden raisins

Garnish:
fresh minced parsley

1. In a large Dutch oven, cook the green onions in margarine just until tender.

2. Add the rice, and cook for 2 minutes or until rice is golden.

3. Add water, bouillon, lemon juice, and turmeric. Bring the mixture to a boil, then reduce heat and simmer covered for 15 minutes.

4. Remove the mixture from the heat. Stir in the raisins, then let stand for 10 minutes. Transfer the rice to a serving bowl, and garnish with parsley.

87 calories per serving: 2 g. fat, 1 g. protein,
18 g. carbohydrate, 0 cholesterol, 17 mg. sodium.
For exchange diets, count 1 starch.

Thai Noodles With Peanut Sauce

Preparation time: 5 minutes
Cooking time: 10 minutes
8 servings—3/4 cup each

2 3-ounce packages oriental-flavor instant ramen noodles
4 cups water
16 ounces frozen broccoli, carrots, and water chestnut mixture
1/3 cup no-added-salt chicken broth
2 tablespoons creamy peanut butter
1 teaspoon sugar
1/4 teaspoon crushed red pepper flakes

1. Remove seasoning packets from noodles.

2. In a large saucepan, bring water to a boil. Add noodles and frozen vegetable mixture. Bring mixture to a boil, and cook for 5 minutes.

3. In a serving bowl, whisk together broth, peanut butter, sugar, red pepper flakes, and reserved seasoning packets. Add noodles and vegetables. Toss to coat, and serve immediately.

85 calories per serving: 2 g. fat, 4 g. protein,
13 g. carbohydrate, 5 mg. cholesterol, 450 mg. sodium.
For exchange diets, count 1 starch.

PINEAPPLE COCONUT BREAD PUDDING

Discover a delicate dessert of Indonesian origin.

Preparation time: 20 minutes
Baking time: 35 minutes
12 servings—1 square each

---

nonstick cooking spray
3 cups cubed white bread
15-ounce can crushed pineapple in juice, drained, reserve juice
3 eggs or 3/4 cup egg substitute
1/3 cup brown sugar
1/2 teaspoon lemon peel
1/2 teaspoon cinnamon
1/2 teaspoon salt
1 cup coconut juice

Garnish:
lemon sherbet or lemon yogurt

1. Preheat oven to 350° F.

2. Spray a 10" x 6" baking dish with cooking spray. Place bread cubes in the pan. Spread drained crushed pineapple over the bread.

3. In a medium mixing bowl, beat eggs until they foam. Stir in brown sugar, lemon peel, cinnamon, salt, pineapple juice, and coconut juice. Pour over the bread cubes and pineapple.

4. Bake for 35 minutes or until a knife inserted in the center comes out clean.

5. Cool slightly, then cut into 12 squares. Garnish with a dab of lemon sherbet or lemon yogurt, if desired.

Nutrient analysis without garnish—162 calories per serving: 5 g. fat,
5 g. protein, 25 g. carbohydrate, 43 mg. cholesterol with real eggs
(0 cholesterol with egg substitute), 185 mg. sodium.
For exchange diets, count 1 1/2 starch, 1 fat.

Chapter Fifteen

Australia

Suggested Australian Menu

Crab Chowder
Carpetbag Steak
Shrimp and Green Bean Salad
Kiwi Tart

Add Fun, Subtract Expense

Crystallized ginger from Australia is now available in spice shops and is perfect for baking.

Do you love kiwifruit? You may be able to grow your own. Originally called the Chinese gooseberry, New Zealanders began to market the fruit to the United States in the 1960s; and soon renamed it to associate it with the kiwi bird. The fruit is now grown in California, and starter plants for several U.S. growing regions are available in most seed catalogs. When ready to eat, kiwifruit are as soft as a ripe peach. If they are firm at the market, ripen at room temperature, uncovered and out of direct sun.

Nectarines are also imported from New Zealand. There are more than 10 varieties, including Firebrite, Red Diamond, Flavor Top, Summer Grand, Flamekist, and Red Gold. Choose nectarines that have an orange-yellow background color between the red areas. They should give to gentle pressure, but are not as soft as a ripe peach. Ripen nectarines at room temperature out of direct sun and uncovered.

Passion fruit is an egg-shaped 2-inch-long fruit with a thick, hard purple shell. The fruit is ripe when the skin is shriveled and dented. The gelatinous, yellow-orange pulp with soft edible seeds has a sweet-tart exotic flavor. To prepare it, simply cut it in half crosswise and scoop out the pulp and seeds with a spoon.

Whenever you eat a meringue shell, think of Anna Pavlova. She was a famous Australian ballerina for whom the classic meringue basket dessert ("Pavlova") is named.

Australian food is quite like mainstream European or American cooking. Basil, parsley, thyme, and onion are often used. Kiwifruit is a must in an Australian meal. Now, if you ever go to the Outback, be sure and try the delicacy of grubworm!

CRAB CHOWDER

Preparation time: 15 minutes
Cooking time: 25 minutes
8 servings—2/3 cup each

1 tablespoon margarine
2 slices bacon, diced
2 tablespoons flour
2 cups chicken broth
1 large potato, cubed
8 ounces crabmeat or imitation crabmeat
1 teaspoon Worcestershire sauce
1/4 teaspoon pepper
1 cup skim milk
1 cup evaporated skim milk
1 ounce reduced-fat cheddar cheese, grated

1. Melt margarine in a large saucepan. Add diced bacon, and cook until crisp. Stir in flour until smooth. Gradually stir in chicken broth with a whisk.

2. Add potato, crabmeat, Worcestershire sauce, and pepper.

3. Reduce heat, and simmer for 15 minutes. Remove from heat. Stir in skim milk and evaporated milk. Heat through, but do not boil.

4. Ladle into soup bowls, and garnish with grated cheese.

137 calories per serving: 5 g. fat, 12 g. protein,
12 g. carbohydrate, 36 mg. cholesterol, 561 mg. sodium.
For exchange diets, count 1 skim milk, 1 fat.

SHRIMP AND GREEN BEAN SALAD

Preparation time: 10 minutes
Cooking time: 20 minutes
4 servings—1 1/2 cups each

1 pound fresh green beans, cleaned and cut into 1-inch sections
1/2 pound cooked shrimp, chilled
1/2 cup fat-free French dressing

Garnish:
celery seed

1. Place green beans in a large kettle, and cover with water. Bring beans to a boil, and cook for 20 minutes. Drain well, and cool to room temperature.

2. In a large salad bowl, combine cooked beans with cold shrimp and French dressing. Toss to mix. Dish onto 4 chilled serving plates, and sprinkle with celery seeds.

110 calories per serving: 2 g. fat, 17 g. protein,
6 g. carbohydrate, 193 mg. cholesterol, 226 mg. sodium.
For exchange diets, count 1 vegetable, 2 very lean meat.

AUSSIE LUNCHEON SALAD WITH ENDIVE

Preparation time: 15 minutes
8 servings—1 1/2 cups each

2 ripe pears, cored and chopped
1/4 cup walnut halves
6 ounces Gorgonzola cheese, cubed (This is a soft mild blue-veined cheese. Substitute blue cheese if you have trouble finding it.)
1 tablespoon chopped fresh parsley
8 ounces artichoke hearts, drained well
2 heads Belgian endive, cleaned and torn into bite-sized pieces

Dressing:

1 tablespoon cider vinegar
1 tablespoon vegetable oil
1/4 teaspoon pepper

1. Combine ingredients for the salad in a salad bowl. Sprinkle vinegar, oil, and pepper on the salad. Toss and serve on 8 salad plates.

148 calories per serving: 8 g. fat, 8 g. protein,
11 g. carbohydrate, 16 mg. cholesterol, 324 mg. sodium.
For exchange diets, count 1/2 fruit, 1 vegetable, 1 lean meat, 1 fat.

CARPETBAG STEAK

Surf and turf lovers, dig in!
Preparation time: 15 minutes
Marinating time: 30 minutes; Broiling time: 25 minutes
8 servings—4 ounces each

1 1/2 pounds sirloin steak, trimmed of excess fat and cut for
  pocket opening
1/2 pound cooked shrimp
Marinade:
  1/4 cup red wine
  1/2 teaspoon salt
  1/4 teaspoon pepper
  1/2 teaspoon dried thyme
  1/2 teaspoon dried sage
  1 tablespoon vegetable oil
  1 tablespoon lemon juice
  1 tablespoon chopped parsley
  1 tablespoon dry sherry

1. Stuff shrimp into the pocket of the prepared steak.

2. Combine marinade ingredients in a shaker container, and pour
over steak. Cover and marinate at least 30 minutes.

3. Broil or grill for 12 minutes on each side or until steak is cooked to
desired doneness. Slice into 8 servings.

236 calories per serving: 12 g. fat, 31 g. protein,
1 g. carbohydrate, 200 mg. cholesterol, 320 mg. sodium.
For exchange diets, count 4 lean meat.

363

SOURDOUGH STEAK SANDWICH

Preparation time: 15 minutes
Cooking time: 25 minutes
8 servings—1 sandwich each

2 tablespoons vegetable oil
1 pound fresh mushrooms, sliced
8 sirloin steaks
1/4 teaspoon pepper

Sauce:

16-ounce can spinach, drained and squeezed well
1/4 cup no-added-salt beef broth
1 large carrot, diced
1 rib celery, diced
1 large onion, diced
1 cup red wine
1 bay leaf
1/2 pound loaf sourdough bread, cut into 8 thick slices

1. Sauté mushrooms in vegetable oil until tender, then set aside.

2. Season steaks with pepper. Broil for 5 minutes on each side for medium-well-done steaks.

3. Combine ingredients for the sauce in a medium saucepan. Simmer uncovered for 10 minutes. Remove the bay leaf.

4. Grill or toast bread slices. To assemble sandwiches, place a piece of toast on each plate, then top with a steak, sautéed mushrooms, and sauce. Serve hot.

342 calories per serving: 14 g. fat, 27 g. protein,
27 g. carbohydrate, 71 mg. cholesterol, 599 mg. sodium.
For exchange diets, count 4 lean meat, 1 starch, 2 vegetable.

KIWI TART

Preparation time: 15 minutes
Cooking time: 5 minutes; Chilling time: at least 2 hours
8 servings—1 slice each

1 1/2 cups skim milk
1 package cook-style (not instant) lemon pudding mix
1 whole egg or 1/4 cup liquid egg substitute
4 large kiwifruit, peeled and sliced thin
1 reduced-fat prepared graham cracker crust

Topping:
1/2 cup all-fruit raspberry or currant preserves

1. In a medium saucepan, combine skim milk and pudding mix. Cook over medium heat, stirring constantly, until bubbles just start to form around the side of the pan.

2. In a small bowl, beat egg well. Transfer 3 spoonfuls of the hot pudding mixture into the egg, and beat well. Transfer the egg and pudding back into the pan, and continue cooking. Boil mixture for 1 to 2 minutes according to package directions until mixture is thick. Remove pan from heat, and cool to room temperature.

3. Fold sliced kiwi into the pudding mixture. Pour into the prepared crust. Refrigerate at least 2 hours.

4. Slice kiwi tart, and serve on dessert plates with all fruit preserves as a topping.

220 calories per serving: 4 g. fat, 4 g. protein,
42 g. carbohydrate, 22 mg. cholesterol, 315 mg. sodium.
For exchange diets, count 1 fruit, 1 starch, 1/2 skim milk, and 1 fat.

PAVLOVA

Preparation time: 15 min.
Baking time: 1 hour
8 servings—1 wedge each

4 large egg whites
1/4 teaspoon salt
1/2 cup granulated sugar
1/2 cup powdered sugar
1 teaspoon cornstarch
1/2 teaspoon vinegar

1. Preheat oven to 250° F.

2. Separate eggs; pour the egg whites into a large mixing bowl. Add the salt, and beat on low speed until foamy. Continue beating until soft peaks form. Gradually add the sugar, one tablespoon at a time.

3. Measure the powdered sugar and the cornstarch into a sifter. Slowly sift into the egg whites, using a spatula to carefully blend. Finally, fold in the vinegar.

4. Place a piece of waxed paper on a baking sheet. Spread the egg whites in a circle on the paper. Build up the meringue to form the sides of a shell. Bake for 1 hour or until the shell is crisp and just very lightly colored. Remove from the oven, and cool.

5. Remove the paper from the shell. Place the shell on a serving platter, and fill with your favorite pie filling or frozen yogurt. Slice into 8 wedges.

80 calories per serving: 0 fat. 2 g. protein,
28 g. carbohydrate, 0 cholesterol, 92 mg. sodium.
For exchange diets, count 1 1/2 fruit.

Chapter Sixteen

the South Pacific

Suggested South Pacific Menus

Salsa Pacifico
Tropical Nut Bread
Fresh Veggie Salad With Green Salad Dressing
Luau Pork Roast
Pineapple Rice
Hawaiian Iced Tea

Add Fun, Subtract Expense

Create an island mood any time with a tape or CD of the tunes from the musical *South Pacific*.

We all taste a bit of the palm breezes when we eat pineapple. Named for its resemblance to a pine cone, the pineapple is second only to the banana as the most popular of tropical fruits. Pineapples were introduced to the South Pacific in the late 18th century.

Look for the jet-shipped label to be guaranteed of fruit at the peak of ripeness and flavor. Once picked, a pineapple may get softer and juicier, but it will not get sweeter. Don't rely on color to tell you when a pineapple is ripe—the rind may be anywhere from green to golden. Your best bet is to select a large, plump, fresh looking pineapple with fresh green leaves and a sweet fragrance. Avoid fruit that has soft spots, areas of decay, or a fermented, overripe odor at its base. Once you get home, store the pineapple at room temperature for up to 2 days.

Try crushed pineapple on French toast or pancakes.

Use pineapple sherbet as a simple dressing on leftover fruits.

South Pacific cuisine can be duplicated by cooking with citrus juices, garlic, ginger, Maui (sweet) onion, coconut syrup and milk, nutmeg, soy sauce, and taro leaves.

Try a Polynesian Cocktail:
Shake 1 1/2 ounces vodka, 3/4 ounces wild cherry brandy, and the juice of 1 lime with cracked ice. Strain into a 4-ounce cocktail glass. Frost the rim of the glass by rubbing with lime and dipping in powdered sugar.

HAWAIIAN SUN TEA

Preparation time: 5 minutes
Sun time: 4 hours
16 servings—8 ounces each

1/2 gallon water
12 tea bags
4 fresh mint sprigs
1 2/3 cups sugar
12 ounces pineapple-orange-banana juice
6 ounces lemon juice

Garnish:

pineapple spears

1. Pour water into a 1-gallon sun tea jar. Add tea bags and mint. Cover and place outside in the sunlight for several hours or until tea is dark.

2. While tea is still warm, add sugar and juices; stir until sugar is dissolved. Add enough water to make 1 gallon. Chill.

3. Garnish with pineapple spears.

91 calories per serving: 0 fat, 0 protein,
23 g. carbohydrate, 0 cholesterol, 1 mg. sodium.
For exchange diets, count 1 1/2 fruit.

BLUE HAWAII

Preparation time: 5 minutes
2 servings—6 ounces each

1 ounce white rum
2 ounces pineapple juice
1 ounce blue curacao
1 ounce cream of coconut
splash lime juice
2 cups ice cubes

Garnish:

pineapple wedges

1. Combine all ingredients in a blender; blend until smooth. Pour into 2 tall glasses. Garnish with a pineapple wedge if desired.

132 calories per serving: 3 g. fat, 0 protein,
13 g. carbohydrate, 0 cholesterol, 11 mg. sodium.
For exchange diets, count 2 fruit.

RUM PUNCH

Imagine the beach, swaying palm trees, a little
reggae music, and working on a tan.

Preparation time: 5 minutes
1 serving—5 1/2 ounces

---

1 ounce dark rum
2 ounces pineapple juice
2 ounces orange juice
1/2 ounce lime juice
1/8 teaspoon bitters

1. Shake all ingredients together in a covered container.

2. Pour into a tall glass filled with ice. Garnish with an orange wheel, a pineapple spear, and a paper umbrella, if desired.

132 calories per serving: 0 fat, 1 g. protein,
16 g. carbohydrate, 0 cholesterol, 1 mg. sodium.
For exchange diets, count 2 fruit.

SALSA PACIFICO

Try this tropical salsa with crackers or serve over grilled chicken or fish.

Preparation time: 20 minutes
6 servings—3/4 cup each

1 cup chopped pineapple
1 cup peeled, chopped mango
1 cup peeled, chopped papaya
1/2 cup chopped red pepper
1/2 cup peeled, chopped kiwifruit
1/2 cup finely chopped red onion
2 tablespoons finely chopped fresh cilantro
2 tablespoons chopped green chilies
1 minced garlic clove
1 teaspoon lime juice
1/8 teaspoon black pepper
1/8 teaspoon salt

1. Combine all ingredients in a medium bowl.

66 calories per serving: 0 fat, 1 g. protein,
17 g. carbohydrate, 0 cholesterol, 2 mg. sodium.
For exchange diets, count 1 fruit.

DILLED GARLIC SHRIMP

Preparation time: 10 minutes
Marinating time: 24 hours
16 servings—2 ounces each

---

3 quarts water
2 pounds peeled and deveined medium shrimp
Marinade:
    1 1/2 cups fat-free mayonnaise
    6 tablespoons ketchup
    3 tablespoons Worcestershire sauce
    4 crushed garlic cloves
    3 tablespoons capers
    3 tablespoons dill pickle juice
    1 tablespoon dill weed

1. Boil water in a large saucepan. Add shrimp, and return water to a boil for 1 minute. Immediately drain and rinse shrimp under cold water. Do not overcook or the shrimp will be tough.

2. In a medium bowl, mix all ingredients for marinade.

3. Add shrimp to marinade; cover and refrigerate for 24 hours.

4. Use a slotted spoon to remove shrimp from marinade and serve on a bed or fresh greens as an appetizer.

86 calories per serving: 1 g. fat, 12 g. protein,
6 g. carbohydrate, 87 mg. cholesterol, 485 mg. sodium.
For exchange diets, count 2 very lean meat, 1 vegetable.

TROPICAL NUT BREAD

Preparation time: 20 minutes
Baking time: 1 1/4 hours; Cooling time: several hours
16 servings—1 slice each

2 cups flour
2 teaspoons baking powder
1 teaspoon baking soda
1/2 teaspoon salt
8-ounce can undrained crushed pineapple
1 cup mashed banana
1/3 cup orange juice
1 cup sugar
1/2 cup soft margarine
1/2 cup liquid egg substitute or 2 eggs
1/2 cup chopped macadamia nuts
nonstick cooking spray

1. Preheat oven to 350° F.

2. In a medium bowl, sift together flour, baking powder, soda, and salt; set aside.

3. In a small bowl combine pineapple with juice, banana, and orange juice; set aside.

4. In a large bowl, cream sugar and margarine; add eggs, and beat well. Stir in flour mixture and fruit mixture alternately just until flour is moistened. Fold in nuts.

5. Pour batter into a 9" x 5" x 3" loaf pan that has been sprayed with cooking spray. Bake for 1 1/4 hours. Cool several hours before slicing.

229 calories per serving: 11 g. fat, 3 g. protein,
31 g. carbohydrate, 0 cholesterol with egg substitute
(21 mg. cholesterol with eggs), 187 mg. sodium.
For exchange diets, count 2 starch, 1 1/2 fat.

GREEN SALAD DRESSING

Preparation time: 10 minutes
Chilling time: 2 hours
12 servings—2 tablespoons each

3 tablespoons chopped parsley
3 tablespoons chopped green onion
2 teaspoons tarragon vinegar
2 teaspoons chopped chives
2 teaspoons anchovy fillets (optional)
1 teaspoon capers
1 clove garlic
1/8 teaspoon salt
1 cup fat-free mayonnaise

1. Combine all ingredients except mayonnaise in a food processor or blender. Process until fine.

2. Add mayonnaise, and process just until mixed. Chill for 2 hours.

3. Serve on your favorite mixed green salad.

17 calories per serving: 0 fat, 0 protein,
4 g. carbohydrate, 0 cholesterol, 292 mg. sodium.
For exchange diets, count 1 vegetable.

BANANA CHUTNEY

Serve over chicken, pork, or fish.

Preparation time: 15 minutes
Cooking time: 15 minutes
12 servings—1/2 cup each

3 peeled and sliced kiwifruit
2 peeled and sliced bananas
1 cup diced red onion
3/4 cup wine vinegar
1/4 cup dark brown sugar
3 minced cloves garlic
2 teaspoons minced fresh ginger
1/4 teaspoon cayenne pepper
1/4 teaspoon allspice
1/4 teaspoon cloves
1/4 teaspoon salt

1. Combine all ingredients in a large saucepan. Cook over low heat, stirring occasionally, for 15 minutes or until mixture is thickened.

2. Allow chutney to cool to room temperature; refrigerate.

53 calories per serving: 0 fat, 0 protein,
13 g. carbohydrate, 0 cholesterol, 48 mg. sodium.
For exchange diets, count 1 fruit.

LUAU PORK ROAST

Preparation time: 15 minutes
Marinating time: 30 minutes; Grilling time: 2 hours
8 servings—4 ounces each

2 pounds lean pork, well trimmed
Marinade:
    1 teaspoon minced garlic
    1/2 cup white wine
    2 tablespoons soy sauce
    1 small onion, chopped
    1/4 cup lemon juice
    2 tablespoons brown sugar
    1 tablespoon dry mustard
    1 teaspoon ginger
    1/4 cup water

1. Place roast in a casserole dish.

2. In a small mixing bowl, combine ingredients for the marinade. Pour over the roast. Marinate at least 30 minutes.

3. Grill the roast at least 4 inches away from the flame for 2 hours or until a meat thermometer registers 170° F.

221 calories per serving: 5 g. fat, 32 g. protein,
6 g. carbohydrate, 87 mg. cholesterol, 340 mg. sodium.
For exchange diets, count 4 lean meat.

GRILLED MAHIMAHI

Preparation time: 10 minutes
Marinating time: 4 hours; Grilling time: 15 minutes
6 servings—4 ounces each

1 cup orange juice
1 cup grapefruit juice
1/2 cup dry sherry
2 tablespoons lemon juice
2 tablespoons lime juice
1 teaspoon thyme
1/4 teaspoon cayenne pepper
1/4 teaspoon salt
1 1/2 pounds mahimahi steaks
paprika

1. In a shallow dish, combine all ingredients except fish and paprika. Add fish; cover and refrigerate for 4 hours, turning fish after 2 hours.

2. Lightly oil barbecue grill. Remove fish from marinade. Grill 5 to 7 minutes on each side or until fish is just cooked. Sprinkle with paprika.

195 calories per serving: 1 g. fat, 50 g. protein,
10 g. carbohydrate, 33 mg. cholesterol, 474 mg. sodium.
For exchange diets, count 1/2 fruit, 5 very lean meat.

PINEAPPLE RICE

Preparation time: 10 minutes
Cooking time: 8 minutes
8 servings—3/4 cup each

2 cups instant rice
2 cups pineapple juice
1 cup pineapple tidbits
1/2 cup raisins
2 tablespoons chopped almonds
2 green onions, finely chopped
1/4 teaspoon allspice

1. Combine all ingredients in a microwave-safe casserole dish. Cover and cook on high power for 8 minutes or until rice is fluffy. Toss and serve at once.

139 calories per serving: 2 g. fat, 3 g. protein,
28 g. carbohydrate, 0 cholesterol, 6 mg. sodium.
For exchange diets, count 1 starch, 1 fruit.

Appendix

Around the World Low-Fat/No-Fat

Guide to Spices

Spice/Herb	Flavor	Cooking Use
Allspice	cinnamon, nutmeg, cloves	desserts, stews, pickling, main dishes
Anise	licorice	desserts
Basil	clove-licorice, aromatic	soups, stews, tomato sauces, salads, soups
Bay leaf	pungent, aromatic	stews, sauces
Caraway seed	intense, pungent	breads, cabbage, cheese, pickling, soups, stews
Cardamom	menthol-like	sauces, coffee, curries, breads
Cayenne pepper	very hot, peppery	meat, main dishes, sauces, vegetables, soups
Chili powder	hot, spicy, combination of chili peppers, garlic, onion, cumin, and other spices	Mexican cooking, soups, stews, eggs
Cilantro	lemony	Mexican & oriental cooking, sauces, pasta, fish, poultry
Cinnamon	sweet, aromatic	all dishes
Cloves	hot, yet sweet; aromatic	baking, stews, desserts, pickling
Cumin	nutty, aromatic	Mexican cooking, soups, stews, curries, meat salads
Curry Powder	blend of turmeric, fenugreek, coriander, ginger, red pepper, other spices	Indian cooking, meat, fish, sauces, vegetables, soups, stews
Dill Weed	tangy, pungent, lemony	meat, fish, vegetables, salads, picking, breads
Fennel	licorice, aromatic, minty	pizza sauce, breads, fish, sausage
Fenugreek	maple-like	curry powder, chutney
Garam masala	sweet, spicy blend of cinnamon, cardamom, cloves, coriander, pepper	Indian cooking

Spice/Herb	Flavor	Cooking Use
Ginger	pungent, spicy	oriental cooking, soups, sauces, pickling
Mace	outer covering of nutmeg seed, sweet, intense	desserts, fruit, salad, soups
Marjoram	mild, oregano-like	stuffings, meat, tomato dishes
Mint	sweet, cool, refreshing	beverages, desserts, sauces, fish, lamb
Nutmeg	sweet, spicy, nut-like	baking, desserts, sauces, meat, stews
Oregano	pungent, strong, slightly bitter	Italian cooking, vegetables, meat, sauces, stews
Oriental five-spice	spicy, sweet, combination of anise, cinnamon, pepper, fennel, and cloves	Oriental cooking
Paprika	sweet to hot	garnish, eggs, meat, fish, sauces, soups
Parsley	mild, slightly pepper-like	garnish, sauces, soups, stews
Rosemary	pine-like	lamb, fish, seafood, soups
Saffron	strong, yet mellow	Indian cooking, rice, curries, tomatoes, fish, lamb, chicken
Sesame seed	rich, nut-like	Oriental and Middle Eastern cooking, breads
Tarragon	strong, anise-like	sauces, dressings, eggs, fish, poultry
Thyme	pungent, aromatic	sauces, chowders, meat, poultry, tomato dishes
Turmeric	musk-like, aromatic	mustards, pickling, seafood

Appendix

Around the World Low-Fat/No-Fat

Food Product/ Frozen Dinner Guide

In a hurry for healthy international taste? This food product guide lists common foods found in supermarkets that will help you fill out your menus. If you've made the Sauerbraten and run out of time to bake the rye bread, just browse this list before shopping and add items that will quickly add authenticity to your worldly menu without excessive fat. Or concoct an entire meal, from appetizer to dessert, from this list of reduced-fat ethnic treats.

Product Name	Serving size	Calories per serving	Fat (g.)	Sodium(mg.) per serving
American South				
New Orleans Jambalaya Mix	1 cup prepared	150	0	590
Negros Brand Black Bean Creole	1 ounce	70	0	20
British				
Wheetena Wheat Cereal	2 Tbsp.	120	1	130
Thomas English Muffins	1 muffin	140	1	135
Wolferman's Crumpets	1 crumpet	80	0.5	240
Wolferman's English Muffins	1 muffin	240	2	310
Wheatabix Wheat Cereal	2 biscuits	120	1	130
Hershey's Irish Creme Hot Cocoa Mix	1 envelope	150	3	160
French				
Healthy Choice Chicken Fettuccine Alfredo	8 ounces	250	3	370
Healthy Choice Beef Tips Français	9.5 ounces	280	5	520
Sans Sucre de Paris Chocolate or Lemon Mousse	1/2 cup	75	3	45
Bread du Jour French Loaf	3-inch slice	130	1	300
Alsace International White or Dark Chocolate Mousse	1/4 package	80	4	40

Product Name	Serving size	Calories per serving	Fat (g.)	Sodium(mg.) per serving
Gen. Foods Int'l. Coffee SF French Van. Café	1 1/3 Tbsp.	30	1.5	75
Sourdough Bread	1 ounce	85	1	150
Krusteaz Dill Rye Bread Mix	1/10 loaf	150	2	170

German

Wilson's Black Forest Maple Ham	2 ounces	50	0	550
Alpine Lace Reduced-Sodium Muenster Cheese	1 ounce	100	9	85
Dickinson's Black Cherry Melba Sauce	2 Tbsp.	130	2.5	70
Gen. Foods Int'l. Coffee SF Café Vienna	1 1/3 Tbsp.	30	1.5	75
Shullsburg Low-Cholesterol Swiss Cheese	1 ounce	110	7	80
Gen. Foods Int'l. Coffee SF Swiss Mocha	1 1/3 Tbsp.	30	1.5	75
Swiss Miss Cocoa Mix	1 envelope	140	3	220
Alpen Low-Fat Swiss Cereal	1/3 cup	110	2	20
Alpine Lace Reduced-Fat Swiss Cheese	1 ounce	100	9	35

Indian

Mary's Curry Rice Pilaf Mix	2 ounces	220	0.5	620

Italian

Healthy Choice Vegetable Pasta Italiano	10 ounces	220	1	340
Lean Cuisine	10 ounces	290	8	560
Weight Watchers Penne Pasta	10 ounces	290	9	550
Healthy Choice Zucchini Lasagna	14 ounces	330	1.55	310
Ragu Light Spaghetti Sauce	1/2 cup	50	1.5	390

Product Name	Serving size	Calories per serving	Fat (g.)	Sodium(mg.) per serving
Kraft Italian Nonfat Cheese	2 teaspoons	20	0	70
Hunt's Light Traditional Sauce	1/2 cup	90	1	420
Healthy Choice Spaghetti Sauce	1/2 cup	50	0.5	390
DiGiorno Angel Hair Pasta	2 ounces	160	1	190
Rice a Roni Fried Rice	2.5 ounces	320	2	1490
Rice a Roni Beef and Rice	2.5 ounces	240	1	700
Healthy Choice Lasagna	1serving	390	5	580
DiGiorno Light Cheese Ravioli	1 cup	280	7	440
DiGiorno Spinach Fettucini or Linguini	2.5 ounces	190	1.5	125
Focaccia	1 ounce	85	1	135
DiGiorno Chunky Tomato Sauce with Basil	1/2 cup	70	0	290
DiGiorno Reduced- Fat Alfredo Sauce	1/4 cup	170	10	600
Alpine Lace Reduced Fat Provolone Cheese	1 ounce	70	5	120
Healthy Choice Fat-Free Pizza Cheese	1/4 cup	45	0	220
Bread du Jour Italian Rolls	1 roll	80	0.5	190
Gen. Foods Int'l. Coffee SF Orange Cappucino	1 1/3 Tbsp.	30	1.5	75
Weight Watchers Italian Cheese Topping	1 Tbsp.	20	0	60
Krusteaz Italian Herb Bread Mix	1/10 loaf	150	2	250

Mediterranean

Product Name	Serving size	Calories per serving	Fat (g.)	Sodium(mg.) per serving
Pam Virgin Olive Oil Spray	1 spray	0	0	0
Millelacs Saffron Rice	1/4 cup dry	160	0	730

Product Name	Serving size	Calories per serving	Fat (g.)	Sodium(mg.) per serving
Mexican				
Lipton Spanish Rice	1/2 cup dry	240	1	940
Healthy Choice Chicken Enchiladas Suiza	10 ounces	270	4.9	440
Chi-Chi's Salsa	2 Tbsp.	10	0	140
Buena Vida Flour Tortillas	1	80	2	290
Fajita Cooking Sauce	1 Tbsp.	10	0	230
Baked Tostitos	1 ounce	110	1	140
Lawrey's Fajita Sauce	2 Tbsp.	15	0	600
Pillsbury Cornbread Twists	1 twist	140	6	330
Tequila Lime Grilling Sauce	1/8 bottle	60	3	710
Novi Black Bean Dip Mix	1/16 pkg.	10	0	170
Vigo Black Beans and Rice	1/3 cup	190	0	950
Middle Eastern				
Kashi Breakfast Pilaf	1/2 cup	170	3	15
Kangaroo Pocket Bread	1 pita	180	0	250
Ak-Mak Original Sesame Crackers	5	120	2	210
Mary's Chicken Pilaf Mix	1 ounce	190	0.5	890
Fancy Foods Tabouli	1/4 cup dry	120	0.5	450
Oriental				
Teriyaki Cooking Sauce	1 Tbsp.	25	0	400
Hot and Spicy Szechuan Seasoning Mix	2 tsp.	15	0	260
Girard's Honey Soy Marinade	1 Tbsp.	30	0	360
Mori Nu Silken Tofu	3 ounces	50	2.5	30
Port Arthur Hot Chinese Mustard	1 tsp.	0	0	80

Product Name	Serving size	Calories per serving	Fat (g.)	Sodium(mg.) per serving
Taste of Thai Garlic Chile Sauce	1 tsp.	10	0	230
Kikkoman Light Soy Sauce	1 Tbsp.	10	0	280
Sweet and Sour Stir Fry Sauce	1 Tbsp.	35	0	50
Lucia Fancy Mixed Chinese Vegetables	2/3 cup	15	0	30
La Choy Bean Sprouts	1 cup	10	0	20
La Choy Sweet and Sour Sauce	2 Tbsp.	60	0	120
Girard's Teriyaki Marinade	1 Tbsp.	20	0	620
Lean Cuisine Sweet and Sour Chicken	10 ounces	260	2.5	440
Healthy Choice Mandarin Chicken	10 ounces	280	2.5	520
Healthy Choice Beef Pepper Steak	9.5 ounces	250	4	470

Scandinavian

Product Name	Serving size	Calories per serving	Fat (g.)	Sodium(mg.) per serving
Wasa Light Rye Crackers	2	225	0	40
Weight Watchers Swedish Meatballs	9 ounces	280	8	510
Finn Crisp Dark Crackers with Caraway	3	60	0	100
Havarti Light Cheese	1 ounce	80	5	120
Morey's Smoked Salmon	2 ounces	80	2	490
Lascco Smoked Salmon	3 ounces	120	6	1070
Norman's Cringle	1 piece	120	3.5	150
Olson Potato Lefsa	1 sheet	60	1	140

Around the World Low-Fat/No-Fat

Restaurant Dining Guide

American

Ask for:
Shrimp cocktail
Broth-based soups
French onion soup with croutons and cheese on the side
Salad dressings on the side
Reduced-fat/fat-free salad dressings
Reduced-fat/fat-free sour cream on the side
Broiled, charbroiled, or baked entrées
Grilled items made with spray shortening only
Oil-free marinated meat, fish, and poultry entrées

Mexican

Ask for:
Black bean soup
Albondigo soup (vegetables and meatballs)
Cerviche (marinated seafood and salsa)
Seafood salads
Grilled chicken salad
Shrimp or chicken fajitas grilled with spray shortening only
Reduced-fat/fat-free sour cream
Salsa
Baked tortilla chips
Pasta and fagioli soup
Gazpacho
Chili with or without meat
Chicken tacos
Chili verde
Chicken tostadas
Green corn tamales
Enchiladas or burritos with half the cheese

Caribbean and Central & South American

Ask for:
Grilled chicken with pico de gallo and pineapple
Grilled tuna with green onions

French

Ask for:

Escargot in mustard sauce
Artichokes à la vinaigrette
Salade Niçoise
Salade de crustaces (seafood)
Salade d'épinards (spinach)
Veal Normande
Salmon papillotte (baked salmon)
Roast game hen with vegetables
Veal forestiere (veal with artichokes)
Veal parmentier (veal with potatoes and mushrooms)
Jambon de parme et melon (ham and melon appetizer)
Truite fumée (trout appetizer with apples and horseradish)
Champignons Francais a crab (mushroom appetizer stuffed with crab)
Vichyssoise with no added fat
Crab Louis (crab meat salad)
Poulet a poivre (chicken in brandy peppercorn sauce)
Scampi matelot (shrimp with tomatoes and mushrooms)
Sole de douvres (sole poached in white wine)
Merou a la sauce d'homard (groups in lobster sauce)
Perch rouge Veronique—snapper with no added fat
Veal Oscar—veal with crab
Veal Picaata (veal in lemon and sherry sauce)
Veal Montueux (veal with spinach and tomatoes)
Cotelettes d'Agneau (lamb chops)
Coq au vin (chicken in red wine sauce)
Shrimp Napoleon (shrimp in sherry)
Berries Flambé

German

Ask for:

Rye bread with no butter
Steamed potatoes with butter on the side
Lean pork or ham entrées
Fat-free brown gravy
Sweet and sour vegetable salads
Sauerkraut
Applesauce
Roasted poultry (leave the skin on your plate)
Steamed vegetables
Marinated fruits in wine for dessert

Scandinavian

Ask for:

Smoked salmon appetizers
Grilled salmon entrées prepared with spray shortening only

Italian

Ask for:

Frutte de mare (marinated seafood on fresh greens)
Marinated mushrooms
Sicilian eggplant (lightly sautéed eggplant in tomato sauce)
Antipasto plates (avoid the fatty sausages or fish in oil)
Tomato Florentine soup
Pasta primavera
Minestrone soup
Vegetarian pizza
Part-skim mozzarella cheese on pizza
Half of the cheese on pizza
Veal Italian (veal in red wine sauce)
Chicken marsala
Chicken cacciatore
Chicken vesuvio (chicken with garlic and lemon)
Italian pepper steak
Sherbet
Stewed fruits
Italian ice
Espresso

Oriental

Ask for:
Steamed dumplings
Hot and sour soup
Sizzling rice soup
Wonton soup
Green pepper steak
Hunan beef
Hunan chicken
Moo Goo Gai Pan
Chicken with broccoli
Hunan shrimp
Princess chicken
Shrimp with vegetables
Rice
Thai chicken curry
Chow mein noodles that are not fried
Szechuan dishes prepared with very little fat
Fortune cookies and tea

Appendix

Glossary

Glossary

Absinthe substitute—anise-flavored liqueur. Original absinthe is distilled from wormwood. It is reputed to be an aphrodisiac. Original absinthe is banned in many countries since it is purported to be habit-forming.

Anchovies—small fish that are salt-cured and packed in oil. True anchovies come from the Mediterranean. Use sparingly, as they are quite flavorful.

Balsamic vinegar—Italian wine vinegar which has been aged several years in wooden barrels. Much stronger and smoother than regular wine vinegar, which can be used as a substitute.

Bitters—liquid flavor made from the distillation of aromatic herbs and spices. Bittersweet in flavor, it is used in small amounts to flavor beverages or foods.

Blue curaçao—blue-colored, orange flavored liqueur used to flavor tropical drinks.

Bok choy—Chinese chard. A type of cabbage resembling celery.

Bulgur—wheat kernels that have been steamed, dried, and crushed. It is the main component of wheat pilaf and tabbouleh.

Capers—unopened green flower buds from a shrub native to the Mediterranean. Capers are sun-dried, then pickled and used as a seasoning.

Cellophane noodles—clear white noodles made from mung beans. Also known as bean threads.

Ceviche—raw fish marinated in citrus juice. Only fresh fish can be used for this dish.

Cilantro—also known as Chinese parsley or coriander. Cilantro is a large leaf parsley with a pungent, lemon-peppery flavor. Used in salsas and Mexican cooking, as well as in oriental, Indian, and Caribbean cooking.

Claret—British term for red Bordeaux wine.

Coconut milk—creamy white liquid extracted from fresh coconut. Used in Thai cooking.

Coconut syrup—made from freshly grated coconut, coconut milk, and sugar. Used in beverages and desserts.

Colcannon—an Irish side dish made of mashed potatoes and shredded cabbage.

Couscous—very fine semolina, also called cracked wheat. Couscous also refers to the dish which contains couscous, steamed vegetables, and/or meats and spices.

Creme de banana—banana flavored liqueur.

Daikon—Japanese white radish.

Dolma—stuffed grapevine leaves. Found especially in Greece, although different variations are found throughout the entire Middle East.

Garam masala—Indian sweet spice mixture. There are many variations, although most include cinnamon, cardamom, cloves, coriander, nutmeg, and black pepper.

Mahimahi—dolphinfish (not to be confused with the porpoise or dolphin which is a mammal); large whitefish with delicate, firm flesh.

Oriental five-spice-mixture—used in oriental cooking. Made from star anise, pepper, cinnamon, fennel, and cloves. Mainly used in Chinese cooking.

Oyster sauce—concentrated flavor made from cooked oysters and soy sauce. Used in oriental cooking.

Pickled ginger—pungent, sliced baby gingerroot that has been sliced and pickled in sweet vinegar.

Red curry paste—seasoning made from red chilies, spices, vinegar, and sometimes ghee (clarified butter). Used extensively in Thai cooking.

Rice vinegar—made from fermented rice. It's lighter and sweeter than regular vinegar.

Roasted red pepper—red bell pepper that has been grilled or broiled until charred, then placed in a tightly sealed bag for about 10 minutes. Charred skin is then rubbed off.

Saké—Japanese wine made from rice. Used as a beverage and for cooking. In cooking, dry sherry can be substituted.

Sesame oil—oil pressed from sesame seed. Used to flavor oriental dishes.

Tahini—sesame seed paste. Used in Middle Eastern cooking.

Tofu—soybean curd. White custard-like consistency. Used in Japanese cooking and as a substitute for meats and cream cheese.

Star anise—star-shaped dried spice with a mild licorice flavor.

Thai fish sauce—dark anchovy-based sauce used to flavor Thai food.

Tomatillos—small green tomato-like fruit used in Mexican cooking. Remove husk before using. Tomatillos should be firm. They impart a lemony, herbal flavor.

Appendix

References

Bielunski, Marlys. *Recipe Format Survey.* Chicago: National Live Stock and Meat Board, 1995.

Cotton, Leo. *DeLuxe Official Bartender's Guide.* Boston: Mr. Boston Distiller Inc., 1965.

Elving, Phyllis. *Sunset Fresh Produce, A to Z.* Menlo Park: Lane Publishing Company, 1987.

Herbst, Sharon. *Barron's Food Lover's Companion.* Hauppauge, New York: Barron's Educational Series, Inc., 1990.

Kissel, Renate. *Delights of Scandinavian Cooking.* Surrey, England: Anglo-Nordic Imprints Ltd., 1990.

Maxwell, Sonia. *Scandinavian Cooking.* London: The Apple Press, 1995.

Pearson, Marina. *The King Edward VII Hospital Cookery Book.* Stanbridge, England: Dovecote Press Ltd, 1993.

Simmons, Amelia. *The First American Cookbook.* New York: Dover Publications, 1958.

Index